Vices And Virtues

Vices and Virtues,

BEING

A Soul's Confession of its Sins,

with

Reason's Description of the Virtues.

A MIDDLE-ENGLISH DIALOGUE

OF ABOUT 1200 A.D.

EDITED, WITH AN INTRODUCTION, TRANSLATION, NOTES,
AND GLOSSARY, FROM THE STOWE MS. 240
IN THE BRITISH MUSEUM,

BY

FERD. HOLTHAUSEN, Ph.D.

PART I.—TEXT AND TRANSLATION.

LONDON:

PUBLISHED FOR THE EARLY ENGLISH TEXT SOCIETY,
BY N. TRÜBNER & CO., 57 AND 59 LUDGATE HILL, E.C.

M DCCC LXXXVIII.

———

Price Eight Shillings.

Early English Text Society.

Vices and Virtues,

BEING

A Soul's Confession of its Sins,

with

Reason's Description of the Virtues.

A MIDDLE-ENGLISH DIALOGUE
OF ABOUT 1200 A.D.

*EDITED, WITH AN INTRODUCTION, TRANSLATION, NOTES,
AND GLOSSARY, FROM THE STOWE MS. 240
IN THE BRITISH MUSEUM,*

BY

FERD. HOLTHAUSEN, Ph.D.

PART I.—TEXT AND TRANSLATION.

LONDON:

PUBLISHED FOR THE EARLY ENGLISH TEXT SOCIETY,
BY N. TRÜBNER & CO., 57 AND 59 LUDGATE HILL, E.C.
M DCCC LXXXVIII.

Price Eight Shillings.

Early English Text Society.

Committee of Management.

Director: DR. FREDERICK J. FURNIVALL, M.A.

Treasurer: HENRY B. WHEATLEY, ESQ.

Hon. Sec.: W. A. DALZIEL, ESQ., 67 VICTORIA ROAD, FINSBURY PARK, LONDON. N.

Hon. Sec. for America: PROF. F. J. CHILD, HARVARD COLL., CAMBR., MASS., U.S.A.

(With power to add Workers to their number.)

Bankers:

THE UNION BANK OF LONDON, 2 PRINCES STREET, LONDON, E.C.

Half the Publications for 1866 (13, 14, 15, 16, 18, 22) are out of print, but will be gradually reprinted. Subscribers who desire the issue for 1866 should send their guineas at once to the Hon. Secretary, in order that other Texts for 1866 may be sent to press.

The Publications for 1864–1871 (one guinea each year, save those for 1866 now half out of print, two guineas) are:

1. Early English Alliterative Poems, ab. 1360 A.D., ed. Rev. Dr. R. Morris. 16s. 186
2. Arthur, ab. 1440, ed. F. J. Furnivall. M.A. 4s.
3. Lauder on the Dewtie of Kyngis. etc., 1556, ed. F. Hall, D.C.L. 4s.
4. Sir Gawayne and the Green Knight, ab. 1360, ed. Rev. Dr. R. Morris. 10s.
5. Hume's Orthographie and Congruitie of the Britan Tongue, ab. 1617, ed. H. B. Wheatley. 4s. 186
6. Lancelot of the Laik, ab. 1500, ed. Rev. W. W. Skeat. 8s.
7. Genesis and Exodus, ab. 1250, ed. Rev. Dr. R. Morris. 8s.
8. Morte Arthure, ab. 1440, ed. E. Brock. 7s.
9. Thynne on speght's ed. of Chaucer, A.D. 1599, ed. Dr. G. Kingsley and Dr. F. J. Furnivall. 10s.
10. Merlin, ab. 1440, Part I., ed. H. B. Wheatley. 2s. 6d.
11. Lyndesay's Monarche, etc., 1552, Part I., ed. J. Small. M.A. 3s.
12. Wright's Chaste Wife, ab. 1462, ed. F. J. Furnivall, M.A. 1s.
13. Seinte Marherete, 1200–1330, ed. Rev. O. Cockayne. 186
14. Kyng Horn, Floris and Blancheflour, etc., ed. Rev. J. R. Lumby, B.D.
15. Political, Religious, and Love Poems, ed. F. J. Furnivall.
16. The Book of Quinte Essence, ab. 1446–70, ed. F. J. Furnivall.
17. Parallel Extracts from Forty-five MSS. of Piers the Plowman, ed. Rev. W. W. Skeat. 1s. [In print.]
18. Hali Meidenhad, ab. 1200, ed. Rev. O. Cockayne.
19. Lyndesay's Monarche, etc., Part II., ed. J. Small, M.A. 3s. 6d. [In print.]
20. Hampole's English Prose Treatises, ed. Rev. G. G. Perry. 1s. [In print.]
21. Merlin, Part II., ed. H. B. Wheatley. 4s. [In print.]
22. Partenay or Lusignen, ed. Rev. W. W. Skeat.
23. Dan Michel's Ayenbite of Inwyt, 1340, ed. Rev. Dr. R. Morris. 10s. 6d. [Re-printing.]
24. Hymns to the Virgin and Christ; the Parliament of Devils, etc., ab. 1430, ed. F. J. Furnivall. 3s. 186
25. The Stacions of Rome, the Pilgrims' Sea-voyage, with Clene Maydenhod, ed. F. J. Furnivall. 1s.
26. Religious Pieces in Prose and Verse, from R. Thornton's MS. (ab. 1440), ed. Rev. G. G. Perry. 2s.
27. Levins's Manipulus Vocabulorum, a ryming Dictionary. 1570, ed. H. B. Wheatley. 12s.
28. William's Vision of Piers the Plowman, 1362 A.D.; Text A, Part I., ed. Rev. W. W. Skeat. 6s.
29. Early English Homilies (ab. 1220–30 A.D.). Part I. Edited by Rev. Dr. R. Morris. 7s.
30. Pierce the Ploughmans Crede, ed. Rev. W. W. Skeat. 2s.
31. Myrc's Duties of a Parish Priest, in Verse, ab. 1420 A.D., ed. E. Peacock. 4s. 186
32. Early English Meals and Manners; the Boke of Norture of John Russell, the Bokes of Keruynge, Curtasye, and Demeanor, the Babees Book, Urbanitatis, etc., ed. F. J. Furnivall. 12s.
33. The Knight de la Tour Landry, ab. 1440 A.D. A Book for Daughters, ed. T. Wright, M.A. 8s.
34. Early English Homilies (before 1300 A.D.). Part II., ed. R. Morris, LL.D. 8s.
35. Lyndesay's Works, Part III.: The Historie and Testament of Squyer Meldrum, ed. F. Hall. 2s.
36. Merlin, Part III. Ed. H. B. Wheatley. On Arthurian Localities, by J. S. Stuart Glennie. 12s. 186
37. Sir David Lyndesay's Works, Part IV., Ane Satyre of the Three Estaits. Ed. F. Hall. D.C.L. 4s.
38. William's Vision of Piers the Plowman, Part II. Text B. Ed. Rev. W. W. Skeat, M.A. 10s. 6d.
39. Alliterative Romance of the Destruction of Troy. Ed. D. Donaldson and G. A. Panton. Part I. 10s. 6d.
40. English Gilds, their Statutes and Customs, 1389 A.D. Ed. Toulmin Smith and Lucy T. Smith, with an Essay on Gilds and Trades-Unions, by Dr. L. Brentano. 21s. 187
41. William Lauder's Minor Poems. Ed. F. J. Furnivall. 3s.
42. Bernardus De Cura Rei Famuliaris, Early Scottish Prophecies, &c. Ed. J. R. Lumby, M.A. 2s.
43. Ratis Raving, and other Moral and Religious Pieces. Ed. J. R. Lumby, M.A. 3s.
44. The Alliterative Romance of Joseph of Arimathie, or The Holy Grail: from the Vernon MS.; with W. de Worde's and Pynson's Lives of Joseph: ed. Rev. W. W. Skeat, M.A. 5s. 187
45. King Alfred's West-Saxon Version of Gregory's Pastoral Care, edited from two MSS., with an English translation, by Henry Sweet, Esq., B.A., Balliol College, Oxford. Part I. 10s.
46. Legends of the Holy Rood, Symbols of the Passion and Cross Poems, ed. Rev. Dr. R. Morris. 10s.
47. Sir David Lyndesay's Works, Part V., ed. Dr. J. A. H. Murray. 3s.
48. The Times' Whistle, and other Poems, by R. C., 1616; ed. by J. M. Cowper, Esq. 6s.

1 March, 1888. With this, go out four of the Society's volumes, bringing its issues up to time. These four are the two Texts of the Original Series for 1887,—1. Dr. Horstmann's re-edition of Henry Bradshaw's Life of St. Werburghe, A.D. 1521 ; 2. Dr. Horstmann's edition of the earliest MS. and form of the well-known set of Saints' Lives, &c., contained in the Laud MS. (see p. 4 below) ; 3. the third and last Text of the Extra Series, 1887, The Torrent of Portyngale, re-edited by Dr. E. Adam (with Prof. Kölbing's help) ; 4. the first Text of the Original Series for 1888: Part I, the text and translation of Dr. Holthausen's edition of an early treatise on the Vices and Virtues from the Stowe MS. 240, ab. 1200 A.D.

The other Original-Series Texts for 1888 will be Mr. Rhodes's re-edition of the Anglo-Saxon Glosses and Latin text of Bede's Liber Scintillarum, and Mr. Harsley's edition of Eadwine's early 12th century Canterbury Psalter, as to which see below. Both these Texts are all in type.

For the Extra Series, 1888, Bullein's Dialogue on the Feuer Pestilence, 1573, has been for a long while all in type and revised ; and it will go out as soon as its Editors, Messrs. A. H. and Mark Bullen, allow. The second book for this year will be a new edition of the first English Anatomie of the Body of Man, by Thomas Vicary, Serjeant of the Surgeons, and Chief Surgeon to Henry VIII, Edward VI, Q. Mary, and Q. Elizabeth, five times Master of the Barber-Surgeons' Company, and Chief Surgeon to St. Bartholomew's Hospital after its refoundation in 1547 by Henry VIII and the City of London. No copy of the first edition of this little book in 1548 is now known ; and therefore the unique copy of it, re-issued by the Surgeons of Bartholomew's in 1577, has been reprinted. Diligent efforts have been made to secure all accessible details of Vicary's life in its various aspects of—1. 'a meane practiser at Maidstone' ;

2. the head Court-Surgeon for over forty years; 3. a member (1527–62) and Master of the Barber - Surgeons' Company; 4. a Governor of the recreated Bartholomew's Hospital; and 5. a private citizen. But though fair success has attended the searches under sections 2 and 5, little has been attained under 1; while for 3 and 4, delay is still needful. Mr. D'Arcy Power has, by the kind leave of Mr. South's widow, lent the Society Mr. South's full extracts from the earliest Minute-Book of the Barber-Surgeons' Company; but the consent of the Governors of the Company has not yet been obtained to the printing of part of the extracts. And it is probable that this consent will be given in only a partial form : as a member of the Company has long been compiling its history from its records, his fellow-members will probably not wish any of these printed before his book is publisht, which will be some years hence. With regard to Bartholomew's Hospital, its Records are now printing; and till Part I of these is out, the Society's book cannot appear. Meantime all Vicary's work, with its many illustrative Documents, Extracts from MSS., etc., is in type, as well as the full Forewords up to the Barbers' Company Section. The remainder is partly in draft, and will be in type before the Bartholomew's section—the old Surgeon's life at the Hospital in 1548–62—can be written. The New Shakspere Society has sold the Early English Text Society the right to print copies of its plates of Edward VI's Coronation Procession through the City of London in 1547, and Norden's Plan of London in 1593; and other illustrations will be given. The Editors are the Director, and his son Mr. Percy Furnivall, a student of St. Bartholomew's Hospital. It is hoped that the book will be ready by May, at latest; but this, as above mentioned, depends on the appearance of Part I of the Bartholomew's Records.

Mr. Alexander J. Ellis has already in type over a hundred pages of Part IV of his great work on *Early English Pronunciation*, dealing with our modern dialects. This will be issued by the Philological and Chaucer Societies jointly with the Early English Text Society; but the date of publication must depend on the progress of the very intricate and laborious work, and the funds of the several Societies. This Part will undoubtedly be finisht this year.

The Large Paper issue of the Extra Series is stopt, save for the completing of unfinisht works in it.

Dr. Aldis Wright, many years ago, undertook the editing of the MS. Anglo-Saxon Psalters for the Society. As a preliminary, he copied the 12th century (? about 1150 A.D.) Trinity MS. of Eadwine's Canterbury Psalter, which has transitional forms like the change of A.Sax. *c* to *ch* (*wyrchende* for A.Sax. *wyrcende*), the weakening of full vowels in the endings, *senfullen* for A.Sax. *synfullan*, &c. Dr. Aldis Wright also made notes of all the other A.Sax. Psalters from the 9th to the 12th century, and tentatively classified them by the Roman and Gallican versions which they respectively glost. Meantime Dr. Hy. Sweet edited the oldest MS., the Vespasian, in his *Oldest English Texts* for the Society. The next step should have been to collate six or eight Psalms from all the MSS., and see whether one or (at most) two texts, with collations, would not have sufficed for the whole body. But as Mr. Harsley, to whom Dr. Aldis Wright kindly handed his whole material, wanted one text printed forthwith for his Doctor's Dissertation, leave was given for the late Canterbury Psalter to go to press; and now the text of it is all printed. Dr. Logeman then raised the question of how the other MSS. should be treated; and he was authorised to prepare a Parallel-Text edition of the first ten Psalms from all the MSS., to test whether the best way of printing them would be in one group, or in two—in each case giving parts of all the MSS. on one page—under their respective Roman and Gallican Latin originals. If collation proves that all the MSS. cannot go together on successive pages, there will be two Parallel-Texts, one ƒf the A.Sax. MSS. following the Roman version, and the other, of those glossing the Gallican; but every effort will be made to get the whole into one Parallel-Text. This Text will be an extravagance; but as the Society has not yet committed one in Anglo-Saxon, it will indulge in one now. And every student will rejoice at having the whole Psalter material before him in the most convenient form. Dr. Logeman and Mr. Harsley will be joint editors of the Parallel-Text. The Early English Psalters are all independent versions, and will follow separately in due course.

Through the good offices of Prof. Arber, the books for the Early-English Examinations of the University of London will be chosen from the Society's publications, the Committee having undertaken to supply such books to students at a large reduction in price. The profits from these sales will be applied to the Society's Reprints. The *Ayenbite of Inwyt* is now reprinting under the supervision of its Editor, Dr. Richard Morris. Members are reminded that fresh Subscribers are always wanted, and that the Committee can at any time, on short notice, send to press an additional Thousand Pounds' worth of work.

Our *Jubilee Reprint Fund,* for which Mr. M. T. Culley, of Coupland Castle, has sent a Letter of Appeal to every Member, has as yet received but little support, tho' Mr. Mortimer Harris started it with a cheque for two guineas. Further Donations will be welcome. They should be paid to the Honorary Secretary, Mr. W. A. Dalziel, 67 Victoria Road, Finsbury Park, London, N.

The Subscribers to the Original Series must be prepared for the issue of the whole of the Early English *Lives of Saints,* under the editorship of Dr. Carl Horstmann. The Society cannot leave out any of them, even though some are dull. In many will be found interesting incidental details of our forefathers' social state, and all are worthful for the history of our language. The Lives may be lookt on as the religious romances or story-books of their period.

The Standard Collection of Saints' Lives in the Corpus and Ashmole MSS., the Harleian MS. 2277, &c. will repeat the Laud set, our No. 87, with additions, and in right order. The differences between the foundation MS. (the Laud) and its followers are so great, that, to prevent quite unwieldy collations, Dr. Horstmann decided that the Laud MS. must be printed alone, as the first of the Series of Saints' Lives. The supplementary Lives from the Vernon and other MSS. will form one or two separate volumes. The Glossary to the whole set, the discussion of the sources, and of the relation of the MSS. to one another, &c., will be put in a final volume.

When the Saints' Lives are complete, Trevisa's Englishing of *Bartholomaeus de Proprietatibus Rerum,* the mediæval Cyclopædia of Science, &c., will be the Society's next big undertaking. Dr. Holthausen has kindly said that he will probably edit it. Before it goes to press, Prof. Napier of Oxford has been good enough to promise that he will edit for the Society all the unprinted and other Anglo-Saxon Homilies which are not included in Thorpe's edition of Ælfric's prose [1], Dr. Morris's of the Blickling Homilies, and Prof. Skeat's of Ælfric's Metrical Homilies.

For 1889, Dr. Holthausen's Part II, the Introduction, Notes, and Glossary to the Stowe MS. *Vices and Virtues,* will probably be ready in January. What other books will follow, must depend on when any editor of one of the many works in preparation for the Society has a Part or the whole of it ready for issue. Lists of these Works are on the last page of the Cover and the first of this inside quarter-sheet.

---

[1] Of these, Mr. Harsley is preparing a new edition, with collations of all the MSS. Many copies of Thorpe's book, not issued by the Ælfric Society, are still in stock.

In case more Texts are ready at any time than can·be paid for by the current year's income, they will be dated the next year, and issued in advance to such Members as will pay advance subscriptions.   Last year's delay in getting out Texts must not occur again, if it can possibly be avoided.

OTHER SOCIETIES.

Wyclif, founded by Dr. Furnivall in 1882, for the printing of all Wyclif's Latin MSS.   *Hon. Sec.,* J. H. Standerwick, General Post Office, London, E.C. One Guinea a year.

Chaucer, founded by Dr. Furnivall in 1868, to print all the best Chaucer MSS., &c.   *Editor in Chief,* F. J. Furnivall.   *Hon. Sec.,* W. A. Dalziell, 67 Victoria Road, Finsbury Park, N.   Subscription, Two Guineas a year.

New Shakspere, founded by Dr. Furnivall in 1873, to promote the intelligent study of SHAKSPERE, and to print his Works in their original Spelling, with illustrative Treatises.   *President,* Robert Browning.   *Director,* F. J. Furnivall.   *Hon. Sec.,* K. Grahame, 65 Chelsea Gardens, Chelsea Bridge Road, London, S.W.   Subscription, One Guinea a year.

Ballad, founded by Dr. Furnivall in 1868, to print all Early English MS. Ballads, and reprint the Roxburghe, Bagford, and other collections of printed Ballads. *Editor in Chief,* The Rev. J. W. Ebsworth, M.A., F.S.A.   *Hon. Sec.,* W. A. Dalziel, 67 Victoria Road, London, N.   One Guinea a year.

Shelley, founded by Dr. Furnivall in Dec. 1885, to promote the study of Shelley's Works, reprint his original editions, and procure the acting of his *Cenci. Chairman of Committee,* W. M. Rossetti.   *Hon. Sec.,* T. J. Wise, 127 Devonshire Road, Holloway, London, N.   Subscription, One Guinea a year.

Browning, founded by Dr. Furnivall and Miss Hickey in 1881, for the study and discussion of Robert Browning's Works, to print Papers on them, illustrations of ·them, and to procure the performance of the poet's plays.   *President,* Dr. Furnivall.   *Hon. Sec.,* W. B. Slater, 249 Camden Road, London, N. Subscription, One Guinea a year.

Philological, founded in 1842, to investigate the Structure, Affinities, and the History of Languages.   *Hon. Sec.,* F. J. Furnivall, 3 St. George's Sq., Primrose Hill, London, N.W.   One Guinea entrance, and one a year. Parts I, II, III, of the Society's English Dictionary, for which material has been collecting for 30 years, have lately been issued, edited by Dr. J. A. H. Murray, and publisht by the Clarendon Press, Oxford.   Part IV (nearly ready) will complete vol. i (A–B), and start vol. ii (C–D).   Mr. Henry Bradley is now joint Editor, and has begun vol. iii with E.

Wagner, to promote the study of his Musical and other works, and the performance of his Operas at Bayreuth.   *Hon Sec.* for England, B. L. Mosley, 55 Tavistock Square, London, W.C.   Subscription, Ten Shillings a year.

Shakspere Quarto Facsimiles, issued under the superintendence of Dr. Furnivall, 10s. 6d. each, or 6s. if the whole series of forty-three is taken, edited by F. J. Furnivall, Prof. Dowden, Mr. P. A. Daniel, Mr. H. A. Evans, Mr. Arthur Symons, Mr. T. Tyler, and other Shakspere scholars.   B. Quaritch, 15 Piccadilly, London, W.   (Thirty-five Facsimiles have been published, and eight more will be ready soon.   The Series will be completed in 1888.)

Vices and Virtues.

(PART I.)

Agents for the sale of the Early English Text Society's
Publications.

DUBLIN: WILLIAM MᶜGEE, 18 Nassau Street.
EDINBURGH: T. G. STEVENSON, 22 South Frederick Street.
GLASGOW: OGLE & Co., 1 Royal Exchange Square.
BERLIN: ASHER & Co., Unter den Linden 20.
NEW YORK: C. SCRIBNER & Co., LEYPOLDT & HOLT.
PHILADELPHIA: J. B. LIPPINCOTT & Co.

Vices and Virtues,

BEING

A Soul's Confession of its Sins,

with

Reason's Description of the Virtues.

A MIDDLE-ENGLISH DIALOGUE
OF ABOUT 1200 A.D.

*EDITED, WITH AN INTRODUCTION, TRANSLATION, NOTES,
AND GLOSSARY, FROM THE STOWE MS. 240
IN THE BRITISH MUSEUM,*

BY

FERD. HOLTHAUSEN, Ph.D.

PART I.—TEXT AND TRANSLATION

LONDON:
PUBLISHED FOR THE EARLY ENGLISH TEXT SOCIETY,
BY N. TRÜBNER AND CO., 57 AND 59 LUDGATE HILL.
MDCCCLXXXVIII.

Oxford
HORACE HART, PRINTER TO THE UNIVERSITY

VICES AND VIRTUES.

A SOUL'S CONFESSION OF ITS SINS,

WITH

REASON'S DESCRIPTION OF THE VIRTUES,

A MIDDLE ENGLISH DIALOGUE OF ABOUT 1200 A.D., FROM THE
STOWE MS. 240 IN THE BRITISH MUSEUM.

[*Translation.*]

... any man may do. They all are refused by God's own mouth, which says thus: *Vade prius reconciliari fratri tuo,* 'Go first and be reconciled with thy brother. No offer is so dear to Me as the love of God and of all men.'

Of sorrow.

Again, there is another secret sin that has deceived me and many other souls. It is called *tristitia,* that is, sorrow. This is one of the cardinal sins, although it be secret. It is called sorrow—*tristitia mortem operante,* 'sorrow working death'—because all good which is begun to be done for God's love displeases it. This cursed spirit makes the religious man, who has renounced all worldly things for God's love, sorrowful and dreary and heavy in God's works, and often causes [him] to regret that he ever has done so. So he does the men who have promised to forsake sins, and so he does also the men who have promised God to do good, or to seek saints, or to fast, or to do some other good thing. In every wise he tries how he may hinder good works, or cause them to be done with displeasure, and with sorrow, and unblithely.

Of sloth, listlessness.

Again, this deceptive sin has a sister, who is called *accidia,* that is, sloth, who has deceived me many times through my negligence. It has made me heavy and slow in God's works through idleness; it has often caused me to consume other people's sore toil quite unearned. Often it has made me sleep where I ought to have been awake in God's service by day and by night. Such [as I], no other might be. This cursed sin is one of the cardinal sins,

[*The beginning of the MS. is lost.*]

æni mann mai don. Alle hie bieð forsakene on godes awene muðe, ðe ðus seið: Vade prius reconciliari fratri tuo[2], 'Ga arst and seihtle wið ðine broðer. Nis me nan ofrende swa lief swa 4 godes luue and alre mannes.'

Of sorinesse.

GIET is an oðer derne senne ðe me and maniȝe oðre saule hafð beswiken. Hie hatte tristicia, þat is, sarinesse. Þes is an 8 of ðe heued-sennes, ðeih hie dierne bie. Hie is icleped sarinesse, tristicia mortem[3] operante, 'sarinesse deað wurchende,' for ðan hire ofþingþ of alle gode ðe aȝunnen bieð for godes luue te donne. Þes awerȝede gast, hie makeð ðane religiuse man, ðe alle 12 woreld-þing for godes luue hafð forlaten, sari and drieri and heui on godes workes, and ofte doð ofþenchen þat he æure swo haueð[4] idon. Al swo he deð þo men ðe sennen habbeð forhaten te laten, and swa h(i)e[5] doð iec ðo menn ðe habbeð gode behaten god te 16 donne, oðer halȝe to sechen, oðer to fasten, oðer sum oðer god te donne. On alle wise he fandeð hu he muȝe gode weorkes letten, oððe mid ofðanche and mid sarinesse and unbleðeliche[6] hes don [don]. 20

Of a-solknesse. Vnlust.

ÐIES swikele senne haueð ȝiet ane suster, ðe is icleped accidia, ðat[7] is, asolkenesse, ðe me haueð ðurh mire ȝemeleaste maniȝe siðes beswiken. Hie me haueð imaked heuy and slaw on 24 godes weorkes ðurh idelnesse; hie me haueð ofte idon eten oðer-mannes sare swink all un-of-earned. Ofte hie me haueð idon slæpen ðar ic scolde wakien on godes seruise be daiȝe and be nihte. Swilch hit non oðer bien ne mihte. Ðies awerȝede senne is on of 28 ðe heued-sennes, and hie beswikð mucheles ðe mare ðe me of hire

---

[1] page 1.　　　　　　　　　　　　[2] Evangelista. red at side.
[3] Sanctus Paulus. red at side.　　　[4] haued MS.
[5] The ( ) mean that the letter they enclose is a correction over the line or in the margin.　　　[6] and unbleðeliche on erasure by another hand.
[7] ðat corrected from ðad, the d being crossed red and a red t added.

and it deceives much the more as one takes little heed of it.
That is the end of this sin, that it would that one should take no
heed of oneself, but that he should lead his life in sloth and in
idleness even up to his last day, and that he should therefore be
condemned to the pain of hell. This is sooth, take heed who will!

Of pride.

After this comes another, which is called *superbia*, that is,
pride. It was the beginning of all sins, and it brought the
brightest angel from the height of Heaven down into the depth
of hell. Concerning it is written: *Deus superbis resistit,* ' God
withstands all proud men.' Because all those who will exalt themselves are adversaries of God. God Himself says that they shall
be lowered. Therefore I am low and powerless, because I have
been proud and haughty, and have thought much of myself. Neither
ever hated I this cursed cardinal sin, nor shunned [it] as I should,
but I often did on account of it what God would not. Woe to me
for that ! This same pride, though it has lot and part among all
other sins, nevertheless has one, that is very near to it and very
compliant, which has very often deceived me, that is, *vana gloria,*
vain glory or vain boasting. This makes the man who is deceived
by it, double his sin; just as the man who has slain a man against
God's prohibition, boasts then that he is well avenged on his
enemy; or if he has deceived a maiden, or a rich lady who is
wedded, thereby he thinks all the better of himself, and so becomes
deceived. Because he never wept over this, but still adds more
thereto, that is, if he for his sins goes out of the country to seek
saints, or if he fasts much, or gives alms, then he often boasts,
or does them in such wise, that he has praise thereof and so loses
[the merits of] them. Thereof says the Gospel: *Receperunt mercedem suam,* ' They have received their reward.' These are all who
do any good, and like praise thereof. Think hereof ye that do
your good [deeds] before men ! Some others leave the world
and take the clothes of a religious order, and soon esteem themselves holy, and think unworthily of others. They nevertheless

litel ȝeme nimþ. Þat is þe ænde of ðessere senne, ðat hie wolde
ðat man none ȝieme ne name of him seluen, ac ðat he on slauþhe
and on ydelnesse his lif ladde anon to his ande-daiȝe, and ðat he
herfore wurðe fordemd into helle pine. Ðis is soð, neme ȝeme se 4
ðe wile !

¹ Of modinesse. pride.

H IERAFTER cumþ an oðer, ðe is i-cleped superbia, þat is,
modinesse. Hie was anȝinn of alle sennes, and hie brohte 8
ðane brihteste angel fram ðare heuene heinesse niþer into helle
depnesse. Of hire is ȝewriten : Deus superbis resistit, ' Godd
wiðstant alle modi mannen.' Forðan hie bieð godes wiðerwinen,
alle ðo ðe willen hem seluen heiȝin. Godd seið him self ðat hie 12
sculen bien ineðerede. Hierfore ic am neðer and unmihti, forðan
ic habbe (ȝeben) prud and modi, and michel ilaten of me seluen.
Ne ðese wereȝede heaued-senne ic næure ne hatede ne ne scunede
swa swa ic scolde, ac ofte ich dede ðurh hire ðat ðe godd nolde. 16
Wa me ðas ! Dies ilche modinesse, ðeih hie habbe hlot ² and dale
mang alle oðre senues, naðelæs hie haueð ane, ðe is hire swiðe
neih and swiðe hersum, ðe me haueð swiðe ofte beswiken, þat is,
Vana Gloria, idel wulder ³ oðer idel ȝelp. Dies dieð ðe manne 20
ðe ðurh hire is beswiken ðat he twifealdeð his senne ; alswo ðe
man ðe haueð islaȝe anne mann aȝeanes godes forbode, ðanne ȝelpð
he ðat he is wel iwreken of his unwine ; oðer ȝif he hafð beswiken
an maiden, oðer an riche lafdi ðe is bewedded ⁴, ðar ⁵ of he lat ðe 24
bett of him seluen, and swa he wurð beswiken. For ðan he næure ⁶
ðis ne beweop ⁷, ac ȝet ðar to more he ecð, ðat is, ȝif ⁸ he for his
sennes farð ut of lande halȝen te seken, oðer he michel fast, oðer
almesse doð, ðat he ofte biȝelpð, oðer on swilche wise hes dieð, ðat 28
he herienge ðar of hafð and swa hes forliest. Darof seið ðat godspell : Receperunt mercedem suam, ' Hie habbeð inumen here
lean.' Dat bieð alle ðe ani god doð, and ðar of herienge luuieð.
Ðencheð herof ȝe ðe doð ȝewer god teforen mannen ! Sume oðre 32
forlæteþ ðe world and nimeð ðe cloðes of religiun, and sone hem
seluen healdeð for hali, and unwurð healdeþ of oðre⁹, ðe neure ȝiete

---

¹ *page* 2.   ² loth *MS.*   ³ wu *on erasure.*   ⁴ dd *corrected from* dd.
⁵ r *on erasure.*   ⁶ e *on erasure.*
⁷ *a small red* ð *inserted above between* p *and* a.   ⁸ Gif *MS.*   ⁹ odre *MS.*

[do not repent] their own sins with humility nor with true repentance. Some think well of themselves, if they are of high family,
or if they are of a high office, or if they have some high com-
mand [authority], or if men of the world esteem them holy men;
they forget too much themselves within, and hearken to the idle
works without. Hereof I am conscious myself that this cursed
spirit has made me [such], that I have greatly sinned against my
Lord God Almighty.

*(Here ought to be put ill-will, which this soul seems to forget in
its confession. Envy should not be forgotten, because death entered
the earth through the devil's cunning and ill-will.)*

Of disobedience.

Again, I have much misdone through another sin which is called
inobedientia, that is, disobedience. As the angel was driven out of
the kingdom of Heaven for pride, so was Adam, our forefather, out
of Paradise for this disobedience. For that, he suffered death—and
afterwards, all mankind—and the pain of hell more than five
thousand winters [years], until Christ released him by obedience.
All who see, and read, or hear this, I beg and warn, for the love of
God and for your dear soul, that you hate and shun, above all
things, this cursed sin. For it we shall all suffer death, as those
have done who were before us. It is the key of all the other sins;
no sin can be done but through disobedience. So deeply has God
forbidden us all the cardinal sins, as he did Adam the tree of
Paradise, both by the old law and also by the new one. What shall
I do, wretched soul, that am guilty through disobedience, because
I never have been obedient, neither to God, nor to my spiritual
fathers, nor to my baptism, nor ever yet kept obedience well? But
pray we all our Lord Christ, who was obedient to His Father even

[bieteð] here aȝene sennen mid eadmodnesse ne mid soðre berewsinge.
Sume læteð[1] wel[2] of hem seluen, ȝif hie bieð of heiȝe kenne, oðer[3]
ȝif he bie of heiȝe menstre, oðer ȝif he hafð sum hei obedience, oðer
ȝif menn of ðe world hes healdeð for hali menn; hie[4] forȝiteð to
swiðe hem seluen wið-innen, and harkieð to ðe idele werkes wið
-uten. Her-of ic am becnawe me self ðat ðie[s] iwerȝede gast me
hafð idon, ðat ic am swiðe forȝelt aȝeanes mine laferde god almihtin.

4

8

[The following comment is written at the top of the page.]

(Hic deberet poni inuidia, quam uidetur obliuisci hec
anima in sua confessione. **Nith nere nohutt te forȝeten,**
quia sapientia et inuidia diaboli, mors intrauit in orbem
terre, et cetera.)

12

Of vnbuhsumnesse[5].

GIET ic habbe muchel misdon ðurh ane oðre senne þe is
ȝecleped inobediencia, þat is, unhersumnesse. Al swa ðe
angel was ȝedriuen ut of heuene riche for modinesse, swa was
Adam, ure forme fader, ut of paradise for ðessere unhersumnesse.
For hire he ðolede deað, and seððen all mankenn, and ðe pine of
helle ma ðanne fif ðusend wintre, al hwat Crist him liesde wið
hersumnesse. Alle ðe ðis isieð, and radeð, oðer ȝehiereð, i bidde
and warni, for ðe luue of gode[6] and for ȝuer lieue saule, þat ȝie hatien and scunien, ouer alle þing, ðes awerȝhede senne. For hire
we sculen alle deað þolien, al swo habben idon ðe te-foren us wæren.
Hie is kæie of alle oðre sennes; non senne ne mai bien idon bute
ðurh unhersumnesse. Al swo diepliche hafð godd us forboden
alle heaued-sennes, swo he dede Adame ðe treu of paradise, aiðer
ðurh ðare ealde laȝwe and iec ðurh ðare n(i)ewe. Hwat do ic,
wrecche saule, ðe am forgilt ðurh unhersumnesse, for ði ðat ic[7]
naure hersum ne habbe ibien, ne gode, ne mine gastliche faderes, ne
min cristendom, ne obedience nauerȝiete wel ne h(i)eld ? Ac bidde
we alle ure lauerd Crist, ðe was hersum his fader anon to ðe deaðe[8],

16

20

24

28

32

---

[1] læted MS. [2] page 3. [3] ð on erasure. [4] h on erasure.
[5] Originally vnhersumnesse, h altered to b; uh written above er, er underlined by a different hand. [6] g corr. from d.
[7] ic wrecche saule MS., the last two words underlined. [8] d corr. from ð.

unto death, that, as we lose this short life by disobedience, He will give us might that we may be obedient to Him in all good works even until death, and so may go forth into the eternal life which He has promised us through His mercy.

Of swearing oaths.

Again, here is more of the evil kind of seed, that has often made me forswear God's own name and also His saints, and in many ways to curse myself, or one of my friends whom I helped to swear, and in such wise fancied to help both of us, and brought both of us into much harm. This I did against God's commandment, which says: *Nolite jurare, neque per coelum neque per terram,* 'Do not swear, neither by Heaven nor by earth, nor by any other thing, but yea, yea, nay, nay.' All that we swear more, is evil and sin. Some fancy to be guiltless of this sin, because they are compelled to the oath. Though one compel me to the oath, one does not compel me to forswear, but to say the truth concerning what I am accused of. If I were a true Christian, I would rather suffer the death of the body, than kill the wretched soul so piteously.

Of lying.

Often I have committed another sin, since I could speak, up to this day, that is *mendatium* by name, that is, lying, which has polluted all the offspring of Adam, who could or might speak, save Christ alone, who is rightly called Truth, and Saint Mary, His mother. The same devil is rightly called father of lying, when he said: *Ero similis altissimo,* 'I shall be like the Highest.' This was the first lie that ever was found. There thou liedst, thou false devil! and so thou doest still, concerning all that thou ever promisest. Thou thinkest well to accuse me before God for this sin; but I accuse myself now before God and before all His saints, and forsake thee and all thy leasings. There is nothing more contrary to Christ, who is called Truth, than lying is. Beware who will!

þat, al swo we forlieseð ðis scorte lif ðurh unhersumnesse, ðat he us ʒiue mihte ðat we moten him bien hersum on alle gode [1] woerkes anaon to ðe deaðe, and swa cumeð forð in to ðe eche liue ðe he hafð us behoten ðurh his mil(d)ce.   4

Of oðe(s) [2] sueriingge.

GIET hier is mare of ðe eueles kennes sade, ðe me hafð ofte idon godes aʒwene name forsweren [3] and ec his halʒen, and a manies kennes me seluen to weriʒen, oðer sume of mine friende 8 ðe ic halp to sweriʒen, and on swilche wise wende helpen unc baðe, and brohte unc baðe in to muchele harme. Þis ic dede aʒean godes [4] bebode, ðe seið : Nolite iurare, neque per celum neque per terram, ' Ne sweriʒeð, naiðer ne be heuene ne be ierðe, ne bie 12 nan oðer ðing, bute ia, ia, næi, nai.' Al þat we more sweriʒeð, swo it is euel and senne. Sume weneð bien sacleas of ðessere senne, for ðan ðe me nett hem to ðan aðe. Þeih me niede me to ðan aðe, me ne net me noht te forsweriʒen, ac soð te seggen 16 of ðan ðe ic am bicleped. ʒif ic ware riht cristeneman, ic wolde bliðelicor poliʒen ðas lichames deað, ðanne ic wolde ðe wrecchede saule sa rewliche acwellan.

Of lesinge.   20

OFT ic habbe beuolen an oðer [5] senne, fram ðat ic cuðe speken, ʒiet to ðese daiʒe, ðat is mendatium be name, ðat is, leasinge, ðe all Adames ofspring hafð be-smiten, ðe speken cuðen oðer mihten, wið-uten Crist ane, ðe is mid rihte icleped soðh, and sæinte 24 Marie, his moder. De selue dieuel is icleped mid rihte fader of leasinge, ða ða he sade : Ero similis altissimo, [6] ' Ic scal bien ʒelich ðan heisten.' Ðis was ðe forme leasinge ðe æure was ʒefunde. Dar ðu luʒe, ðu lease dieuel, and swa ðu diest ʒiet, of al 28 ðat tu aure behatst. Ðu me þen(c)st wel to wreiʒen to-fore gode for ðessere senne ; ac ic wreiʒe me nu te-fore gode and teforen alle his halʒen, and te forsake and alle ðine leasinges. Nis nan ðing mare aʒeanes Criste, ðe is icleped soð, ðanne is leasinge. Bie war 32 se ðe wile !

---

[1] page 4.   [2] o corr. above a.   [3] another s inserted over the first r.
[4] ʒodes MS.   [5] oder MS.   [6] page 5.

Of evil backbiting.

Another sin is called *detractio*, which reaves God's love from man's heart, that is, evil backbiting. It has often made me guilty against God's prohibition, that forbids me all evil speeches, and reproves me thus: *Sedens adversus fratrem tuum loquebaris,* ' Thou satst,' He said, ' over against thy brother, and both of you each day cry to Me, who am your Father, and say: *pater noster.* Before him thou spokest good, behind him evil, so that he did not hear it. Thus thou didst, and I was still; and therefore thou thoughtst that I was like thee, that it pleased Me as it did thee. But thou shalt stand before Me on Doomsday, and before all mankind, where I shall reprove thee with the same words which thou often hast heard in order to warn thee, and thus say: *Dilexisti malitiam super benignitatem.* That is: ' Thou lovedst evil more than good, to speak unrighteousness more than righteousness; therefore God Almighty shall destroy thee, both body and soul. Go away from Me, thou cursed, forth with the devil!' Who is there that is not adread of this great thunderclap that comes out of God's own mouth? Take heed who will! How great danger it is to break God's prohibition!

Of deceit.

Again, I have committed more bad practices. I have deceived my fellow-Christian with fair words which I have spoken unto him, and have shown him otherwise by my works, and have often promised him upon my word of honour, what I never afterwards accomplished for him. If I bought from him or sold him any-thing, it was always more preferable to me, that I should gain and he lose, than that our bargain should be given up. God for-bids us to have twofold weights or twofold measures, but [bids us] give and lend joyfully, without earthly meed, to all that have need and beseech us, for His love, for the same goods that He has lent us. Sooth to say, I do not know whether I ever yet did any-thing that I would not have some kind of reward thereof, either

Of heuele [1] bafte(s)pache.

DETRACTIO hatte an oðer senne, ðe reaueð godes luue of
mannes hierte, ðat is, euel bafte-spache. Hie me haueð ofte
ȝemaked forȝielt aȝeanes godes forbode, ðe me forbett alle euele 4
spaches, *and* ðus me undernemð: Sedens aduersus fratrem
tuum loquebaris, 'Ðu sate,' (he seið), 'aȝeanes ðine broðer,
ðe ælche dai baðe clepieð to me, ðe am ȝure fader, *and* seggeð:
pater noster. Aȝeanes him ðu spake (god), bafte him euele, þat 8
he it ne herde. Ðus ðu dedest, *and* ic was stille; *and* for ði ðu
wendest þat ic ðe ware ilich, *þat* hit likede me swa swa hit dede
ðe. Ac ðu scalt stonden tefore me a domesdaiȝe, *and* teforen all
mankenne, ðar ic ðe scal undernemen mid ða ilche wordes ðe ðu 12
ofte hafst ȝeherd for ðe te warnien, *and* ðus cweðen: Dilexisti
maliciam super benignitatem. Ðat is: 'Ðu luuedest euelnesse
mare ðanne godnesse, unrihtwisnesse more to spekene ðanne rihtwisnesse; for ði ðe scal god almihti [2] forliesen, baðe lichame *and* 16
saule. Ga awei fram me, ðu ȝewereȝede, forð mid te dieule!'
Hwa is ðat nis ofdradd of ðese mu-[3]chele ðþunresleiȝ [4] ðe cumþ
ut of godes auȝene muðe? Nime ȝieme se ðe wile! Hu michel
haht hit is godes forbod te brekene! 20

Of swicedome.

GIET ich habbe ma vnðeawes beuolen. Ic habbe beswiken
min emcristen mid faire wordes ðe ic to him habbe ȝespeken,
and oðerlicor mid weorkes him ȝekydd, *and* uppe mine lahfulnesse 24
ofte him behet, þat ic næure eft him neȝelæste. Gif ich at him
ani þing bouhte oðer him sealde, æure me was leuere þat ic biȝate
and he forlure, ðanne unker chepinge bileafde. Godd us forbett
ðat we ne sculen habbe twifeald wæiȝe ne twifeald imett, ac ðat 28
we sculen bliðeliche ȝiuen *and* leanen, wið-uten erðliche mede, alle
ðe niede habbeð *and* us for his luue besecheð of ðan ilche gode ðe
he us hafð ilænd. Soþ to seggen, ic not ȝif ich [5] auerȝete ani ðing
dede ðat ic nolde habbe sumes kennes (lean), oðer [6] of ðouhtes 32

---

[1] *The first* e *corrected above* u. [2] almihtin *MS.* [3] *page* 6.
[4] a ç *above* re. [5] ich *corrected over* hit.
[6] *Before* oðer *is* ðer *of underdotted, behind it one word erased.*

of thoughts or of words or of works; and if I had not, methought
that it was not well bestowed, when I had done it.

Of cursing.

Again, we find that the apostle says: *Maledici regnum Dei non
possidebunt*, that is, ' The cursing men, who so blithely will curse,
they never may dwell in the kingdom of Heaven,' because they
curse God's handiwork, that He has blessed.   Hereof I am guilty,
and acknowledge that I have cursed, both clerics and laymen, relations and strangers, and many things which I should not curse.

Of impatience.

Another sin is named *impatientia*, that is, unbearingness [im-
patience].   It seizes the man whom it overpowers, that he may not
control himself neither in thoughts, nor in words, nor in works.
So it has done me always too oft.   Through it I am guilty against
God, who gave me example, first of Himself, and afterwards
with holy words instructed me : *Qui te percusserit in maxillam,
praebe ei et aliam*, ' Who smites thee under the ear, turn to him the
other,' He said, ' and do good for evil.   If he cursed thee, do thou
bless him.'   This I never did ; but if my Lord God would chastise
me with any rod, as a father does his son, I was impatient at it, and
both thought and said : ' Why should such mishaps come to me ? Many
another was there who had misdone more, and no mishap came,
but he had all bliss and rest enough.'   Therefore said God Almighty
of me and my like : *Et dimisi eos secundum desideria cordis eorum*,
' I let them [go],' He says, ' after their own will ; after what their
heart lusted, I followed them.'

Of self-will.

Through this sin I, unhappy soul, fell into another sin, which is
called *propria voluntas*, that is, self-will.   Certainly, God has rejected that same man who omits to do God's and his spiritual fathers'

oðer of wordes oðer of weorkes; *and* ȝif ic nadde, me ðuhte þat hit
nas naht [1] wel betowen, ðar ic hit idon hadde.

Of werȝhinde.

EFT we findeð ðat ðe apostel seið: Maledici [2] rengnum dei 4
non possidebunt, ðat bieð: ' Ða werȝinde menn, ðe swa
bleðeliche willeð werȝien, þat hie naure on heuenriche wuniȝen ne
muȝen,' for ði ðat hie werȝieð godes handiwerc, ðe he hafð iblesced. Herof ic am sceldi, *and* wel am becnawe ðat ic ȝewerȝed 8
habbe aiðer ȝe hodede ȝe leawede, sibbe *and* framde, *and* mani þing
ðe ic werȝi ne scolde.

Of vnðolemodnesse.

INPACIENCIA hatte an oðer senne [3], þat is, unþolemodnesse. Hie 12
benemð ðe manne [4] ðe hie ouermai, ðat he ne mai wealden
him seluen ne a þouhtes, ne on wordes, ne on weorkes. Swa hie
haueð me idon aure to ofte. Þurh hire ic am forȝelt aȝeanes gode,
ðe me forbisne ȝaf, arst of him seluen, *and* seððen mid haliȝe wordes 16
me wissede: Qui te percusserit in maxillam, (prebe [5]) ei *et*
aliam, ' Se ðe smit under ða eare, want to ðat oðer,' he sade, ' *and*
do god aȝean euel. Gif he ðe wereȝede [6], ðu hine blesci.' Ðis ne
dede ic næure; ac ȝif min lauerd godd me wolde swingen mid ani 20
swinge [7], al swa fader doð [8] his sune, ic was ðar aȝean unþolemod,
and aiðer ðohte *and* ec sæide: ' Hwi me scolde cumen swilche un-
ȝelimpes ? Mani oðer was ðe more hafde misdon, *and* non unȝe-
limp ne cam, ac hadde alle blisse *and* reste inowh.' For ði saide 24
god almihti [9] be me *and* be mine i-liche [10]: *Et* dimisi eos secundum desideria [11] cordis eorum, ' Ich hem let,' he seið, ' after
here awene wille; after ðan ðe here herte leste, ic hem folȝede.'

Of aȝen-wille.   28

DURH ðessere senne ic, unȝesali saule, fel in to an oðer senne,
ðe is icleped propria voluntas, þat is, auȝen-wille. Ȝewiss
hafð godd forworpen ðan ilche mann ðe lat godes (wille) *and* his

---

[1] *Corrected from* naltt.   [2] ditci *or* dicci *MS.*   [3] sennne *MS.*   [4] *page* 7.
[5] *Added over the line and twice at side.*   [6] d *barred red ; and* ðu *MS.*
[7] swinke *MS.*   [8] *Corrected from* deð.   [9] almihtin *MS.*
[10] *an erasure between* i *and* l.   [11] s *on erasure.*

will, unless He again through His great mercy take it [this sin] away from him, before he goes out of this life. No creature that is rational, as are angels and men, ought to have their self-will, because they are not, nor ever can be, righteous nor good, save they follow God's will in all ways. Therefore we find in the holy Writ : ' The man that will follow his self-will, he is hostile to God, as is the man who is hostile to the king and wishes to deprive him of his crown.' Christ Himself says in His Gospel : *Non veni facere voluntatem meam,* ' I came not to give you an example of doing My own will, but I came in order to do My Father's will.' When Christ was born, the angels of Heaven came and sang that precious song, *Gloria in excelsis Deo,* and proclaimed peace to all those men who have good will, that is, to none but those who love and follow God's will. Alas and well-a-day, that I have followed my own self-will, so that I have to suffer for my obstinacy evermore, except God's holy mercy deliver me !

Of unrighteousness.

Another sin is called unrighteousness, which has ever too long deceived me with its treacherous vices. It is always against righteousness, because no man can be saved, except he be righteous and not twofold [double-faced], neither in speeches nor in deeds. Other have I been than I have shown myself. Men see me outside. I and my like, we are on the outside like the dead man's tomb, that without is whited, and within is stinking and full of worms. So have I been full of evil thoughts. Woe to me for this ! *Mea culpa !* Because I have not had right belief, nor fast hope, nor true love to our Lord God as I should, therefore I have been unmighty and un-strong against all these foresaid sins. I cannot number nor tell all the sins, nor all the vices, nor all the wonders that I, wretched sinful one, have done and committed, since I first could sin. But of Him who alone knows them, the Almighty God, I beg mercy and forgiveness.

gastliche faderes (wille[1]) to donne, bute he eft ðurh his muchele
mildce hes him benime, ær ðane he of ðese liue fare. Non scafte ðe is
scadwis, al swo bieð angles *and* menn, ne aȝeð te hauen here aȝen
-will, forðan hie ne bieð, ne ne muȝen bien, næure riht-wise ne gode, 4
bute hie folȝin godes wille *on* alle[2] wisen. Forðan we findeð on
hali write: 'Se ma*nn* ðe wile folȝin his aȝen wille, he is aȝeanes
gode, alswa is ðe mann ðe is aȝeanes ðe kinge *and* wile his
curune him benemen.' Crist self seið on his godspelle : Non 8
ueni facere uoluntatem meam, 'Ne cam ic noht te ȝiuen ȝew
for-[3]bisne of mire aȝene wille to donne, ac i cam for to donne mines
fader wille.' Ða ðe Crist was ȝeboren, ða comen ða aingles of
heuene *and* sunge ðane derewurðe sang, Gloria in exselsis deo, 12
and bodeden sibsumnesse to[4] alle ðo mannen ðe god wille habbeð,
ðat nis non bute ðo ðe godes wille luuieð *and* folȝið. Weilawei
and walawa, ðat ic min aȝen iwill swa habbe ifolȝed, ðat im min
unȝewill awh aure ma te poliȝen, bute godes hali mildse me aliese[5]! 16

Of hunrihtwisnesse.

UNRIHTWISNESSE hatte an oðer senne, ðe me haueð æure to
longe ȝedweld mid hire swikele unðeawes. Hie is æure aȝean
rihtwisnesse, forðan no man ne mai bien ȝeborȝwen, bute he bie 20
rihtwis and naht twifeald, ne on speches ne on dades. Oðer ic
habbe ibie*n* ðanne ic habbe me i-sceawed. Me*nn* me isieð wiðute*n*.
Ic *and* mine iliche, we beoð wiðuten al swa ðe deade man[n]es þruh,
þe is wiðuten ihwited, *and* wið-inne stinkende[6] *and* full of wermes. 24
Swa ic habbe ibie*n* full of euele þohtes. Wa me þas! Mea
culpa!

Forði ðat ich nabbe ihafd rihte ileaue, ne faste hope, ne soðe
luue to ure lauerde gode swa swa ic scolde, forði ic haue bien 28
unmihti and unstrong onȝeanes alle þese forenam*m*de sennes. Ic
ne mai rime*n* ne tellen alle ðo sennes, ne alle ðo unðeawes, ne alle
ðo wundren ðe ich, wrecche senfulle, habbe idon *and* beuolen,
seðð*en* ic arst mihte seneȝin. Ac him ðe hes one wat, almihti 32
god, ic bidde are *and* forȝiu[en]esse.

---

[1] *Added over the line and at side.*   [2] *Corrected from* allt.   [3] *page 8.*
[4] *Corrected from* do.   [5] *es corr. from* ss.   [6] *de corr. from* dr.

Of the five senses.

Again, my heart accuses me of the five senses that God assigned me to look after my wretched body, that is, *visus, auditus, gustus, odoratus, et tactus;* that is, sight, hearing, taste, and smell, and touch. These five senses, betoken the five golden Bezants [talents] which the Lord entrusted to his thrall in order to gain therewith. So did the good servant that gained five others. Therefore his Lord said to him : ' Well then, good servant ! Over little things thou wast true ; over great things I shall set thee. Go into thy Lord's bliss !' This I have not earned, that have done no good with the same Bezants of the five senses, but through them and through my carelessness I have lost my Lord's property. Each day messengers come into my thoughts that I shall soon come before Him, and give Him answer, what I have done with His property. He will have it well coined, and by right weight well weighed, and of well refined gold ; and except I have this, in those days when He sends after me, I shall hear rueful tidings. ' Answer Me now, thou unhappy soul,' He will say, ' what hast thou so long done in the world ? A long respite I gave thee well to do if thou wouldst, and little good thou hast gotten with the five Bezants of the five senses I entrusted to thee. More than five thousand Bezants of good thoughts, and of good words, and of good works, thou mightst have gained if thou wouldst, in the long space I gave thee ; but thou, poor soul, wouldst not think of thy departure, when thou shouldst separate thyself from thy body, and come before Me, and answer Me for all thy deeds.' Then He calls His tormentors, and bids them take me, and bind me, both hands and feet, and throw me into the uttermost darkness. The inmost darkness is in the heart which will not foreshow whither he shall go when he goes hence. The uttermost is the darkness of hell, where never yet light came, save those nights when Christ's soul came therein after His chosen ones. But always there is weeping and wailing through the great heat

Of ðа fif wittes.

GIET me wreið min herte of ða fif wittes ðe god me (be)tahte
to lokin of mine wrecche[1] lichame, þat is[2], visus, audit*us*,
gust*us*, odorat*us*, *et* tact*us*, þat is, ȝesihthe, ȝeherhþe, smac, *and* 4
smell, *and* tactþe.   Das fif wittes, hie tacniþ ða fif gildenene besantes ðe ðe hlauerd betahte his þralle (for)[3] to biȝeten ðar mide.
Swa dede ðe gode þrall ðe biȝatt oðer fif.   For ði his hlauerd him
sede : 'Wel ðe, gode ðrall !   Ouer litel þing ðu ware trewe ; ouer 8
michel þing ic ðe scal setten.   Ga in to ðine lauerdes blisse !'   Þis
ne habbe ic nauht[4] ofearned, ðe no god ne habbe idon mid ðo
ilke besantes of ðe fif wittes, ac ðurh hem and þurh mine ȝemeleaste ic habbe mines lauerdes eihte forloren.   Ælche dai me 12
cumeð sonden on mine þohtes þat ic scall neuliche cume*n* te-foren
him, *and* ȝiue*n* him and-sware, hwat ic habbe mid his eihte ȝed*on*.
He wile hes habben wel imotet[5], *and* bi rihte wæiȝe wel i-wæiȝen,
and wel imered gold ; *and* bute ich þis habbe, ðas daiȝes ðe he after 16
me sant, ic scal iheren reuliche tidinge.   'Andswere me nu, þu
un-ȝesælie saule,' he wile seggen, 'hwat hafst ðu swa lange ido*n*
on ðare woreld ?   La[n]gne first ic ðe ȝaf wel to donne ȝif ðu
woldest, *and* litel god ðu hafst biȝeten mid ða fif besantes of ðe 2ɔ
fif gewittes ðe ic þe betahte.   Mo ðanne fif ðusende besantes of
gode þohtes, *and* of gode wordes, *and* of[6] gode woerkes, ðu mihtest
habben biȝeten, ȝif ðu woldest, on ða lange firste ðe ic ðe ȝaf ; ac ðu,
earme saule, noldest þenchen of ðine for(ð)siðe, þat tu fram ðine 24
lichame[7] scoldest skelie*n*, *and* tefore me cume*n*, *and* me andswerie*n*
of[8] alle ðine dades.'   Ðanne çlepeð he his pinères, *and* hat he*m* me
nemen, *and* binden me, baðe han[8]-den *and* fiet, *and* werpen me in ðe
uttreste þiesterneƨƨe.   Þe inreste[9] þesternesse[10] (is) in[11] ðare hierte 28
ðe ne wile forsceawin h(w)ider[12] he scal ðanne he henen farð.   Þe
uttreste (i)s[13] se þiesternesse of helle, ðar næure ȝiete liht ne cam,
bute ðas nihtes ðe Cristes saule ðar inne cam after his ȝekorene.
Ac æure ðar is wop *and* woninge for ðare michele hæte *and* unȝe- 3ɔ

---

[1] *The under dotted letters are scarcely legible.*   [2] *page 9.*   [3] *On the margin.*
[4] nauth *MS.*   [5] *So has the MS.*   [6] os *MS., the f not being crossed.*
[7] *Only* li . . . me *still legible.*   [8] *page 10.*
[9] *The final* e *on erasure and an* s *erased behind it.*   [10] *On erasure.*
[11] i *corrected into* ñ.   [12] w *red above the line.*   [13] s *corr. from* i.

and immeasurable burning, and there is gnashing of teeth through
the immeasurable chill ; and there is sorrow and pain through the
great despair that comes at the thought that they never more shall see
God nor one of His saints, nor relation or strangers who will be saved,
but evermore shall dwell with the awful devils, who are so loathsome and so grisly to look at, that if a man now saw one just as he
is in his proper shape, he would soon be out of his wit, and endure
this [madness] evermore without end.   I cannot think, nor say with
mouth, nor write in a book, all the pains of hell. Woe to them that
they ever were created, who deserve these pains! Understand, all who
read or hear this, and have wit to understand, God's great forbearance
towards us in this life, how He admonishes us each day, and says to
us : *Convertimini ad me, et agite poenitentiam,* ' Turn to Me,' He
says, ' ye that are turned away from Me, through the devil's lore,
take and do penance, each after what his sin is ; and speed,
because your end-day is near, and comes unawares as a thief by
night. Fast, and keep vigil, and turn from evil, and do good, weep
and wail, sigh and yearningly beg mercy and forgiveness, the
little while we dwell here. Because, unless ye earn it here, mercy
will never betide you elsewhere.' Those who will not listen to nor
observe these, God's holy words, listen to what the Holy Ghost says
through the prophet David : *Maledicti qui declinant a mandatis
tuis, Domine,* ' Cursed be all they, Lord, who will not hold Thy
commandments!' Those who are not adread of this awful cursing,
that all ordained each day curse the while they sing God's praise
at prime, listen to another cursing that comes out of God's own
mouth, because this curse is nothing but an earnest of the last
[curse], when God shall say Himself with much awe : *Discedite a
me, maledicti, in ignem æternum,* ' Go away from Me, ye cursed by
all ordained heads, into everlasting fire, ye that would not listen
to My counsel, nor love My commandments, nor hold them. Be
gone away from Me, forth with the devils, where ye never more
again shall see Me !' All ye that have Christ's charity, that is, God's

mæte brene [1], *and* ðar is chiueringe of toðen for ðe unmate chele ;
and ðar is sorwȝe *and* sarinesse for ðare muchele ortrewnesse ðe
cumþ of ðan ȝeþanke ðe hie næure mo godd [2] ne sculen isien ne nan
of his halȝen, ne sibbe ne framde ðe iborȝen sculen bien, ac aure [4]
ma wunien mid ða eifulle dieulen, ðe bieð swa laðliche *and* swo
grislich [3] an to lokin, ðat ȝif a mann iseiȝe nu anne [4] al swilch al
se he is on his ȝekynde, he scolde sone bien ut of his iwitte, *and*
ðis þoliȝen æure ma wið-uten ande. Ne mai ic þenchen, ne mid [8]
muðe seggen, ne on boke write, alle ðo pinen of helle. Wa hem
ðatt h(i)e æure iscapene waren, ðe ðo pinen of-earniþ ! Vnder-
standeþ, alle ðe ðis radeþ oðer ihereð, *and* witt habbeð to understonden, þe muchele ðolemodnesse of us on ðeſe liue, hv godd us [12]
meneȝeð alche dai, *and* to us seið : Conuertimini ad me, *et*
agite penitenciam, 'Wandeð to me,' he seið, 'ȝie ðe berð iwant
fram me, ðurh dieules lare, *and* nemeð *and* doð scrift [5], [æll]ch after
ðat his senne is ; *and* spedeð ȝeu, forðan ȝure ænde-dai neihȝeð, *and* [16]
cumð unȝewares al swa þief be nihte. Fasteð *and* wakieð *and*
buȝeð fram euele *and* doð god, we[p]eð [6] *and* wanið, sihteþ *and*
ȝeorne biddeð are *and* forȝiuenesse, ða litle hwile ðe we her
wuniȝið. For-ðan, bute ȝif ȝe [7] hier (hit) ne of-earniȝeð, ne [20]
wurþ ȝeu næure milce elleshwar.' Ða ðe nelleð ðese godes hali
(wordes) hlesten ne healden, harkið hwat ſe haligast seið ðurh ðe
profiete Dauið : Maledicti qui declinant a mandatis tuis,
domine, 'ȝewerwed bien hie, lauerd [8], alle ðe ðine behode healden [24]
nelleð.' Ða ðe ne bieð ofdrad of ðessere eisliche werȝinge, ðe
alle hadede [9] ællche dai werȝið ðar hwile ðe h(i)e singeð godes
lofsang at prime, harkieð an oðer wariȝing ðe cumþ ut of godes
awene muþe, forðan ðes werȝinge nis bute erres of ðare laczste, [28]
ðanne god seið him self mid muchele eiȝe : Discedite a me, maledicti, in ignem eternum, 'Gað aweiȝ fram me, ȝie iwerȝede of
alle hadede hafde, in to ðan eche fiere, ȝie ðe nolden mine rad
hlesten, ne mine bebode luuien ne healden. Witeð awei fram me, [32]
forð mid ða dieulen, ðar ȝie naure ma eft me ne ȝesien !' Alle
ðe habbeð Cristes kariteð, ðat is, godes luue *and* mannes, wepeð

---

[1] n *written over a blotted-out letter.*   [2] gode *MS.*   [3] e *erased after* h.
[4] añne *MS.*   [5] *The following three or four letters are totally destroyed.*
[6] w *half,* p *totally destroyed.*   [7] *page* 11.   [8] l *corrected from* h.
[9] i *scratched out before* h.

and man's love, weep and wail ever with me, and let us try to cool God's wrath with tears, which are very agreeable to Him with other sacrifices of bitter sorrow ! He who knows all things knows that they sorely pain me. To you I cry also who are dwelling in fellowship with the Lord God, and to our Lady St. Mary. Mother of mercy, I beg thee, through thy great mercy, that thou beseech for me forgiveness of my sins of Jesus Christ, thy dear son, that has might to forgive all sins, through the same love He has to my kind which He had from thee without a .... thereof has given as lot and part His flesh and His blood, through which I believe firmly that I should have mercy and pity, if I received it as worthily, as it was worthy. To all the saints who here were born in this life, and now are dwelling with our Lord God, I cry and beg through the great charity that is in you, that ye think of us who are here in this wretched life, where the way is slippery, and we are easy to fell, and where many foes are, before and behind and on each side. We thank God and praise Him after our might, who has brought you out of this great wretchedness. Pray ye that we may come to you, not through our deserving, but through God's great mercy and through your [merits]. So truly as He had mercy and pity on you, and sent you the gift of the Holy Ghost without merits, as truly may He have mercy and pity on us, who are His handiwork as well as you, and may grant us that we may, with your help and with His holy grace, so lead here this short life, that we may ever abide with you in bliss, and evermore love Him and praise Him in eternity. Amen.

Now, dear friend, thou that raisedst me, sinful soul, from death, [and] through God's grace instructedst and warnedst [me] to do well, —may God requite thee !—and taughtst me to be conscious of my sins, now thou hast heard [by] my bemoaning that I am so very guilty: for the love of God I beseech thee that thou teachest me still, in what wise I might best be reconciled to my Saviour Christ,

and wanieð forð mid me, *and* fondie we te kelien gode(s) wraððe
mid teares, ðe him bieð swiðe icueme mid oðre loke [1] of sare birewnesse! He hit wat ðe wat alle þing, ðat sare hie me reweð. To
ȝeu ic clepiȝe iec ðe bieð wuniȝende mid ȝemaneliche hlauerde gode, 4
[and] to ure lafdi sainte Marie. Moder of mildcę [2], ðę ic bidde, for ðine
muchele mildze, ðat tu me besieke [3] forȝiuenesse of mine sennes
to Iesu Criste, þine lieue sune, ðe hafð [4] mihte te forgiuene alle
sennes, for ðare ilke luue ðe he hafð [5] to mine ikynde ðe he nam of 8
ðe wið-uten a [6] . . . . ðarof iȝiuen hafð lott *and* dale, his flesc
and his blod, ðurh hwan ich [7] ilieue fastliche are *and* mildze to
habben, ȝif ic hit swa wurðliche underfenge, swa hit wurðe wære.
To alle ðo halȝen ðe hier on liue waren iboren, *and* nu mid ure 12
lauerde gode wuniȝende bieð, ic clepie *and* bidde for ðo muchele
kariteð ðe is an ȝeu, ðat ȝie ðenchen an us ðe bieð hier on ðese
arme [8] liue, ðar ðe wei is slider *and* we lihtliche to fællen, and
fele unwines, teforen *and* baften *and* on alche side. We ðankieð 16
gode *and* herieð after ure mihte, ðe ȝew haueð of ðessere (michele)
wrecchade ibroht [9]. Biddeþ ðat we moten to ȝew cumen, naht for
ure earninge, ac for godes muchele mildce *and* for ȝewer! Al swa
soðliche swa he hadde are *and* mildze of ȝeu [10], *and* ða giue of ðe 20
hali gaste ȝew sænte wiðuten earninge, sa soðliche habbe he are
and mildce of us, ðe bieð his handeweorc al swa ȝie, *and* us unne
ðat we moten, mid ȝeure helpe *and* mid his hali grace, swa ðis
scorte lif her laden, ðat we moten forð mid ȝew on blisse wuniȝen, 24
and him eure ma luuien *and* herien on ecnesse. Amen.

NV, lieue friend, ðu ðe me, senfulle saule, aweihtest of deaðe,
ðurh godes grace wissedest *and* warnedest wel te donne,
—ȝielde þe godd!—and lardest ðat ic scolde bien icnawe of mine 28
sennes, nu ðu hafst iherd mine bemone þat ich am swa swiðe forȝelt [11]: for ðe luue of gode ic ðe besieche ðat [tu] [12] me wissi ȝiet, an
hwælche wise ic mihte betst sahtlin wið mine halend Criste, ðe

---

[1] ðe—bieð and icueme—loke *repeated, but this time is written* icweme *and*
lake.　　　[2] *cp. page* 17, *note* [1].　　　[3] b *and* k *not distinct.*
[4] lieue : : : : : h : fð *(scarcely visible).*
[5] *Only* ilke...he h...ð *clear.*　　　[6] *Half a line illegible*　　　[7] *page* 12.
[8] *A letter before a scratched out.*　　　[9] *Corrected from* ibroltt.
[10] *Corrected from* ȝeli.　　　[11] *Corrected from* fortelt.　　　[12] *Erased.*

whom I chose as Lord through His own mercy, if I sinful might
have mercy in this short time.   And I will blithely listen to thy
counsel, and all the more blithely, if thou wouldst show me thy
unknown name.

How Reason answers and says to the soul.

Almighty God be thanked that thou so well understandest
thyself! *Haec mutatio dextrae excelsi,* 'This turning is truly through
God's right hand.'   Now as thou wilt so eagerly know my name,
I will tell thee forsooth.   I am a gleam of God's face that was
shaped in thee, dear, dear soul, *Ratio* by name, that is, Discernment.
I left thee, because thou followedst more thy self-will than thou
didst my counsel.   When I went from thee, then went forth with
me the same good will and that good mind which God had shaped
in thee, all three of us after His own likeness to help thee.   Then
thou couldst do no good nor any of the holy virtues that God
had shaped to help thee.   They all went away from thee, because
thou followedst thy self-will and leftst God's own likeness.   Thus
the devil betrays many other souls that prefer to follow their
bodies' will, than to learn God's lore or follow it.   When the
cursed spirits saw that thou wast naked and helpless, they spoke
between themselves and said : 'Let us go to this idle and empty
soul, since it has let discernment go from it, and follows the will
of its flesh.   It desires all that we desire.   Let us keep together
with it against all the holy virtues that ever strive against us!'
Afterwards came to thee the cursed spirits of greed, of drunken-
ness, of lechery, of covetousness, and many others, all too many, and
have ruled thee after their own will in their thraldom ever too
long.   Now as thou hast forsaken them through God's grace, now
is great need to thee that thou understandest with sharp wit what
these virtues are, which can shield thee from these cursed
spirits, and with God's help and with theirs may bring thee

ihc cheas to lauerde ðurh his awene mildce, ʒif[1] ic senfulle are
mihte habben on ðese scorte timę. *And* įç bliðeliche ðine rad
wile hlesten, *and* micheles ðe bliðe[2]-liker, ʒif ðu me ðin uncuðe
name[3] woldest kyðen.   4

Hu andswereð Ratio *and* syeð to þare saule.

ALLMIHTI godd bie ʒeþanked ðat tu swa wel understan(c)st ðe
seluen! H*ec* m*u*tac*io* dext*ere* excelsi, 'Ðies wændinge
is iwi(s) ðurh godes swiðere hand.' Nu ðu[4] wilt mine name swa 8
ʒiernliche witen, soð ic ðe wile seggen. Ic am an leme of godes
anlicnesse ðe was iscapen on ðe, lieue, lieue[5] saule, R a c i o be name,
þat is, scadwisnesse. Ic ðe forliet, for(ðan[6]) ðu folʒedest mare ðin
aʒen iwill ðanne ðu dedest mine rad. Ða ðe ic wænte fram ðe, 12.
ða[7] wente forð mid me ðe ilche gode wille *and* ðat gode imiend
ðe godd hafde iscapen on ðe, us alle ðrie after his aʒen anlicnesse
ðe to helpe. Ða ne mihtest ðu nan god don ne nan of ðe hali
mihtes ðe godd hadde iscapen ðe to helpen. Alle hie wanten awei 16
fram ðe, for ðan ðe ðu folʒedest ðin aʒen(e) wille *and* forliete
godes an(ʒ)ene anlicnesse. Ðus beswikð ðe deuel maniʒe oðre
saules ðe willeð folʒin bleðelicher here lichames wille, ðanne hie
willen godes lare liernin oðer folʒin. Ða ðe werewede gastes 20
iseiʒen ðat ðu naked ware *and* helpleas, ða spaken hie hem be-
twienen *and* seiden: 'Wuten we fare te ðessere idele saule *and*
amti, seððen hie hafð forlaten scadwisnesse fram hire, *and* folʒeð
hire flesches wille. All hie wile ðat we willeð. Healde we forð 24
mid hire aʒeanes alle ðe hali mihtes ðe æure winneð aʒeanes us!'
Seððen comen[8] to ðe ða werʒede gastes of giuernesse, of drunkenesse,
of galnesse, of ʒitsinge, *and* manie oðre, alles to fele, *and* þe habbeð
iwelt after here aʒene wille on here þewdome æure to longe. Nu 28
ðurh godes grace þu hes hafst forsaken, nu is þe michel nied þat
ðu understande mid scarpe witte hwat hie bien, þese mihtes, ðe
ðie muʒen scilden fram ðese ʒewerʒede gaste(s), *and* mid godes
fultume *and* mid here ðe muʒen bringen ham to ðin earde, ðar ðu 32

---

[1] Gif *MS.*   [2] *page* 13.   [3] name me *MS.*   [4] ð *corrected from* w.
[5] li *looks like* k.   [6] *On the margin.*   [7] ð *corr. from* o.   [8] *page* 14.

home to thy land, whereto thou wast shaped. And know that forsooth, without them thou wilt never come there! This too few souls ever understand, and therefore they often are bereft of many good things, and in the end often deceived.

Of right belief.

One holy virtue is called *fides recta*, that is, right belief. It is the beginning of all Christianity, it can earn much happiness from our Lord God, because it believes what it never saw. Therefore said Christ: 'Blessed are the men who believe in Me and never saw Me!' This holy virtue makes thee believe that Father and Son and Holy Ghost are called one true Almighty God in three persons, and in oneness ever honoured with the Holy Trinity. Thou shalt believe that the Father is unbegotten, the Son begotten by the Father, as His Wisdom, in Heaven without mother, and on earth without father. The Holy Ghost comes from both of them, as the Love of both of them. These three are even in age and in wisdom, and in goodness and in strength, and in every wise after their godhead. This I believe. This one true God, He is without beginning in Himself, even although He is the beginning of all things which are shaped. So much He loved mankind, that He sent His own Son, who took our kind in soul and in body without sin, and is both true God and true man. He took this manhood as He who was God's Wisdom, very wonderfully from St. Mary the holy virgin, through the Holy Ghost. Through His manhood He suffered death, and through His godhead He arose from death, and ascended into Heaven, and sitteth on His Father's right hand, whence He shall come on Doomsday to judge all mankind. *Qui bona egerunt ibunt in vitam aeternam, qui vero mala in ignem aeternum.* 'Then shall they all who have done good go into eternal life, and they that have done evil and not atoned, they shall go into eternal fire.' If thou wilt be sure of right faith, confess with St. Peter: 'Thou art the Christ, the Son of the living God,' and hearken what He to gescapen were[1]. *And* ðat wite ðu to soþe, wið-uten hem ne cumst ðu ðar naure! Ðis understandeþ auer to feawe saules, *and* for ði hie bieð ofte bireaued of maniȝe gode, *and* at ten ænde ofte beswiken.

4

Of rihte ȝeleaue.

AN hali mihte is icleped fides recta, *þat* is, rihte ȝeleaue. Hie is anginn of alle cristendome, hie mai michele eadinesse of-earnin at ure lauerde gode, for ðan ðe hie iliefð ðat hie næure 8 niseih. For ði sade Crist: 'Eadi bieð ða menn ðe on me belieuen *and* næure me ne seiȝen !' Ðis hali mihte ðe dieð ilieuen ðat fader *and* sune *and* hali gast is an soþ almihti godd on þrie hades inammned, *and* an annesse ȝewurðed forð mid ðare hali ðrinnesse. 12 Ðu scalt ilieuen þat þe fader is un-akenned, ðe sune of ðe fader akenned, al swa hiswisedom, on heuene wið-uten moder, *and* on ierðe wið-uten fader. Þe hali gast, he cumþ forþ of hem bam, al swa here beire luue. Ðese ðrie bieþ emliche on ielde [2] *and* on 16 wisdome, *and* on godnesse *and* on strengþe, *and* on alles kennes wisen after here godd-[3]cundnesse. Ðis ic ilieue. Ðies an soð godd, he is wiðuten anginne on him seluen, *and* þeih he is anginn of alle ðing ðe iscapene bieð. Swa muchel he luuede mannkynn, 20 þat he his awene sune sænte, ðe nam ure ȝekynde on saule *and* on lichame wið-uten sennen, *and* is baðe soð godd *and* soð mann. Ðese manniscnesse he nam alswo he ðe was godes wisdom, swiðe selcuð-liche of sainte Marie ðe hali maiden, ðurh ðe hali gaste. Ðurh his 24 mannisnesse he þolede deað, *and* ðurh his goddcundnesse he aras of deaðe, *and* steih in to heuene, and sitt on his fader swiðre, ðanen he cumþ a domesdai al mann-kenn to demen. (Qui bona egerunt ibunt in uitam eternam, qui uero mala in ignem eternum[4]). 28 'Ðanne sculen hi alle ðe god habbeð idon to ðan [5] eche liue, *and* þo ðe euele habbeð idon *and* naht ibett, he sculen in to ðan eche fiere.' Gif ðu wilt bien siker of [6] rihte ileaue, ðane sei ðu forð mid seinte Petre: Tu es Chrīstus [7], filius (dei uiui)[4], *and* harke hwat 32 he him andswarede: Beatus es, Simon Bariona, 'Eadi art þu,

---

[1] were *corr. from* wore. [2] ilelde *MS.* [3] *page* 15. [4] *On the margin.*
[5] dan *MS.* [6] eche li *blotted out.* [7] x͞p͞c *MS.*

answered him: *Beatus es, Simon Barjona,* 'Blessed art thou, because
no earthly man taught thee this, that I am Christ, the Son of the
living God; but My Father in Heaven revealed it unto thy heart.
And upon this stone that thou here hast named, Christ, God's Son,
I will rear My Church, in order that all they who ever believe this
which thou believest, shall be My limbs, and I their head.   And
so we shall be one body and one Church, *et portae inferi non prae-
valebunt adversus eam,* 'The gates of hell may not have any
strength against this faith.'   The gates of hell are the cardinal
sins assuredly, for through them one goes into hell.   But no
sin nor any devil may have strength against this good faith,
that Christ, God's Son, can and will forgive all sins to them
who believe in Him and work thereafter.   In this little lesson
I cannot say all that were good to hear of this holy virtue.   But
what our holy Fathers wrote before us, and taught in the *Credo
in Deum* and in *Quicunque vult,* all that believe thou firmly, else
neither thou nor any man may be saved except we believe all that.
But nevertheless I will, on God's behalf, that thou be warned,
so that thou follow not any heretics, who misbelieve much.   Of
all such whom he had turned to Christ with much labour said
the apostle : *Timeo ne frustra laboraverim,* 'I am afraid,' he
said, 'that all my trouble on you has been lost, who take heed of
days, what one day can be better than another to begin something,
or a new moon better than an old moon to go into a new house or
to lead home a wife.'   Except the doctor who watches the new or
old [moon], after man's nature, and the carpenter who carves his
timber according to the moon, which is a natural thing; all
else is error, which has been retained from heathendom, or except
it be of sowing seed on account of the nature of these seeds of
the earth.   But do as the apostle teaches thee, who says: *Quaecunque vultis facere, in nomine Domini facite,* 'All that ye have to
do, do it in God's name, with good belief, and it shall go well with
you.'   Again, know forsooth, and believe it well, that nothing
may happen nor betide thee, neither evil nor good, nor in right nor

forðan ðe ðis ne tahte ðe non eor(ð)lic[1] mann, þat ic am Crist,
godes liuiendes sune; ac min fader on heuene hit openede in to
(þine) herte. *And* uppe þese stane ðe ðu hier hafst ჳenamd, Crist,
godes sune, ich wille araren mine cherche, (ðat alle) ðe aure ðis 4
(be)lieueð[2] þat tu ჳeliefst, hie sculen bien mine lemen, *and* ich here
heaued[3]. And swa we sculen bien an lichame (*and*) an cherche,
et porte inferi non preualebunt aduersus eam, ' Ðo ჳaten
of helle ne muჳen hauen none strengþe aჳean ðessere ileaue.' Ða 8
ჳaten of helle, ðat bieð ðo heuedsennes fulliwis, (for) ðurh hem
me farð in to helle. Ac ne mai non senne ne non dieuel habben
strengþe aჳean ðessere gode[4] ileaue, þat Crist, godes sune[5], mai
and wille alle sennes forჳiuen hem ðe on him belieueð *and* ðar 12
after wercheð. On ðessere litle radinge ic ne mai al seggen þat
god ware to iheren of ðessere hali mihte. Ac ðat ðe ure hali
faderes teforen us writen, *and* tahte on ðe credo in deum *and*
on quicunque uult, all ჳelief ðu fastliche, elles ðu ne namann 16
ne mai bien ჳeboreჳen bute we all ðat ilieuen. Ac naðelas ic wille,
a godes half, ðat tu bie ჳewarned, ðat tu ne folჳhi none dwelmenn,
ðe muchel misleueð. Of al swi(che)[6] sade ðe apostel, þe he mid
muchele iswinke hadde iwant to Criste: Timeo ne frustra lu- 20
borauerim, ' Ic am ofdrad,' he sæde, ' ðat[7] ich habbe al forloren
min ჳeswink on ჳeu, ðe nemeð ჳeme of daჳas, hwilch an dai bie
betere ðan an oðer to anginnen sumþing, oðer newe mone betere
ðan æld-mone in to newe huse te wænden oðer wif ham to leden.' 24
Wið-uten ðe læche ðe loceð (after)[8] mannes ikynde[9] þe newe oðer
elde, *and* ðe wrihte his timber to keruen after ðare mone, ðe is
ikyndelich þing; elles hit is al ჳedwoll *and* of haðenesse ჳiet wiðhealden, bute hit bie eft of sade te sawen for ðas sades ჳekinde 28
of ðare eorða. Ac do al swo ðe apostel ðe tachþ *and* seið : Que-
cunque uultis facere, in nomine domini facite, ' All ðat ჳe
habbeð to donne, an godes name doþ hit, mit gode ჳeleaue, *and* ჳew
scal wel ჳelimpen.' Eft wite ðu to soðe, *and* wel hit ilief, ðat na 32
þing ne mai ðe ჳelimpen ne to-cumen, neiðer ne euel ne god, ne on

---

[1] eor(d)lic *MS.*   [2] be *put above an underdotted* i.
[3] u *put above an underdotted* f, *the second* e *corrected from* o.
[4] *page* 16.   [5] sune ne *MS.*   [6] che *over erasure.*   [7] ð *corr. from* o.
[8] *On side, a word in the text scratched out.*   [9] y *written over* r.

in wrong, nor in health nor in sickness, nor through fire nor through water, nor through man nor through devil, nor through any of the things which both of them may do, except as God will allow it to them. When good comes to thee, and it well befalls thee, thank thy Lord God for it, and believe that it is through His great goodness, and not through thy merit. Again, when some evil or some mishap betides thee, in whatsoever wise it comes, believe not as some, who never well believed, say that they met evil foot, priest or monk; or some other error they entertain, and say that he had not good handsel who sold him that. Whatsoever harm or mishap befalls thee, think that thou art well deserving of the evil, because thou hast well earned it, that and much more; and thank thereof God very willingly, and so thou mayst make that all this evil may turn out to be of much good to thee.

Christ Himself says a remarkable thing of this blessed virtue: *Omnia possibilia sunt credenti,* 'All the things which ever the well-believing man wishes have done, they are granted him by God's own mouth through this holy virtue.' Again, He said of it a parable, that it is like the mustard-corn, which is little in sight and great in strength. The more one beats and stamps it, the stronger and better is it. Just so is it concerning the man who has with him this blessed virtue: the more he is troubled with griefs, temptations of the devil or of man, the stronger and better is he in good works. Again, it is written about it: *Fides sine operibus mortua est,* 'Faith without works is dead.' 'Many believe with words,' said the apostle, 'with works they forsake.' So does the devil, he believes, but he nevertheless does no good. And so there are all too many men that believe, and do not work accordingly. Beware who will!

Of firm hope.

After this comes another holy virtue that is called *firma spes,* that is, firm hope in God Almighty. All that her sister, the right faith, says to her, she trusts in it all firmly. This same holy virtue, where it comes and is with man, makes worthless to him all the fair things which in the deceptive world seem fair; he does

wele ne on wauӡhe, ne on hale[1] ne on unhale, ne ðurh fier ne ðurh
water, (ne ðurh manne ne ðurh dieule), ne ðurh nan ðare þinge ðe
hie baðe muӡen don, bute al swo godd hit wile hem þoliӡen. Þanne
ðe cumþ god, and þe wel ilimpþ, þanke ðar of ðine lauerde gode, 4
and ilief ðat hit is for his muchele godnesse, and noht for ðin earninge. Ðanne ðe cumþ eft sum euel oðer sum unӡelimp, an hwil-
che(s) kennes wise ðe hit æure cumþ, ne ӡelief ðu naht al swa sume,
ðe naure wel ne ӡeliefden, seggeð þat hie imetten euel fot, priest 8
oðer munec; oðer sum oðer dwel hie driueð, and seggeð þat he
nafde naht gode han(d)sselle ðe him þat sealde. Hwilch harm
oðer hwilc unӡelimp ðe ðe to-cumþ, þench ðat ðu art wel wurðe
ðes eueles, for ðan ðe ðu hit hauest wel ofearned, þat and michele 12
more; and ðanke ðerof gode swiðe ӡierne, and swa ðu miht don
ðat all ðat euel ðe mai wanden te michele gode.

Crist self seið an selcuð þing of ðessere eadi mihte: Omnia
possibilia sunt credenti, 'Alle ðo þing ðe æure ðe wel beliefde 16
(mann)[2] wile habben ӡedon, hie bieð him iteiþed of godes auӡene
muðe ðurh ðessere hali mihte.' Giet he sade of hire ane forbisne, ðat
hie is ӡelich ðe seneueies corne, ðe is litel an sei(ht)þe and michel
on strengþe. Æure ðe mann ðe hit more bat and stampeþ, ðe hit 20
strengere and betre is. Also is of ðe manne ðe ðese eadi mihte mid
him haueð: ðe he more is swaint mid deules, fondinges of dieule
oðer of manne, ðe he strengere and betere is on gode werkes. Eft
is iwriten bie hire: Fide(s) sine operibus mortua, 'Ileaue 24
wið-uten werkes, hie is dead.' 'Maniӡe ilieueð mid wordes,' sæde
ðe apostel, 'mid werkes he forsakeð.' Swo deð deuel, liefð, ac he
ðar after no god ne deð. And swa bieð alle(s) to fele menn ðe
ӡelie[3]-ueð, and noht ðar after ne wercheþ. Bie ӡewar se ðe wile ! 28

Of feste hope.

HIER after cumþ an oðer hali mihte ðe is icleped firma spes,
þat is, fast hope to godalmihti. All ðat hire suster, ðe rihte
ӡeleaue, hire seiӡeð, all hie hit fastliche hopeð. Ðies ilke haliӡe 32
mihte, ðar ðe hie cumeð and bieð mid ðe manne, hie makeð him
unwurð alle ðo faire þinges ðe on ðare swikele woreld[4] faire þen-

---

[1] page 17. [2] On side. [3] page 18. [4] r corrected from l. '

not account it more than filth, compared with the great mirth
he hopes to have in the kingdom of Heaven. That is the same that
St. Paul teaches us in his Epistles, who says thus: *Apparuit gratia
Dei omnibus hominibus erudiens nos,* 'God's grace,' he says, (which
he called it), 'God's Son showed Himself to all men, and He taught
us that we should forsake the frail belief of heathendom, and all
worldly evil lusts, and live moderately, and rightly, and piously,
awaiting the blessed hope and the coming of the great bliss of Christ,
God's Son, when He comes again to show Himself, and to repay
all the promises He promised us, that is, that He will turn the
body of our humility into great brightness, so that it shall shine
as bright as the sun, like the angels with God evermore in mirth
and in bliss.' Nobody may have this blessed hope, unless he well
believe it and love it truly. Therefore, said David, the prophet :
Multi dicunt: quis ostendit nobis bona ? 'Many say,' he said,
' who do not believe well : Who is he, that can show us the good
things that ye promise us ? Here we may see all the world's weal
and have it, but it is a mere assumption whether we may have what
ye promise.' What doest thou say, David ? Hast thou any cer-
tainty hereof ? Teach us, instruct us, it is need ! *Signatum est super
nos lumen vultus tui, Domine; dedisti laetitiam in corde meo.* 'Yes,'
he says, ' we are all sure of God's promise, because the light of His
face is marked right upon us. I know Him, and believe well by
a token He has given me.' *Dedisti laetitiam in corde meo,* 'Thou,
O Lord, gavest bliss into my heart, so that to me there is naught of
all the world's bliss. And Thou hast given me this as an earnest
of that eternal bliss.' Dear soul, if thou hast this bliss in thy heart,
which does not come from any world's bliss, then thou mayst be sure
of God's grace; and if thou hast not, do not cease neither night
nor day ere thou have it. But listen to what this same prophet
says of him who had got it : *Dilexisti justitiam et odisti iniquitatem, propterea unxit te Deus Deus tuus oleo laetitiae;* 'Because,' he

cheð; ne telþ hie namore ðarof ðanne of horewe, aʒeanes ðare
michele[1] merhþe ðe hie hopeð te habbene on heuene riche. Þat is
se ilke ðe san[c]tus Paulus us takð on his pisteles, *and* þus
seið: Aparuit gratia dei omnibus hominibus erudiens 4
nos, 'Godes grace,' he seið, *þat* he clepede her, 'godes sune hine
sceawede alle mannen, *and* he us tahte ðat we scolden forsaken ða un-
wraste ileaue of hæðen-dome, *and* alle woreldliches euele lustes, *and*
maðliche libben, *and* rihtliche, *and* arfastliche, anbidende ða eadi 8
hope *and* ðane to-cyme of ðare[2] michele blisse of Criste(s), gode(s)
sune, þanne he cumþ eftsones to sceawien *him* seluen, *and* to ʒielden
alle ðo behotes ðe he us behiet, *þat* is, þat he wile þane lichame of
ure e(a)dmodnesse *in* to michele brihtnesse[3] wanden, ðat he scal 12
scinen swa brïht swa sunne, emlich ðo aingles mid gode æure mo
on merhþe *and* on blisse.' Ne mai no man ðese eadi hope habben,
bute he hit wel ilieue and soðliche luuie. For ði sade Dauið, ðe
profiete: Multi dicunt: quis ostendit nobis bona? 'Maniʒe 16
seggeð,' (he) sade, ' ðe noht wel ne belieueð: Hwo is, þat us muʒe[4]
sceawin ða gode ðe ʒe us behoteð[5]? Hier we muʒen isien al ða
werdles wele *and* habben; of ðan ðe ʒie behoteþ is a wene hweðer
we it habben muʒen.' Hwat seist þu, Dauið? Hafst þu aniʒe 20
sikernesse herof? Tach vs,[6] wisse us, hit is nied! Signatum
est super nos lumen uultus tui, domine; dedisti leticiam
in corde meo. ' ʒise,' (he) seið, ' we bieð all siker of godes
behate, forðan ðat liht of his ansiene is (ʒe)marked riht uppen 24
us. Ich hine icnawe, *and* wel ilieue be are tacne ðe he hafð iʒiuen
me.' Dedisti leticiam in corde meo, 'Ðu, hlauerd, ʒaue blisse
on mire herte, ðat me nis naht of alles woreldes blisse; and þese ðu
hauest iʒiuen me to earres of ðare eche blisse.' Lieue saule, ʒif ðu 28
ðese blisse hauest on ðine hierte, ðe ne cumþ of nanes woreldes
blisse, ðane miht þu bien siker mid[7] godes grace; *and* ʒif ðu ne
hafdst, ne swic ðu naure niht ne dai ær ðu hes habbe. Ac hærce
hwat tes ilke profiete seið be him ðe hes hadde biʒeten: Dilex- 32
isti iusticiam *et* odisti iniquitatem, propterea vnxit te

---

[1] hope *blotted out.*   [2] r corr. from s.   [3] Before h an s blotted out.
[4] muʒen MS.   [5] teð on erasure.   [6] page 19.
[7] mid corrected over of.

said, 'thou lovedst righteousness and hatedst unrighteousness, therefore thy Lord hath anointed thee with the oil of bliss.' Oil has three qualities in it: it will float over all liquids (so will God's love be over all other loves); it will burn in the lamp brightly (so will this virtue give good example to all them that dwell in God's house); it softens all hardness (so does this holy bliss all sorrow for sins). Well [is] him that may get it! All the men who labour in this toilsome world, they all labour for some hope they have, which often deceives them in the end. David: *In illa die peribunt omnes cogitationes eorum,* 'At their end-day all their thoughts they had thought to carry out will perish.' But those who labour for this blessed hope, they are not deceived. Have thou no trust in gold nor in silver, nor in any possessions of the world, nor even in man. It is written: *Maledictus homo qui confidit in homine,* 'Cursed be the man who hath his trust in man, who turneth his heart and his thoughts more to man's service than to God's.' Let all thy trust be upon our Saviour Christ, who will raise thee and thy body from death as truly as He Himself arose from death, and will bring thee unto eternal life! If thou shouldst live as long as this world lasteth, and always sufferdst pain, thou couldst not earn so much happiness as is promised to thee. But thy Lord earned it on the holy cross; therefore thou hast to bear thy cross after His instruction, who said: *Qui vult venire post me, tollat crucem suam et sequatur me,* 'Who will come after Me into Heaven, let him bear his cross on earth as I did, and so he may follow Me and come where I am.' The cross betokens pain. Pain thyself for His love who suffered pain for thee unto death, in fasting, and in watching, and in patience, and in restraining thy self-will. If thou thus doest, then thou bearest thy cross. Never let it seem to thee so bitter, that this hope does not sweeten it. So it did all the holy martyrs. All the kinds of pains men might do to them men did to them; this holy virtue made them all sweet to them. So it did [make sweet] to all

deus deus[1] tuus oleo leticie, 'Forðan,' he sade, 'ðat tu luuedest rihtwisnesse *and* hatedest unri(h)twisnesse, for ði haueð ðin
lauerd ismered þe mid ða ele of blisse.' Ele hafð þrie ʒekynden
on him : hit wile flotten oue'r[2] alle wætes, swa wile godes luue ₄
bien *ouer* alle oðre luuen ; hit wile *on* lampe berne*n* brihte[3], swa
wile ðes mihte gode forbisne ʒiue*n* alle he*m* ðe on godes huse wunien;
hie liþegað (alle [h]ardnesse), swa dieð ðies haliʒe blisse alle
sarinesses of sennes. Wel him ðe hes biʒete*n* mai ! Alle ðo men*n* ₈
ðe swinkeð *on* ðessere swinkfulle[4] world, alle hie swinkeð for sumere hope ðe hie habbeð, ðe hem ofte aten ande beswikð. Dauið :
In illa die p*e*ribunt[5] *omnes cogita*c*iones eor*u*m, 'On here
ænde-daiʒe forwurðeð alle here þohtes ðe hie hadden iþoht to ₁₂
don*n*e.' Ac ðo ðe swinkeð for ðessere eadi hope, hie ne bieð
naht becaht. Ne haue ðu hope te golde ne to seluer, ne to none[6]
wor(d)lles eihte, ne forðen te man*n*e. Hit is iwrite*n* : M a l e-
dict*u*s homo q*u*i c o n f i d i t i*n* h o m i n e, 'ʒewerʒed bie ðe ₁₆
man*n* þe haueð his hope te man*n*e, þe[7] want his herte *and* his
(ʒeþanc[8]) more to man*n*es seruise ðanne te godes.' All bie ðin
hope uppen ure halende Criste, þe wile arare*n* þe *and* þine[9] lichame
of deaðe swa soðliche swa he hi*m* self aros of deaðe, *and* bringe þe ₂₀
to ðan eche lif ! Gif ðu liuedest swa la*n*ge swa ðes woreld ilast,
and æure þoledest pine, ne mihtest ðu of-earnin swa michel eadinesse swa ðe is behaten. Ac ðin lauerd hes ofearnede *on* ðare
hali rode ; for ði ðu aust te berene ðine rode after his wissinge, ðe ₂₄
sade : Qui uult uenire post me, tollat crucem suam *et* se-
q*u*atur me, 'Se ðe wile cumen after me i*n* to heuene, bere his
rode on ierðe swa ic dede, *and* swo he mai me folʒin *and* cume*n*
ðar ic am.' Rode tacnieð pine. Pine ðe selue*n* for his luue ðe ₂₈
ðolede pine for ðe anon to ðe deaðe, on fasten *and* on wacchen
and on þolemodnesse, *and* on ðine awene wille to laten. ʒif[10] ðu ðus
dost, ðanne berest þu þi*n* rode. Ne þinche hit te næure swa bitter,
ðat þies hope hit ne sw(i)eteð. Swa hie dede alle ðo halie martirs. ₃₂
Alle ðas kennes pines ðe me he*m* mihte do*n* me he*m* dede ; all ðis
halie mihte hes makede he*m* swiete. Swa hie dede alle ðe hali

---

[1] *deus deus on erasure.*   [2] *Corrected from osier.*   [3] *Five or six words erased.*
[4] fullle *MS.*   [5] b *corrected over* d.   [6] nones *MS.*   [7] *page* 20.
[8] *Written above* seruise.   [9] þ *corr. from* b.   [10] ʒ *corrected from* G.

the holy confessors and the holy virgins all that they suffered through it. So it does still in this time to monks, canons, anchorites, and hermits. For this blessed hope they forsake father and mother, wife and children, house and home, and all the world's weal and bliss. So do pilgrims who forsake their own country, and go into other lands. So ought to do all who ever do any good. They all shall do it in order to have reward from God Almighty in the other world and not here; that be their hope! The holy apostle calls these three holy virtues together, *fidem, spem, caritatem,* and says that this which is called *caritas,* is the highest and best of these three, and so it is above all the others. Therefore it shall last evermore, as well in this world as in the other. Of it, we will tell something by God's grace.

Of charity.

Caritas is very holy, because God Himself is called *caritas,* that is, love of God and man. God dwells within all who have this holy love, and they within God. Understand now well, how God dwells in the man who has this blessed virtue, and so thou mayst know, whether God dwells in thee and whether thou hast this virtue. God dwells in the man who loves Him in such a wise that He kindles his heart and his thoughts with the fire which Christ brought on earth. At first He gives him light in his heart, in order to see the good which he ought to do. Of this blessed light said St. John the Evangelist : *Erat lux vera quae illuminat omnem hominem venientem in hunc mundum.* He said of Christ, God's Son, that 'He was the true light which lighteth every man that cometh into this life.' He is called God's Wisdom. He instructs the man's thoughts to whom He comes, either through holy writings or through holy sermons, which He sends him through some wise man in whom He is dwelling. Then comes the Holy Ghost who is an all burning fire, as He came upon the apostles, and inflames the heart, and reminds it often by day and by night and brings it into good will. If

confessores *and* ðe hali uirgines all ðat hie ðoleden ðurh hire.
Swa hie doð ȝiet on ðese time munekes, kanunekes, ancres, *and*
eremites. For ðessere eadi hope hie forlateð fader *and* moder,
wif *and* children, hus *and* ham, *and* alle worldes wele *and* blisse. 4
Swa doð pilegrimes ðe lateþ her awen eard, *and* fareð *in* to oðre
lande. Swo aweð to donne alle ðe æure ani god doð. Alle hie
hit don for to habben lean of godalmihtin on ðare oðre woreld
and naht hier; þat bie here hope I Ðe hali apostel namneð ðese 8
þrie haliȝe mihtes to-gedere, fidem, spem, karitatem[1], and
seggeð þat þies ðe hatte karitas, is heiȝest *and* betst of ðese þrie,
and swo hie is ouer alle oðre. For ðan hie scal æure mo ȝelasten,
aiðer on ðessere woreld *and* ec on ðare oðre. Of hire we willeð 12
sumdæl keðen be godes grace.

Of charite.

CARITAS is swiðe hali, forðan ðe godd self is icleped karitas, þat is, godes luue *and* mannes. Alle ðe habbeð ðese 16
halie luue, godd wuneð inne hem, *and* hie *inne* gode. Vnderstond
nu wel, hu godd wuneð on ða manne ðe ðese eadi mihte haueð,
and swa ðu miht ȝecnawen, ȝif godd wuneð on ðe *and* ȝif ðu ðese
mihte hafst. Godd wuneð on ða manne ðe him luueð. On ðelliche 20
wise þat is, þat he his herte (*and*) his ȝeþanc on-alð mid ða fiere
ðe Crist brohte on ierðe. Arst he ȝifð (him) liht on ðare hierte, to
ȝesiene ðat god ðat he aw te donne. Of ðesen eadiȝen lihte[2] sade
sanctus Iohannes ðe godspellere: Erat lux uera que illu- 24
minat omnem hominem uenientem[3] in hunc mundum.
He sade be Criste, godes sune, þat 'he was ðat soðe liht þe lihteþ
alche manne ðe cumþ on ðese liue.' He is icleped godes wisdom.
He wisseð ðes mannes iðang[c] ðe he to-cumð, oðer ðurh haliȝe 28
writes oðer ðurh hali sermuns, þe he him ðurh sume wise manne
ðe he is inne wuniende[4], sant. Þanne cumþ ðe hali gast ðe is all
fier barnende, swa he com up ðe apostles, *and* analð[5] ðe hierte,
and meneȝeð hie ofte be daiȝe *and* be nihte, *and* bringþ hie on 32
gode wille. Gif ðe herte bliðeliche underfoð godes hali wordes ðe

---

[1] *page* 21.   [2] *Corr. from* ðese eadiȝe mihte.   [3] u *on erasure*.
[4] wudiende hi*m MS.*   [5] anald *MS.*

the heart blithely receives God's holy words which come from
His Son, who is Wisdom, and receives them with much love
as the Holy Ghost, who is the Love of both of them : then comes
thereafter Almighty God the Father and gives the power to
do all this, and [they] make their abode in this blessed soul.
Thus Christ promised that He and His Father would love the
man and be abiding with him who would love Him and keep
His words. Thus says the Gospel : *Si quis diligit me, sermonem
meum servabit ; et pater meus diliget eum, et mansionem apud
eum faciemus.*

Now, thou hast heard, how God abides in the man who loves
Him; hear now, how the man may abide within God, as St.
John says : *Qui manet in caritate, in Deo manet, et Deus in eo,*
' He that dwelleth in love, dwelleth in God, and God in him.'
Some misunderstand here the holy Writ, [and many a one] assumes,
if he gives blithely to eat and to drink, and of his other property
gives for God's love blithely, and himself lies in some cardinal sin,
which he will not give up, but hopes to be saved through his
doing so much for God's love. Against this says God Himself:
Si recte offers, et non recte dividis, peccasti, ' If thou rightly offerest
and doest not rightly divide, thou sinnest more than thou doest
good.' Thou givest thy own to God, and thyself to the devil.
That is not rightly divided ; for better is a good soul, than all
the world with all its possessions. If thou lovest the same thing
that God firmly forbids thee, how canst thou then abide in charity,
that is, love of God and of men ? How canst thou love thy
neighbour as thyself, when thou lovest not thyself ? The holy
.Writ says : *Qui diligit iniquitatem, odit animam suam,* ' The man
who loves unrighteousness, hates his own soul.' For when he
breaks God's forbidding, then he is unrighteous; and through
his unrighteousness he brings his soul into the pain of hell.
Nevertheless let the man never cease to give alms, because, whatsoever becomes of him, he remains not unrewarded. If thou wilt
surely abide in charity and in God, then do thou as we find it

cumþ fram¹ his sune, ðe is wisedom, *and* hes mid michele luue
underfoð al swa ðane hali gast, ðe is here beire luue : ðanne ðar
after cumþ almihti godd ðe fader *and* ȝifð ðe mihte al² ðis te
donne, *and* makieð here wunienge on ðessere eadi saule. Þus ⁴
behet Crist ðat þe mann ðe him wolde luuiȝen *and* his wordes
healden : þat he *and* his fader hine scolden luuiȝen *and* mid him
wuniende b(i)en. Þus seieð ðat goddspell : Si q*uis* diligit
me, sermonem meu*m* seruabit ; *et* pater me*us* diliget ⁸
eu*m*, *et* mansione*m* apud³ eum faciem*us*. Nu ðu hafst
ȝeherd, hu godd wuneð on ðe manne ðe hi*m* luueð ; harke nu, hu
ðe man mai wuniȝen inne gode, al swo s*anctus* Ioh*annes* seið :
Q*ui* manet i*n* karitate, in deo man*et*, *et* deus⁴ i*n* eo, 'Se ₁₂
ðe wuneð on karite, he wuneð on gode, *and* godd on hi*m*.' Sume
mis-understondet⁵ (hier) ðis hali writt, weneð, ȝif he ȝifð bleðeliche
to eten *and* to drinken, *and* of his oðer eihte doþ for godes luue
bleðeliche, and hi*m* self lið on sume heaued-senne, ne ðo ne wile ₁₆
læten, ac hopeð te bien iboreȝen ðurh ðat he dieð swa michel for
godes luue⁶. Hier aȝean seið god hi*m* self : Si recte offers, *et*
no*n* recte diuidis, peccasti, 'Gif ðu riht offrest *and* noht
riht ne sciftst, ðu senegest mare ðan ðu god do.' Ðu ȝifst⁷ ðine ₂₀
eihte gode, *and* ðe seluen ðe dieule⁸. Þat nis naht riht iscift ;
for ðan betere is an god saule, ðan all ðe woreld mid all hire
eihte. Gif ðu luuest ðat ilke þing ðe godd fastliche ðe forbett⁹,
hu miht ðu ðanne wuniȝen on karite, þat is, luue of gode *and* of ₂₄
mannen ? Hu miht ðu luuiȝen ðine nexte al swa ðe seluen, (ðane
þu ne luuest noht þe seluen ?) Ðat hali writ seið : Q*ui* diligit
iniq*u*itatem, odit anima*m* suam, 'Ðe ma*n* ðe luueð unrihtwisnesse, he hateð his awene saule.' Forðan ðanne he brecþ godes ₂₈
forbod, þanne is he un-rihtwis ; *and* ðurh his unrihtwisnesse he
bri[n]gþ his saule in to helle pine. Naðelas ne læte ðe mann
neure almesse te donne¹⁰, for ðan¹¹, hwat swo æure of hi*m* betide, ne
wurþ hie naht un-forȝolden. Ȝif ðu wilt sikerliche wuniȝen on ₃₂
karite *and* on gode, þanne do ðu alswa we hit a boke finden

---

¹ f *corr. from* a.   ² *page* 22.   ³ apuð *MS.*   ⁴ ðs *MS.*
⁵ t *on erasure.*   ⁶ luuen *MS.*   ⁷ ȝ *corr. from* G.
⁸ ð. d. *on erasure.*   ⁹ forbettt *MS.*   ¹⁰ *page* 23.
¹¹ for ðan *twice in MS., the first crossed red.*

written in the book, that is, that thou shouldst work, with right belief and with firm hope and with true love the good things which thou believest. All thou knowest that God forbids, avoid doing it in every way; and if thou breakest any [of His commandments], do penance anon. Never suffer the devil to reign in thee through any sin, but have thy thoughts fixed in God, and beg His forgiveness, and humbly entreat Him to give thee might and strength to withstand the devil's temptations and the lusts of thy flesh. Then thou wilt truly abide in God, if thou thinkest more of Him than thou doest of any thing in the world, by day and by night, for thou hast great need that He always be thy shield against all evils, and thy helper to all good. If thou hast thus thy love in God, it then behooves thee, if thou wilt have charity in thee, to be well aware that thou shouldst love thy neighbour, that is, every man who bears thy likeness. Of this the holy apostle Paul warns us, who says thus: *Si distribuero omnes facultates meas in cibos pauperum,* 'If I give all that I have to wretched men, and in addition to that give my body to be burned all to dust for God's love, and I hate a single man, then I have not charity, nor may I be saved in any wise, except I have it.' St. Gregory gives an example of this, that just as no web can be woven without two beams, so charity can never be finished without two loves, that is, God's and man's, and just as many threads are necessary ere it be made, so is much reflecting of thoughts and words and works needful to charity during all thy life-time, ere it be ordained in thee as it is necessary. It is a great pity for many a man who is in great error about himself, and presumes that he is wise and that he has with him love of God and man, but has none. Many a man says in words that he loves God. The true love of God is rather in works than in words. If thou lovest nothing in the world by which thou mayst lose God's love or man's; and wrath does not abide with thee one day's length, but thou either forgivest every trespass [against thee] or requitest [it] with love: if thou doest thus,

iwrite*n*, þ*at* is, ðat tu mid rihte ȝeleaue *and* mid faste hope *and*
mid soðe luue bie werchind*e* ðat god ðe ðu iliefst. Al ðat ðu
wast ðat godd forbett, forbuh hit to do*n*ne on alle wise*n* ; and ȝif
ðu au(h)t tebrecst, ano*n* siech ðu ðine bote. Ne ðole ðu naure 4
ðat dieuel rixi on ðe for none senne [1], ac fastliche haue ðin iþanc
te godd, *and* bide hi*m* forȝiuenesse, *and* besiec hi*m* eadmodliche
ðat he ȝiue ðe mihte *and* strengþe to wiðstanden aȝeanes dieules
fo*n*dinges *and* ðine flesches lustes. Ðanne wunest ðu sikerliche 8
on gode, þ*an*ne ðu þen[c]st more of hi*m* ðanne ðu do of aniȝe þinge
of ðare woreld, be daiȝe *and* be nihte, for ðare michele niede ðe
ðu hauest þ*at* he æure bie þi*n* sceld aȝeanes alle eueles, *and* þin
helpend to alle gode. Ðanne ðu ðus hauest ðine luue te gode, 12
ðanne behoueð ðe ðat ðu bie wel warr þ*at* tu luuiȝe ðine nexte,
ðat is, aurich man*n* ðe beıð ði*n* anlicnesse, ȝif [2] þu karite scalt
habbe*n* on ðe. Herof us warneð ðe holi apostel Paul*us*, *and* ðus
seiȝeð: Si dist*r*ibuero omnes facultates meas i*n* cibos 16
paup*er*um, ' Gif ic dale all ðat ic habbe wrecche ma*n*nen, *and*
ȝiet ðar uppe*n* ȝiue mine lichame all to barne*n* to duste for godes
luue, *and* ich hatede anlepine man*n*, ðanne ne habbe ic naht charite,
ne ich iboreȝen a none wise ne mai bie*n*, bute ic hes habbe.' 20
S*anctus* Gregori*us* seið hier on ane forbisne, þ*at* al swa na*n*
webb ne mai bie*n* iweue*n* wið-uten twa beames, al swo ne mai
næure karite bie*n* fulfremed wið-uten twa luues, þ*at* is, godes *and*
ma*n*nes, and alswo [3] ðar behoueð to maniȝe þreades ær hit bie full- 24
wroht, al swo behoueþ to charite on alle ðines liues time michel
embeþanc of þohtes [4] *and* of wordes *and* of werkes, ær hie bie
ȝediht on ðe swa swa hit nied is [5]. Hit is a michel reunesse of
mani ma*n*n ðe is on michele dwele on hi*m* selue*n*, wenþ þ*at* he bie 28
wis *and* ðat he haue mid hi*m* godes luue and ma*n*nes, *and* ne haueð
naht. Mani ma*n*n seið mid wordes þ*at* he godd luueð. Þe soðe
luue of godd, hie is mare on werkes ðanne on wordes. Gif ðu na
þing ne luuest on ðare woreld ðurh hwat ðu miht forliesen godes 32
luue oðer ma*n*nes ; ne wraððe mid ðe ne wuneð ones daiȝes længe,
ac alchne gylt forȝifst oðe mid luue sah(t)lest : ðanne ðu ðus

---

[1] se*n*nns *MS.* [2] ȝ *corr. from* G. [3] *page 24.*
[4] *Corr. from* þoltes. [5] *a letter erased after* s.

then thou hast charity in thee and assuredly God's love and
man's. If thou doest not this, do not deceive thyself by be-
lieving that Christ abides with thee, or thou with Him, whilst
thou hast wrath or envy in thee, or lovest any thing in this
false world against His commandment.   Of this St. John the
Evangelist bears witness, who says thus: *Qui diligit mundum,
non est caritas patris in eo,* 'Whoso loveth this world, the love of
the Father the Almighty God is not in him.'   Woe then to every
man who is so much deprived of understanding, that he, through
this false love of the treacherous world, should lose the sweet love
of Christ and the joy of the everlasting land ! It may happen that
some one, who sees or hears this, thinks: 'How can I dwell in the
world and not love it ?   Or how can I dwell therein, and also be
saved ?' According to what holy Writ says : 'Thou who dwellest
in the world, and art bound therein with house and with wedded
wife and with children, if thou wilt be saved, thou oughtst to
follow the righteous and simple Job, who lived in the world with
wife and with children, and with great property, which was shared
in by all the needful, and who was also tempted with great wealth,
and with great distress, and with great sickness, and with many
evil upbraidings, both from his own wife and also from his own
friends, from relations and from strangers, and from the devil
himself ; but none could bereave him of this holy virtue which we
are speaking about, that is, charity, of God's love or man's, nor
break this patience with one intemperate word.' Listen here, listen
here, ye proud men, the devil's followers, who follow the devil, that
stirs up wrath and strife and bitter words and the forbidden curs-
ings, and will have neither place of rest nor any softness in your
heart, on which the Holy Ghost might rest Himself ! Cease, cease,
if ye will have the Holy Ghost dwelling with you, and drive the
fellowship of the cursed spirit from you. Know forsooth, ye worldly
men, who are bound in the world, that except ye love the

dest, ðanne hafst ðu charite mid ðe *and* iwis godes luue *and*
mannes. Gif ðu ðis ne diest, ne beswic ðu noht ðe seluen ðat tu
ilieue ðat Crist wuniȝe mid ðe, oðer ðu mid him, all ðare hwile
ðe ðu wraððe oðer nið hauest mid te, oðer ani þing *on* ðese lease 4
woreld luuest aȝeanes his bebode. Hier of berþ ȝewitnesse *sanctus*
Iohannes ðe godspellere, *and* þus seið: Qui diligit mundum,
non *est* charitas patris in eo, 'Se ðe luueð ðese woreld, ðes
fader luue god-almihtines nis naht an him.' Wa ðan ilke manne 8
ðe is swa [1] swiðe wittes bedæld, ðat he, for ðessere lease luue of ðe
swikele woreld, scal forliesen ðe swete luue of Criste *and* ðe merhðe
of ðe liuiȝende lande [2] ! Hit mai ilimpen ðat sum mann, ðe ðis
ȝeseðh oðer ȝeherð, þat he þen(c)þ [3] : 'Hu mai ic *on* ðane world 12
wuniȝ*en and* naht hes ne luuiȝen ? Oðer hu mai ic ðær on wuniȝ*en*,
and ec be ȝeborȝ*en* ?' After ðan ðe ðat hali writt seið : 'Ðu ðe
wunest *on* ðære woreld, *and* art ðar inne ibu*n*de mid huse *and* mid
weddede wiue *and* mid childre, swa swa ðu wilt bien ȝeboreȝ*en*, 16
ðu aust te folȝin ðane rih[t]wise *and* onfald Iob [4], ðe was wuniȝende
on ðare woreld mid wiue *and* mid children, *and* mid michelere
heihte, þe was ȝemanlich alle niedfullen, ðe was iec fonded mid
michele wele, *and* mid michelere nafte, *and* mid michel unhæle, *and* 20
mid maniȝe euele upbreides, aiðer of his aȝene wiue *and* ec of his
auene frienden [5], of sibbe *and* of framde, *and* of ðe selue dieule ;
swa nan ne mihte him benem*en* ðas haliȝe mihte ðe we e*m*be
spekeð, þat is, charite, godes luue ne ma*n*nes, ne ðis ðolemodnesse 24
tobrec*en* naht mid one unbehealdene worde.' Hlesteð hider,
hlesteð hider, ȝe modi men*n*, ðes dieules folȝeres, ðe folȝið ðe
dieule [6], ðe ararð upp ðe wraððhes *and* þe cheastes *and* te bitere
wordes *and* te forbodene werȝinges [7], ðe ne willeð nane reste ne 28
nane soft(n)esse on ȝeure h*er*te habben, ðar ðe hali gast him mihte
resten ! ȝeswikeð, iswikeð [8], al swa ȝe willeð ðes hali-gastes
wunienge habben mid ȝeu, *and* ðas ȝewerȝede gaste(s) felauscipe
fram e(u)wȝ driu*en*. Wite ȝe te soðe, ȝe worldmen*n*, ðe bieð *on* 32
ðare woreld ibunden, bute ȝie ðeses rihtwises ma*n*nes lif luuiȝ*en*

---

[1] swa *twice in the MS., the first underlined.*
[2] terra uiuentium, *gloss at the side.*   [3] *page* 25.
[4] iustus et simplex erat, *added at the side.*   [5] friennden *MS.*
[6] d *corrected from* ð.   [7] werȝinginges *MS., the last g corr. from* e.   [8] -d *MS.*

life of this righteous man and follow [it], ye shall never come to
the great happiness which he [Job] has with God Almighty.
Those, who have forsaken this deceitful world and serve our Lord
in orders, follow Daniel, the holy prophet, who is called *vir desi-
deriorum*, that is, the man who was never overcome by the
covetousness of the world, and was never defiled by the lusts of the
flesh, and never yearned or cared for, or loved any of the things
which were in this world, but his neighbour and the lawful things
which God had bidden him to do.   Nevertheless, above all things
he loved after God *abstinentiam, castitatem*, that is, abstinence from
meat, drink, and all kinds of lecheries.   None of them could defile
him.   Although he was long brought up and nourished in [the]
king's retinue, it was more agreeable to him to eat beans and
peas and such coarse meats, and to drink water, than the costly
dishes or the good wines which came from the king.   All who
have forsaken this world for God's sake, must follow this holy
man Daniel in abstaining from all evil things, and in avoiding
all kinds of lecheries, if they will attain the great happiness
which Daniel has with the angels in Heaven.   The spiritual
shepherds, who must both guard and direct those who are in the
world, and also those who are without, follow Noah, the good
steersman, who was very dear and pleasing to God through the
great obedience [with] which he wrought for many years, ere he
could make the ark; and he afterwards steered it in such a way
in the great terrible flood which overflooded all the earth, amidst
strong winds and storms, that he lost none of those whom God
had intrusted him to keep alive and to bring to land.   So ought
the spiritual steersmen to steer the ark of the holy Church in such
a way that they lose neither a body nor a soul of it, through no
wind of human temptation, nor through any storm of devilish
temptation; and again, in fair weather, they should not be too
sure, because so many little drops of various kinds of carelessness
might come into the boat of souls, that they might sink with all

and folȝin, ne cume ȝe næure mo to ðare michele eadinesse ðe he
haueð mid godalmihtin. Ðo ðe ðese swikele woreld habbeð forlaten [1] *and* seruið ure drihten *on* religiun, hie folȝið Daniele, ðe
hali profiete, þe is icleped uir desideri(o)ru*m* [2], ðat is, ðe man*n* 4
ðe naure [3] worldes ȝitsinge n(e) [4] ouerca*m*, ne næure ðe flesliches
lustes hi*m* [5] ne befield*e*, ne no*n* ðare ðinge ðe on ðesse worlde
ware*n* [6] he ne ȝernde, ne he ne rohte, ne he ne luuede, bute his
nexte *and* ðo laȝeliche þing ðe god him hadde ȝehote te don*n*e. 8
Naðelæs, ouer alle þing he luued*e* under gode abstinenciam,
castitatem, þat is, wiðheal[d]nesse of metes *and* of drenches, *and*
of alles kennes galnesses. Ne mihte hi*m* naðer befele*n*. Swa swa he
was on kynges hyrde lange ifedd *and* ȝefostred, leuere hi*m* was tò 12
ete*n* benen *and* pesen *and* swilche unorne metes, *and* ðat wat*er* to
drinken, ðan*n*e hi*m* ware ðo derewurðe sondes ðe come*n* fro ðe
kynge, oðer ðe gode wines. Alle ðe ðese woreld for godes luue
habbeð [7] forlaten, alle hie mote*n* ðisne hali ma*n*n Daniele folȝin 16
mid wiðhealdenesse of alle euele þinges, *and* mid clannesse fram
alles kennes galnesse(s), swa swa hie willeð cume*n* to ðare michele
eadinesse ðe [8] Daniel haueð mid ðo angles on heuene. Ðe gastliche hierdes, ðe sculen boðe loki*n* *and* stieren ðo ðe bieð in ðare 20
woreld, *and* ec (ðo) ðe bieð ute, hie folȝið Noe ðane gode stieresma*n*n, ðe god*e* was swiðe lief *and* ȝecweme for ðare muchele hersumnesse ðe he maniȝe wi*n*tre swanc, ær he (ða) arche mihte habbe*n*
ȝemaked, *and* seððen hie swa stierde on ðe muchele wilde flode ðe 24
ouerȝiede all middeneard, mang stronge windes *and* stormes, ðat
he ðarof ne forleas naþing ðe godd hi*m* hadde betaht to liue *and*
to londe to bringe*n*. Swa scule ða gastlich(e) [9] stieres-men*n* (steren)
ða arche of ðe hali cherche, ðat hie ðarof ne for-liesen ne lichame 28
ne saule, for none wi*n*de of ma*n*nliche fandi*n*ge, [10] ne for none
storme of dieuliche fandi*n*g*e*; *and* eft, on fuire weder*e*, ne bien hie
naht to sikere, forðan swo maniȝe litle dropes of maniȝes kennes
ȝemeleastes mihte*n* cume*n* in to ðe saule bote, ðat hie mihte*n* sinke*n* 32
mid alle hire biȝeates ; ac lokien [11] hie alle ðe wið-i*n*nen scipes borde

[1] *page* 26.   [2] *The last* r *on erasure*.   [3] *After this fourteen letters erased*.
[4] e *red over* no.   [5] i *on erasure*.
[6] was *MS*.   [7] habbed *MS*.   [8] ð *corr. from* o.
[9] e *above erasure*.   [10] *page* 27.   [11] lokieð *MS*.

its contents; but let them all take heed who dwell within the
board of the ship, that they be obedient and buxom to their steersman, if they wish to come to the everlasting land with soul and
with body. And listen what the Lord who owns the ship says
to the steersmen and to all who dwell therein: *Qui vos audit,
me audit,* 'Whoso listens to your counsel,' says He, 'listens to
Myself; and whoso forsakes you and your lore, forsakes full surely
Myself.' This He says to the steersmen. In great peril we all sail
who sail *in hoc mare magnum,* 'in this great sea of the bitter
world.' Of our steersmen is written: *Ascendunt usque ad coelos,
et descendunt usque ad abyssos,* 'They mount up to Heaven' in
their spiritual thoughts in order to view the great joy of the
kingdom of Heaven, in order to view the winds and the evil
storms which come from the devil's blasts, and in order to warn us
lest our ropes break, which are woven of three strings, of right
belief and of firm hope in God and of the true love which is
called charity, which Christ loves most. Again, it is said that
'they go down to the depths' in their thoughts, in order again to
warn us against the stone-rocks of the hard heart which never
will soften with any water of wisdom, but if a ship comes thereto
it breaks up. So does the unwise man who comes to the unbelieving man that neither will nor can understand God's lore
through the hardness of his heart: he [the unwise man] breaks up,
if he has any good will, for he hurts his good will. And he breaks
up with such words: 'What doest thou?' he [the unbelieving
man] says, 'thou givest away all that thou hast! If thou listenest
to preachers and priests and monks and these ordained men, thou
wilt never have any goods. They would swallow all the world, if
they could. Be a faithful man and keep thy goods; thou wilt find
few who will give thee anything, except they do it for a reason.'
The unguarded man who hears this, thinks that he [the unbeliever]
gives him good counsel. If he before did little for God, after that
he does much less; and so he perishes, because he will neither
listen to nor follow his priest's lore nor his counsel. Charity

wuniȝeð, þat hie bien hersum *and* leðebeiȝe here stieres-manne [1],
swa swa hie willeð cumen to ðe liuiende land*e* mid saule *and* mid
lichame.   And hlesteð hwat ðe hlauerd seið, ðe ðat scip auh, to
ðe stieresma*nn*en *and* to alle ðe ðar inne wuniȝeð : Q u i   u o s 4
a u d i t, me a u d i t, ' Se ðe ȝeu(w)er ra(d) [2] hlest,' he seið, ' he hlest
me selue*n* ; *and* se ðe ȝew forsakþ *and* ȝewere lare, he forsakþ fullȝewiss me seluen.'   Þis he seið [3] to ða stieresma*nn*en.   On michele
hahte we fareð alle ðe fareð i*n* h o c m a r e m a g n u m, ' on ðessere 8
michele sea of ðare bitere woreld.'   Of ure stieresma*n* is ȝewriten :
A s c e n d u n t u s q*ue* a d c e l o s, *et* d e s c e n d u n t u s q*ue* a d a b i s s o s,
' Hie stieð up to heuene' mid here gastliche þohtes for to sceawin
ðe michele merhðe of heuene riche, for to sceawin ðe windes *and* 12
ðe euele stormes [4] ðe cumeð of deules blastes, *and* for us te warnin
þat ure ropes ne to-breke*n*, ðe bieð ibroiden mid þrie stræn̄ges, of
rihte ileaue *and* of faste hope te gode and of ðare soðe luue [5] ðe is
ihoten carite, ðe Crist mæst luueð.   Eft hit seið ðat hie stikð ₁6
niðer i*n* to nielnesse [6] mid here ðohtes, for us eft to warnin wið
ðo stanroches of ðe harde hierte ðe næure ne wile nexi*n* for none
wat*ere* of wisdome, ac ȝif ðar cum*þ* scip to hit tobrekð.   Alswo
doð ðat unwise ma*nn* ðe cum*þ* to ðan unbiliefde ma*nn*e ðe ne wile 20
ne ne mai godes lare understa*n*den for his h*er*te hardnesse : he tobrekð [7], ȝif he ani god wille hafð, forðan he hert his gode wille.
And hie tobrecþ [8] mid þelliche wordes : ' Hwat dest þu ? ' he
seið, ' ðu dalst al ðat tu hafst !   Wile ðu hlesten spelleres *and* ₂4
pr(i)estes *and* munekes *and* þese hadede ma*nn*en, ne scalt ðu næure
habben god.   Hie wolden for(i)swelȝen all ðe woreld, ȝif hie
mihte*n*.   Be trewe ma*nn* *and* halt ti*n* god ; þu finst feawe ðe wile
ȝiuen ðe ani þing, bute hie wite*n* hwarfore.'   Ðe unware ma*nn* ðe ₂8
ðis ȝeherð, ðingþ ðat he seið him god rad.   Ȝif [9] he arrer dede litel
te gode, ðar after he doð michel(e) lasse ; *and* swo he forfarð, for
ðan ðe he his priestes lare ne his ræd lesten ne folȝin ne wile.
Carite sprat his bowes [10] on bræde *and* on lengðe swiðe ferr. ₃2

---

[1] *The 2nd e destroyed.*   [2] d *above erasure.*   [3] seid *MS.*
[4] stormes euele *MS., with sign? of transposition.*
[5] *Corr. from* lirue.   [6] abissos *on the margin.*   [7] -d *MS.*
[8] *page 28.—At the bottom of p. 27 in a different hand* : qui cum in forma
dei e(s)set non rapinam arbitratus *est* semet.
[9] ȝ *corr. from* G.   [10] u *altered to* w.

spreads its boughs very far in breadth and in length. It has caused me to speak further than I had intended. But now, by God's help, I will turn to the holy virtues just as I had begun before. But methinks that thou lookest wayward, and appearest heavy, and it is [for] me too much labour to think or to speak about them, unless thou wilt listen to it with good will and understand them.

How the Soul answers and says :

I entreat thee for the same Lord who created thee, to help me, that thou wilt bring forth and teach me these holy virtues just as thou hast begun and laid the ground-work of them. For they are very unknown to me because of the many vices which I have had in me too long. But now I will stop them, and with God's help desist from them, and keep my thoughts in thy teaching. For the holy virtue which is called charity, I beseech and beg thee that thou puttest in writing this hallowed lore, because I ponder much whilst I dwell in this wretched body, and often forget what would be good to me to keep ; and it will also help some other soul.

How Reason answers and thus says :

Methinks that thou wilt blithely understand and learn God's teaching ; and that, I like very well, because it is said in the holy Gospel : *Qui est ex Deo, verba Dei audit,* ' He that is of God heareth blithely God's words.' Now an example comes into my mind which St. Gregory tells us : *Qui virtutes sine humilitate congregat, quasi in vento pulverem portat,* ' He that gathers virtues without humility,' he says, ' he is like the man who bears dust in the wind.' Therefore methinks it is wise, that we first of all things speak of this holy virtue, without which none may be restrained to any advantage or to any good.

Hie me haueð idon speken forðer ðane ic hadde ȝeþouht. Ac nu
ic wile wænden to ðe hali mihtes alswo ich ær hadde iȝunnen be
godes fultume. Ac me þincþ ðat tu lokest aweiward, *and* heui-
liche latst, *and* hit is me to muchel iswinch ðar embe to þenken[1] 4
oðer to speken, bute ȝif ðu woldest mid god wille ðarto lhesten
and hes understanden.

Hu andswereð ðe saule *and* seið:

ICH ðe bidde for ðan ilche hlauerd ðe ðe iscop, me to helpe, ðat 8
alswo ðu hauest ȝegunnen *and* ðane grundwall ileid of ðese
hali mihtes, ðat tu hes forð-bringe *and* me hes tæche[2]. Forðan
hie bieð me swiðe unbecnawe for ðe maniȝe unðeawes ðe ic mid
me to longe habbe ihafd. Ac nu ic hes wile leten, *and* mid godes 12
fultume of hem ȝeswiken, and min ȝeþanc to ðine lore healden.
For ðare hali mihte ðe cariteð is icleped, ic ðe beseche *and* bidde
ðat tu ðese halwende lore *on* write sette, for ðan ic am michel þen-
chind*e* ðar hwile ðe ic *on* ðese wrecche lichame am wuniende, *and* 16
ofte forȝete ðat me god wære te healde*n*; and ec sum oðer saule
hit wile helpe*n*.

[3]Hu andswereð Scadwisnesse *and* þus seið:

ÐAS þe me þincþ þu wilt godes lore bliðeliche understonden *and* 20
liernin; *and* ðat me likeð swiðe wel, forði ðat hit seið on
ðe hali godspelle: *Qui est* ex deo, uerba dei audit, 'Se ðe
is of god*e*, he harkeð bleðeliche godes wordes.' Nu me cumþ on
iþanke an forbisne þe sanctus Gregorius us seið[4]: Qui uir- 24
tutes sine humilitate co*n*gregat, qu*a*si i*n* uento pul-
uer*em* portat, 'Se ðe gadereð mihtes wiðuten eadmodnesse,' he
seið, 'he is ilich ðo ma*n*ne ðe berð dust amidewarde ðe wi*n*de.'
For ði me þingþ þat is wisdom, ðat we alre ðinge arst speken of 28
ðessere hali mihte, wið[5]-uten hwam no*n* ne mai bien wiðhealde*n* te
none freme ne te none gode.

---

[1] *MS.* þennke*n*.　　　[2] o *corr. from* s.　　　[3] *page* 29.
[4] *MS.* seid.　　　　　　　　　　　*MS.* wid.

Of humility.

This holy virtue about which we speak, is called *humilitas*, that is, humility. The holy apostle calls it *virtutem Christi*, 'Christ's own virtue,' because through His manhood, and through the great humility He showed with it, as an example to all mankind, He overcame [the] devil, and all his power over the deceived world. So thou mayst also, if thou wilt learn this virtue of Him, and follow Him. *Discite a me, quia mitis sum et humilis corde, et invenietis requiem animabus vestris*, 'Learn of Me,' says Christ, 'that am meek, and of humble heart: and so ye may find rest unto your souls.' Hear now the first example He showed to mankind and which we can understand. The apostle says about Him: *Qui cum in forma Dei esset, exinanivit semet ipsum, formam servi accipiens*, 'Though Christ, God's Son, was like God, His Father, in age and in power and in every way, He humbled Himself before man's eyes, with His body of a thrall, which He took, and bore therein the burning light which enlightened all His chosen ones who would follow Him.' If thou canst see this light, full surely the higher thou art, the more cautiously wilt thou humble thyself. If thou wilt not humble thyself for this example, know forsooth that thou shalt see little or naught of this light. Woe be to the blind man, who stands amidst the shining sun and sees naught of it! Again, thou mayst learn more examples of this blessed virtue from Christ. He who lifts up with His finger Heaven and earth, and all the things which are therein, like He who created them all, He made Himself as little as is the child of one night's age. He, through whom kings reign, and from whom all power and strength comes, lay wrapt in rags and bound with swaddling bands; and He who is God's Wisdom, from whom come all understanding and all wisdom, and all speaking tongues, He lay as the child which

Of edmodnesse.

ÐIES hali mihte ðe we embe spekeð, hie hatte humilitas, þat
is, eadmodnesse. Ðe hali apostel hes clepeð uirtutem
Christi, 'Cristes awene mihte[1],' forði ðat þurh his mannisnesse, 4
and ðurh ðare michele eadmodnesse ðe he mid hire sceawede, all
mannkyn te forbisne, he ouercam deuel, and all his mihte of ðare
beswikene woreld. Swa ðu niht alswo, ʒif ðu wilt ðese mihte at
him lernin, and him folʒin. Di[s]cite a me, quia mitis sum 8
et humilis corde, et inuenietis requiem animabus uestris, 'Liernið at me,' seið Crist, 'þat ic am softe, and of eadmode
hierte: and swa ʒe muʒen finden reste te ʒeure saule.' Harke nu
ðe formeste forbysne ðe he mankenn sceawede ðas þe we cunnen 12
understonden. Ðe apostel seið be him: Qui cum in forma
dei esset, exinaniuit semet[2] ipsum, formam serui accipiens, 'Ðo ðe Crist, godes sune, was ʒelich godd his fader on
ielde and on mihte[3] and alles kennes wisen, he litlede him seluen 16
to-foren mannes eiʒen, mid his þralles lichame ðe he nam, and ðar
inne bar ðat liht barninde ðe lihte[4] alle his ʒecorene ðe him wolde
folʒin.' Gif ðu ðis liht miht isien, full[5] ʒewiss ðe ðu heiʒer art,
þe warliker[6] ðe seluen wilt neðerin. Gif ðu ðe seluen for ðessere 20
forbisne ne wilt naht neþerin, wite ðu to soðe ðat tu of ðese lihte
litel oðer[7] naht ne ʒesikst. Wa mai bien ðe blinde, ðe stant amidewarde ðe scinende sunne and of hire naht ne isikð! ʒiet[8] ðu
miht of ðessere eadi mihte ma forbisne liernen at Criste. He ðe 24
weiʒþ upp mid his fingre heuene and ierðe and alle ðo þing ðe
ðar inne beoð, al swo he ðe hes alle iscop, he makede him swa litel
swo is ðat child of one niht ielde. He, ðurh hwam kinges rixit,
and alle mihtes and alle strengþes of him cumeð, he lai bewunden 28
on fiteres and mid swaðelbonde ibunden; and he ðe is godes wisdom, ðurh hwam bieð alle wittes and ælle wisdomes and alle tungen
spekinde, he lai alswa ðat child ðe nan god ne cann, ne speken

---

[1] a final s erased.   [2] m corr. over n.   [3] page 30.
[4] At side: erat lux uera que illuminat (the last t corrected from d).
[5] A letter erased before f.   [6] hwarliker MS.   [7] tel o on erasure.
[8] ʒ corr. from G.

E

knows no good, nor can speak, nor see, nor rule itself, through
whom all ears hear, and all men rule themselves, and all eyes see.
He to whom all knees kneel, and all men bow, was obedient [to]
a mortal man, Joseph the carpenter, and His mother. This same
Lord Jesus Christ abode here in this life three-and-thirty winters
[years] and a half among sinful men, very God (whom they could
not see), and very man (whom they could see), and kept all the
laws fully, and was obedient to His Father unto death, for this great
humility which He showed to man as [an] example, and ate and drank,
and rested and slept, and [did] all things as very man, except without
sins. Therefore [the] devil was deceived, and urged the heathen with
his wicked admonitions until they doomed Him to death with great
injustice, and also the most ignominious death, and the most loathly
they could think of, that was on the cross, and also between two
thieves. This they did to increase all the shames and the insults
which they had done to Him before undeservedly. In such wise Christ,
God's Son, overcame the treacherous devil through this blessed
virtue; [He] willed to tear mankind away from him by no force,
because the devil brought him [man] out of Paradise, not by any
force, but by deceiving him; and by right doom of God he [Adam]
was put out, because God had warned him before: *In quacunque
die comederis ex hoc ligno, morte morieris,* 'In the day,' He said,
'that thou eatest of this tree thou art guilty unto death.' All ye
Adam's children who are lustful after new fruits, run, run to the tree
which stands amidst Paradise, viz. of the knowledge both of good
and evil! For your behoof is planted a blessed tree amidst the holy
Church, that is, the holy cross whereon Christ hung, the most
precious fruit which ever yet any tree bore. Use this with
right belief and with firm hope, and with the true love which is
called charity: and to you shall be forgiven the guilt which our
father earned, that is, eternal death. And to increase it, then
ye shall surely have eternal life, all who ever believe in this
true belief, and partake of this holy fruit, which is rightly called
corpus Domini. Take what ye see, bread and wine without;
and in your thoughts believe that which ye see not: that is, Christ's

ne mai, ne isien, ne him seluen wealden, ðurh hwꞓm alle earen
ȝehiereð, and ꞓlle menn hem seluen welden, and alle eiȝene isieð.
He ðat alle cnewes to cnelið, and alle menn to buȝeð, he was
buhsum ane deadliche manne, Iosepe ðe smiðe, and his moder. 4
Ðies ilke hlauerd Iesus [1] Crist, he was her on ðese liue wuniȝende
þrie and þrihti wintre and an half mꞓng senfulle mannen, soð
godd, (ðe hie ne mihten isien [2]), and soð mann, ðe hie isien mihten,
and alle ðe laȝwes fulliche hield, and hersum was his fader anon 8
to ðe deaðe, for ðessere muchele eadmodnesse ðe he sceawede manne
to forbisne, and att and dranc, and reste and sliep, and [3] alle ðiug
alswo soð mann, wiðuten sennen ane. For ði warð dieuel beswiken and beuall þo haðene mid his leðre meneȝinges al hwat hie 12
hine fordemden to deaðe mid muchele unrihte, and ec ðane forcu-
þeste deað, and ðane laðlicheste ðe hie beðenchen mihten, þat was
on rode, and iec betwenen twa þieues. Ðis [4] hie deden to echen alle
ðe scames and ðe bismeres ðe hie arrer him hadde idon un-of- 16
earned.   On ðelliche wise ouercꞓm Crist, godes sune, ðane swikele
dieuel ðurh ðessere iblescede mihte ; nolde mid none strengþe him
binemen mankenn, for ðan ðe ðe dieuel mid none strengþe ut of
paradise hine ne brohte, ac he him beswoc; and mid rihte godes 20
dome he was ut ȝedon, for ði ðat godd hadde iwarned him beforen :
In quacunque die comederis ex hoc ligno, morte morieris, 'Hwilche daiȝe,' he sede, 'se ðu etst of ðese trewe ðu art
deaðes sceldi(h).'   Alle ȝe Adames children ðe bieð lustfull uppe 24
newe wastmes, ierneð, ierneð to ðe trewe ðe stant amidewarde
paradise, witende boðe god and euel! Te ȝewere behofde ys ȝe-
planted an iblesced treu amidde ðare hali chereche, þat is, ðe hali
rode ðe Crist on hangede, ðe derewurðeste wastme ðat æure ȝiete 28
ani treu bar. Notieð hier of mid rihte ileaue and mid faste hope,
and mid ðare soðe luue ðe is icleped kaïite ; and ȝeu scal bien
forȝiuen ðe gelt ðe ure fader of-earnede, þat is, se eche deað. And
to eche, ðan ȝe sculen habben sikerliche ðat eche lif, alle ðe æure 32
belieueð on ðessere soðe beleaue, and of ðese hali wasme notieð,
ðe is mid rihte icleped corpus domini. Notieð ðat ȝe isieð,
bread and win wiðuten ; and on ȝeüre iþanke ilieueð ðat ȝe naht né

---

flesh and His blood.   And know forsooth, as truly as bread and
wine feed the body, while it dwells in this life, so this holy *corpus
Domini* truly feeds both soul and body unto eternal life.   And
as truly as the tree of Paradise was called 'knowledge both
of good and evil,' so this same tree truly bears the fruit which
turns many to life, and also some to death, through misbelief
and for the irreverence with which one takes it as unworthily
as one takes the bread of the board [table], with foul heart and
with foul thought and with foul belly.   Whoever eats this holy
fruit of Him that hung on this tree of life, and is bound with [any]
cardinal sin, who can never be unbound but through the mouth of
a priest or a bishop, so truly may he know, as it is certainly
the flesh and blood of Him who shall judge all mankind, that he there
rightly forejudges himself ere he come to the doom.   Beware whoso
will !   I had thought that I should write nought but of these holy
virtues, though I myself have none as it behoved me ; then I am
led aside sometimes, ere I know anything of it, to another thing :
for if it does not help one, it helps another.   Dear soul, of this holy
virtue humility I cannot stop without letting thee hear more of
it ; because it is so very needful to thee, that thou canst not have
nor keep any other virtue, nor be saved in any wise, unless thou hast
this.   These holy virtues which we speak about are spiritual
and invisible, and therefore it is the more difficult to speak about
them.   They are rightly called God's gifts.   Therefore said the
angel Gabriel to our Lady St. Mary : *Ave, gratia plena !* 'Hail
thou, Mary,' he said, 'full of God's gifts ; thou shalt bear in thy
womb God's own Son.' Well might she then know that she should
be highest over all things in Heaven and on earth (as God's own
mother), except Himself.   But she declared soon that this holy
virtue was in her, when she said : *Ecce ancilla Domini,* 'Look here,'
quoth she, 'God's own servant !' Hark, hark, Eve's daughters, ye
who think so highly of yourselves, that one calls you ladies, go to

ȝesieð: þat is, Cristes flasch *and* his blod! And wite ȝe te soðe,
all swo soðliche swa bread *and* win fedeð ðane lichame, ðar hwile
ðe[1] he on ðese liue wuniȝeð, swa soðliche fett ðis hali corpus
domini baðe saule *and* lichame to ðan eche liue. *And* al swa 4
soðliche swa ðat trew of paradise was icleped 'witinde baðe god
and euel,' swa soðliche berð ðis ilche trew ðat wastme ðe maniȝe
want to liue, *and* ec sume to deaðe, for ðare misbileaue *and* for
ðare unwurscipe ðe me nimð hit al swa unwurðliche swa me nimð 8
ðat bread (of ðæ borde), mid fule herte *and* mid fule þanke *and*
mid fule buce. Hwa se ðis hali wastme of ðan ðe heng on ðese
liues trewe noteð, *and* is mid heued-senne ibunden, (þe naure ne
mai ben unbunden) bute ðurh priestes muðe oðer ðurh biscopes, 12
al swa soðliche wite he, al swa hit is sikerliche his flesc *and* his
blod ðe scal all manken demen, ðat he ðar rihtes for-demþ him
seluen ær he to ðe dome cume. Bie war se ðe wile! Ich hadde
iþoht ðat ic naht ne scolde writen bute of ðese haliȝe mihtes, ðeih 16
ic me selu nono ne habbe swa (swa) me behofde; ðanne am ic
iladd ut oðerhwile, ær ic hit ouht wite, to oðer þinge: for ðan ȝif
hit ne helpð one, hit helpð an oðer. Lieue saule, of ðessore hali
mihte eadmodnesse ic ne mai swa laten ðat tu of hire ȝiet more ne 20
ȝehiere; for ðan hie is þe swa swiðe nedfull, ðat tu ne miht none
oðre mihte habben ne healden, ne on one wise ȝeborȝen bien, bute
þu ðese habbe. Ðese hali mihtes ðe we embe spekeð, hie bieð
gastliche *and* unaseiȝenliche, *and* for ði hit is ðe strengere embe 24
hem to spekene. Hie[2] bieð mid rihte godes ȝiues icleped. For ði
sade ðe angle Gabriel to ure lafdi sainte Marie: Aue, gratia
plena! 'Hail ðu, Marie,' he seide, 'full of godes ȝiues; ðu
scalt beren on ðine wombe godes auwen[3] sune.' Wel hie mihte 28
ða (witen)[4] þat hie scolde bien heiȝest ouer alle þing on heuene *and*
on ierðe, alswo godes aȝen moder, wið-uten him[5] seluen. Ac hie
kedde sone ðat þies hali mihte was on hire, ða hie sæde: Ecce
ancilla domini, 'Loke hier,' cwað hie, 'godes aȝen þralle!' 32
Harkieð, harkieð, Eue dohtren, ȝe ðe telleð swa wel of ȝeu seluen,
þat me[6] clepeð ȝeu lafdies, gað to ðare rihte lafdi *and* lierneð ead-

---

[1] *page* 32. [2] ie *on erasure.* [3] *page* 33.
[4] *added red above.* [5] m *on erasure.* [6] *before* m *an erasure.*

the right Lady and learn meekness! In the time when she was here living in life, it was written : *Maledicta sterilis, quae non peperit,* 'Cursed be the wife who cannot have a child!' They who would not, or could not, bear a child, were very much despised in those days ; and nevertheless she would not on that account forbear, but vowed to keep her maidenhood evermore to her Lord God. She would rather be despised here among men, than lose the great honour among the angels. Therefore she said : *Quia respexit humilitatem ancillae suae. Ecce enim ex hoc beatam me dicent omnes generationes,* 'Because my Lord God regarded the humility of His servant, inasmuch as I had made myself despised among my kin of Israelitish folk, because I would not have man's company nor bear children, but offered Him both my body and soul, and promised Him evermore to keep my maidenhood, therefore all mankind will say that I am blessed that I believed in God's message, which He sent to tell me by Gabriel, His high angel, that I should be, through His great mercy, the mother of God's Son, and also ever remain a maiden. This wonder He did to me, *Quia potens est,* 'because He is mighty and holy,' *et misericordia ejus a progenie in progenies timentibus eum.* 'This great mercy He made known in me. Evermore it lasteth with Him from generation to generation, unto all those men who fear Him.' The holy words which I have written in *magnificat,* know thou forsooth that they are of the holy Gospel, which St. Mary said herself to help men, and to warn all those who fear Him, and for His fear forsake all unrighteousness, to have much hope in God's mercy. And as for those who will not so, she says further again : *Dispersit superbos mente cordis sui, et exaltavit humiles,* 'All who are proud and think much of themselves in the imagination of their hearts, if they do not humble themselves ere they go out of this life ; just as truly as St. Mary said it with her holy mouth, so truly shall God Almighty destroy them, in soul and in body, as those who are against Him and follow

modnesse ! On ðe time ðe hie was[1] hier[2] on liue libbende, hit was
iwriten : Maledicta sterilis, que non (pe)perit, 'ȝewerȝed
bie þat wif ðe child ne mai habben !' Hie ðe child nolden beren
oðer ne mihten, hie waren ihealden swiðe unwurð be ðan daiȝe ; [4]
and naþelæs nolde hie naht ðarfore læten þat hie ne behiet hire
maidenhad æure mo to healden hire lauerde gode. Wolde bliðelicor hier bien unwurðed mang mannen, ðanne[3] hie scolde forliesen
ða michele wurðscipe mang ðo aingles. For ði hie sæide : Quia [8]
respexit humilitatem ancille sue. Ecce enim ex[4] hoc
beatam me dicent omnes generaciones, 'For ði ða(t) mi
lauerd godd lokede to ðare eadmodnesse of his þralle, þat ic me
hadde maked unwurð mang mine kenne of israelisce folke, for þi [12]
ðat ic nolde habben wapmannes imone ne childre beren, ac him ic
ofrede baðe mine lichame and saule, and min maidenhad him behiet eure mo to healden : for ði seggeð all mankynn þat ic am eadi
þat ic beliefde on godes sonde, ðe he me sante seggen bi Gabriel, [16]
his heih ængel, þat ic scolde, ðurh his muchele mildce, bien godes
sunes moder, and ec æure ðurh-wuniȝen maiden. Ðis selcuð he
dede be me, Quia potens est, 'forðan[5] he is mihti and hali,'
et misericordia eius a progenie in progenies timentibus[6] [20]
eum. 'Ðese michele mildce he kedde on me. Eure mo hie ȝelast
mid him fro kenne to kenne, to alle ðo mannen ðe him ondradeð.'
Ðe hali wordes ðe ic habbe[7] iwriten on magnificat, wite ðu te
soðe ðat hie bieð of ðe hali goddspelle, ðe sainte Marie sæde hire [24]
self mannen to helpe, and to warniȝen þat hie michele hope to godes
milce hauen, alle ðe him ondreadeð, and for his eiȝhe alle unrihtwisnesse forlateð. And þo ðe swo ne willeð, hie seið ȝiet forðer :
Dispersit superbos mente cordis sui, et exaltauit humi- [28]
les, 'Alle ðe bieð modi and michel læteð of hem seluen ðurh[8] ðe
þanc of here hierte, bute hie[9] hem seluen neðerien ær ðanne hie
of ðese liue faren : al swa soðliche swa sainte Marie hit sade[10] mid
hire hali muðe, (swa soðliche)[11] scal goddalmihti[12] hes forliesen, [32]
mid saule and mid lichame, al swo ðo ðe bieð aȝeanes him and

---

[1] hie was twice, the middle was hie underlined.   [2] e corr. from o.
[3] ðannne MS.   [4] Corr. from hex by underdotting the h.   [5] page 34.
[6] bus on erasure.   [7] bbe on erasure.   [8] rh corr. from ch.
[9] e corr. from o.   [10] de corr. from ð.   [11] added at side.   [12] almihtin MS.

the devil, who would glorify himself.' But He sent him very low into hell, and all his followers. Again, she says further: *Et exaltavit humiles*, 'Just as He has cast down into the ground of hell all the proud who in this life followed the devil, so He has raised all those who have loved Christ's meekness and kept it, into the joy of the kingdom of Heaven.' Dear soul, call willingly to our Lady St. Mary, that she, for the great meekness which she had in this life, bear thy errand to Christ, her dear Son, that this holy virtue may reign in thee, ere thou departest from thy body ! And how thou mayst know it, I will warn thee. To some men it comes and goes, and with some men it is abiding, and in very few men it is reigning. In the man in whom it is reigning, this is the token : as the worldling lightly laughs at vanities which he sees or hears, so the spiritual man in whom it [humility] reigns, lightly weeps or sobs, sometimes with bitter tears, at other times with very sweet tears, according to what he sees or hears or thinks. Of all the things in which the worldling has consolation and bliss, this spiritual man has nought but grief and sorrow. Though he do better than another, yet let him think worse of himself, than he does of others, who do not so. He thinks in his heart that he is of the same mould as those are who do evil ; and if God had not given it to him, he would full surely do just so or worse ; and as God has mercy and pity on him, He may [also] on them, when it is His will. They are not all humble who live coarsely in meat and in clothes, and go after worldly possessions. Some live coarsely in meat and in clothes, not for God's love, but as it may be natural to them. Reward they shall have, but not such as those shall have who could live exaltedly, but humble themselves in order to have humility and to help God's needy ones. Some others take God's mark upon them, change their clothes and not their manners, judge themselves, and say that they are the most sinful of all men ; but if

dieule¹ folȝieð, ðe wolde him seluen herȝen.' Ac he brohte him
seluen swiðe neðer in to helle, and alle his folȝeres. Ȝiet² hie seið
furðer: Et exaltauit humiles, 'All swa he hafð ineðered
niðer in to helle grunde alle ðe modi ðe hier on liue ðe dieule 4
folȝeden, alswa he haueð iheiȝed alle ðo ðe Cristes eadmodnesse
habbeð ȝeluued and ihelden, in to heuene riches³ merhðe.' Lieue
saule, clepe ȝierne to vre lafdi sainte Marie, ðat hie, for hire
michele eadmodnesse ðe hie hier on ðese liue hadde, ðat hie bere 8
ðin arnde te (Criste⁴), hire lieue sune, ðat ðis hali nihte mote on
þe rixin, ær ðu fram ðine lichame scelie! ¶ And hu ðu miht hes
ȝecnawen, ic ðe wile warnien. To sume menn hie cumð and farð,
and mid sume men hie is wunende, and on swiðe feawe menn hie 12
is rixende. On ða manne ðe⁵ hie is rixende, þis [is] ðe tacne:
al swo ðe woreld-mann lihtliche lei(c)heð of ydelnesse ðe he isieð
oðer iherð, al swa ðe gastliche mann ðe hie on rixeð, lihtliche
wepð oðer sobbeð, oðerhwile mid bitere teares, oðerhwille mid wel 16
swete teares, after ðan ðe he isiecþ oðer iherð oðer þengþ. Of
alle ða þinges ðe ðe woreld-mann hafð frieurenesses and blisses,
nafð ðes gastliche mann bute reunesses and sarinesses. Ðeih he
betere do ðan an oðer, þeih h(w)eðere he læte wers of him seluen, 20
ðanne he do of oðre, ðe swo ne doð. Ðen[c]þ on his herte þat he
is of ðare ilche mo(l)de ðe hie bieð ðe euele doð; and ȝif godd hit
him nadde iȝiuen, he scolde fuliwis⁶ don alswa oðer wurse; and
alswa godd haueð⁸ ore and milsce of him, swa he mai of hem, 24
whanne⁷ his wille⁸ is. Hie ne bieð nauht alle eadmode ðe unorne-
liche libbeð on mete and on claðes, and draȝeð te world-eihte.
Sume libbeð unorneliche on mete and on claðes, naht for godes
luue, ac swilch hit hem bie icynde. Lean hie sculen habben, ac⁹ 28
naht swilch swa sculen habben¹⁰ ðo ðe mihte heiliche libben, ac
hie neðerið hem for eadmodnesse te habben and for to helpen
godes þe(a)ruen. Sume oðre nimeð godes marc (on hem), wandeð
here claðes and naht here þe(a)wes¹¹, diemeð hem seluen, seggeð 32
ðat hi bieð senfullest of alle oðre manne; ac ȝif sum mann hes
undernimþ mid sume unþeawe, hie cyðeð sone mid bitere answere

¹ dieulen MS.   ² G altered to ȝ.   ³ e corr. from o.   ⁴ written above gode.
⁵ page 35.   ⁶ On erasure.   ⁷ w corr. from h.   ⁸ willen MS.   ⁹ a on erasure.
¹⁰ e on erasure.   ¹¹ a letter scratched out between w and e.

anybody reproves them for any vice, they soon show with bitter
answer and with evil words that the doom with which they so
strongly condemned themselves did not come from a meek heart.
Beware, if thou wilt ! Thou hast never true humility in thee, until
thou canst suffer all harms and shame and insults, that any man
may do to thee. And then thou shalt still say, and with the heart
believe it : 'All that I have suffered, I am well worthy to suffer
that and more, for His love who suffered much more for me, all
undeservedly.' Again, beware of one thing ! It is written : *Nimia
humilitas est maxima superbia*, that is : ' If thou behavest thyself
otherwise, than other good meek men, and thou hast [it] not so in
thy heart as thou showest outside, know thou then forsooth that
that is great pride.' Though thou do a great goodness before many
others, it is all lost save humility be with it. Because we have
written here before that God's mercy lasteth evermore on all
men who fear Him, as St. Mary herself bears witness, therefore,
with God's grace, I will tell thee of His fear, after what the holy
scriptures say and reveal to us.

Of fear.

Timor domini is another holy virtue, which, as Solomon said, is
initium sapientiae, ' the beginning of wisdom.' The Holy Ghost
speaks through David the prophet, and says thus : *Venite filii,
audite me, timorem Domini docebo vos*, ' Come children, [ye] who
will learn, and listen to me, and I will teach you the fear of God.'
Quis est homo qui vult vitam ? 'Who is there of you,' he says,
' who will have eternal life, long life, and happy life, who so
dearly love this short life ? ' If thou answerest with heart or with
mouth, and sayst : ' I yearn for it and I will have it very blithely,
if I may,' he teaches thee yet further, and says : *Prohibe linguam
tuam a malo*, ' keep thy tongue from evil, and thy lips that they
speak not guile ;' *diverte a malo et fac bonum*, ' turn from evil
habits, and do good ; seek to have peace with God, so that thou

and mid euele wordes ðat hit ne cam noht of eadmode [1] *herte*, ðe
dom ðe hie swa swiðe fordemden *hem* seluen. Bie war, ȝif ðu
wilt! Ne hafst tu næure soðe eadmodnesse on [2] þe, ær ðu muȝe
poliȝen alle harmes *and* scames *and* bismeres, ðat ani man ðe mai 4
don. *And* ðanne scalt tu ȝiet seggen, *and* mid *herte* hit ilieuen:
' All ðat ic habbe ipoled, ic am wel wurðe ðat *and* more to þolien,
for his luue ðe þolede [3] michel more for me, all un-of-earned.' Giet
bie war of one þinge ! It his ȝewriten: Nimi(a) humilitas (*est*) [8]
maxima superbia, ðat is, ' ȝif ðu latst ðe seluen oðerliker ðanne
oðre gode eadmode menn, *and* tu ne hafst swa on ðine *herte* swa
ðu sceawest wiðuten, ðanne wite ðu te soðe ðat ðat is michel
modinesse.' Ðeih þu do ane michele godnesse teforen maniȝe oðre, 12
all it is forloren bute eadmodnesse bie ðar mide. For ðan ðe we
habbeð hier te-foren writen *þat* godes milsce last æuremo (to) alle
ðo mannen ðe him bieð dradinde, swa swa sainte Marie hire self
berð ȝewitnesse, for ði, mid godes grace, ic ðe wile seggen of his 16
drædnesse, after ðan (ðe) hali writes seggeð *and* us openieð.

Of dradnesse.

TIMOR do*mi*ni is an oðer hali mihte, *þat* ðe Salamun seide
hie is initium sapientie, 'Anginn of wisdom.' Þe hali 20
gast spekð ðurh Dauið ðe profiete, *and* ðus seiþ: Venite fili,
audite me, timorem do*mi*ni docebo uos, 'Cumeð children,
ðe liernien willeð, *and* (h)lesteð me, *and* ic eu wile tachen godes
drædnesse.' Qu*i*s e*st* homo qui uult uitam? 'Hwa is *þat*,' 24
he seiþ, ' ðe wile hauen ðat eche lif, *þat* lange lif, ðat eadi lif of
ȝeu, ðe luuiȝeð swa swiðe ðis scorte lif?' Ȝif ðu andswerest mid
herte oðer mid muðe, *and* seist: ' Ic hit ȝ(i)erne *and* ic hit wile
hauen swiðe bliðeliche, ȝif ic mai,' he wisseð ðe ȝiet forðer, *and* 28
seið: Proibe linguam tuam a malo, 'forbet ðine tunge fram
euele, *and* ðine lippen ðat he ne speken swikedo*m*;' diuerte a
malo *et* fac (bonu*m*) [4], 'wænd fro euel wune, and [5] do god ;
siec ðat tu haue pais aȝeanes gode, *þat* ðu naht ne healde aȝeanes 32

---

[1] *The first* e *on erasure.* [2] *A letter scratched out behind* n.
[3] *page* 36. [4] bonu*m* *above erasure.*
[5] *an erasure before* a.

hold not against His commandments nor against any man, neither
with word nor with deed, which thou canst rule.' When thou
hast found this peace, then thou art righteous: and have always
the fear of God with thee, lest thou lose this. 'Then will God's
eyes be upon thee, that nothing may hurt thee, and His ears open
unto thy cries, that He will deny thee nothing.' Thus the Holy
Ghost advises thee, who speaks still every day through the psalm
which thou seest or hearest. Beware, if thou wilt ! Let him who
will not understand, nor keep this holy lore of the Holy Ghost, listen
what He says thereafter : *Vultus autem Domini super facientes mala,
ut disperdat de terra memoriam eorum,* 'God,' He says, 'looks
wrathfully upon them that do evil, and who will not cease through
His fear. Therefore will God's wrath come upon them, ere they know
it, and cut them off, both body and soul, from this mortal land
wherein they dwell and which they love so much.' So they
shall also lose the everlasting land, which is eternal life, because
they would not listen to God's love nor follow [it]. Again, He
says that their remembrance will be so lost, that men will neither
speak nor think of them. Again, saith holy Writ : *Qui timet
Deum, faciet bona ; qui autem duri cordis est, corruet in malum,*
'He that feareth God, forbeareth always, for awe of Him, to do
evil ; he who is of hard heart, feareth not God, and therefore he
goeth from evil unto evil and from sin unto sin.' Many men are
greatly deceived who fear a mortal man more than they do God
Almighty, [they] who for shame of the world or for their short life,
forswear themselves wholly, and slay their own soul, and lose
eternal life. Therefore Jesus Christ warns us, and says thus :
*Nolite timere eos qui corpus occidunt, animam autem non possunt
occidere,* 'Fear not,' He said, 'them who can kill your body ; but
of Him ye ought to be adread, who can cast both body and soul
into the fire of hell.' Again says the Book of Wisdom : *Deum
time, et mandata ejus observa,* 'Fear God, and keep His commandments !' Every man ought to do this, because nothing will fail
them, neither in this life nor in the other, who fear and love Him

his bebode ne aȝean none manne, ne mid worde ne mid weorke, ðas
ðe ðu muȝe wealden.' Ðanne ðu ðese sibsumnnesse hafst ȝefun-
den, [1] ðanne art tu rihtwis : *and* haue æure godes drædnesse mid
þe, þ*at* ðu ðis ne forlies. 'Ðanne sculen godes eiȝen bien uppe ðe, 4
ðat nanðing ne mai ðe deriȝen, *and* his earen opene to ðine
b(i)enes, ðat naþing he ðe ne wile wærnen.' Ðus ðe ratt ðe halie
gast, ðe spekð ȝiet alche dai ðurh ðene selm ðe ðu ȝesikst oðer
iherst. Bie war, ȝif ðu wile ! Se ðe nele ðese hali lare of ðe hali 8
gast understanden, (ne wiðealden [2]), hlest hwat he seið ðar after :
**Vultus aut*em* domini super facientes mala, ut disperdat
de ter*r*a memoria*m* eo*rum*,** 'Godd,' he [3] seið, 'lokeð wraðliche
uppe he*m* ðe euele doð, ðe for his dradnesse ne willeð iswike*n*. 12
For ði scal godes wraððe cumen on he*m*, ær hie hit aut witen, and
forliesen hem, baðe li(came) [4] *and* saule, of ðese deadliche lande ðe
hie on wunieð *and* swa michel luuiȝeð.' Swa hie sculen iec forliese*n* ðat liuiende land, þ*at* is, ðat eche lif, for ðan ðe hie nolden 16
godes lare hlesten ne folȝin. Giet he seið ðat here ȝemiend scal
swo bien forloren, ðat me of he*m* ne scal neiðer ne speken ne
þenche*n* [5]. Giet seið ðat hali writ : **Qui timet de*um*, faciet
bona; q*ui* aut*em* duri cordis *est*, corruet i*n* malu*m*,** 'Se 20
ðe ondrat godd, he lat æure ðe euel to done for his heiȝe ; se ðe is
of hard*e* hierte, he no*n*dratt noht godd, *and* for ði he farð from
euele to euele *and* fram senne to senne.' Hit bieð maniȝe men
swiðe beswikene ðat more dradeð ane deadliche manne ðane he doð 24
god almihtin, ðe for ðare worldes scame oðer for here scorte liue,
hem al forswerieð, *and* sleað here auȝene saule, *and* forlieseð ðat
eche lif. Forði us warneð Ie*sus* [6] C*ri*st, *and* ðus seið : **Nolite
timere eos q*ui* corpus occidu*n*t, anima*m* aute*m* [7] non** 28
possunt occide*r*e, 'Ne drædeð naht,' he sade, 'hem ðe ȝure [8]
lichame muȝen ofslean ; ac of hi*m* ȝe aweð to ben ofdrad, þe mai
baðe lichame *and* saule werpe*n* i*n* to ðe fier of helle.' Eft seið ðe
boc of wisdome : **Deum time, *et* mandata ei*us* obserua,** 32
'Dræd godd, *and* hald his bebode !' Þis auh(t) elch ma*n*n te
do*n*ne, forðan no þing hem ne scall trukien, on ðese liue ne on

---

[1] *page* 37.　　[2] *On the side.*　　[3] h *corr. from* s.　　[4] came *written above* f.
[5] *On the side :* u*t* disperdat de ter*r*a memoria*m* eo*rum*.　　　[6] iħu *MS.*
[7] *page* 38.　　　[8] *corr. from* ȝeuere *above* here.

in truth. After this fear of pain, comes another which is called *timor sanctus*, that is, holy fear, which shall last for ever, world without end, because it is mingled with the true love which is called charity. This fear is as sweet as the son's who fears his father, not for any pain, but fears him lest he lose his sweet love; and therefore he serves his father with great love, mingled with fear. This same fear is needful to us. *Qui timet Deum nihil negligit*, 'He who feareth God, for his carelessness he omitteth to do nought of what he hath to do.' From this fear of God springs another of God's gifts, which is very needful to every man who will be saved.

Of ruth (pity).

Pietas is called one of these holy virtues, that is, ruth (pity) in English. It comes from the wounded hearts which are wounded with God's arrows. Of them says the prophet: *Sagittae tuae acutae*, 'Lord,' he said, 'sharp are Thy arrows;' they wound the guilty man who fought against Thee through the devil's lore. Thou throwest him down, so that he lies stretched upon the bare earth, and esteems himself as earth, weeps and wails that he ever was shaped to man, that he should have misdone so much against his Creator, for which he deserves the pain of hell. Ruth (pity) causes [him] to do this, which is assuredly God's gift. It causes him at first to have ruth (pity) on himself, and then on his neighbour, for all [the] misfortunes which befall him for his sins. If thou canst get this gift of God's, then thou wilt have a soft and good heart, and compassionate to help thyself, and to save thy soul from the pains which it has deserved. Have thou no hope in father nor in mother, in son nor in daughter, in brother nor in sister, nor in any earthly man, when thy body lies under the earth separated from all living men, alone, foul, stinking, full of worms, and in the darkness [away] from all light, and thou, poor soul, in the boiling heat of the hot fire, and again, sometimes, in the shivering chill, so that thou canst not help thyself, until thou have redeemed all thy sins, and be all cleansed

ðere oðre, ðe him drædeð *and* luuiʒeð inne soðe. After ðesse [1]
drædnesse ðe is of pine, cumð an oðer ðe is icleped timor sanc-
t us, *þat* is, hali dradnesse, ðe æure scal ilasten, on worelde [2] woreld,
forðan ðe hie is imæng(d) mid ðare soðe luue ðe hatte kariteð. 4
Dies dradnesse is swete, al swa ðe (sune ðe) drat his fader, naht
for noɫe pine, ac drat him ðat he forliese his swete luue; *and*
for ði he ðeneð his fader mid muchele luue, imaingd mid dradnesse.
Dies ilke dradnesse us behoueð.　Qui timet *d e*um nich*i l* ne- 8
gligit, 'Se ðe gode on-dratt, for his ʒemeleste ne latt he naht te [3]
donne of ðat he haueð te donne.'　Of ðesere godes dradnesse
springþ ut an oðer godes ʒiue, ðe is swiðe niedfull auriche manne
ðe i-boreʒen scal bien.　　　　　　　　　　　　　　　　12

Of reuhðe [4].

PIETAS hatte on of ðese hali mihtes, *þat* is, reuhðe [4] cn enge-
lisc. Hie cumþ of ðare iwundede herte ðe bien iwunded mid
godes arewen. Of he*m* seið ðe profiete : Sagitte tue acute, 16
'Lauerd,' he sæde, ' scarpe bien ðine arewen'; hie wundieð ðane
forgilte man*n* ðe wan*n* ongeane(s) ðe ðurh dieules lare. Þu wer-
pest him ðer niðer, *þat* he lið istreiht upe ðare bare ierðe, *and* halt
him seluen [5] for ierðe, wepð *and* woneð ðat he æure was to ma*n*ne 20
iscape*n*, ðat he scolde swa michel habbe*n* misdon aʒean his sceppend, for hwat he [6] ofearneð [7] helle pine. Ðis dcð reuhðe don, ðe
is iwis godes ʒiue. Hie dieð hi*m* arst habben reuhðe of hi*m* seluen,
and ðanne of his nexte*n*, of alle unʒelimpes ðe hi*m* for his sennes 24
to-cumeð. Gif ðu ðese godes ʒiue biʒete*n* miht, þan*n*e scalt tu
hauen nexce herte (*and*) gode, *and* riewsiend*e* ðe seluen to helpe,
and ðine saule to aliesen fram ðo pines ðe hie ofearne*il* hafð. Ne
haue ðu hope te fader ne te moder, te sune ne te dohter, te broðer ne 28
te swuster, ne te na*n* ier[ð]lich ma*n*n, ðanne þi*n* lichame lið under
ierðe ʒetwamd fram alle liuiende ma*n*ne, all-ane, fule, stinkende,
full of wermes, *and* on ða þiesternesse fram alle lihte, *and* ðu, earme
saule, on ðe wallende brene of ðe hote fiere, *and* eft, embehwile, on 32
ðe chiurerinde chele, ðat tu ðe selue*n* naht ne miht helpe*n*, ær

---

[1] desse *MS.*　　　[2] *A later hand has inserted* to.　　　[3] t *corr. from* d.
[4] u *corr. from* w.　　　[5] *on erasure.*　　　[6] *page* 39.　　　[7] earned *MS.*

from all thy misdeeds through the pains which thou sufferest, and through masses and prayers and alms which one does for thee. Then thou wilt sorely repent that thou hadst not helped thyself better the while thou couldst. How should God, or any of His saints, or any of thy friends, relation or stranger, have ruth or mercy on thee, since thou thyself hast now here none of thyself? This is God's gift, if thou thus considerest and workest thereafter.

Of knowledge.

After this comes another gift of God, which is called *scientia*, that is, understanding or knowledge. Through it thou canst know all the crafts which are written in books. It teaches thee good manners and to lead [a] good life, how thou shalt turn from evil, and how thou shalt do good works. But there are some who are held very wise through this gift of God, and turn for themselves and also for some others to great harm, what God gave them for their great good. Hereof said the apostle: *Scientia inflat, caritas aedificat.* He says that 'this sharp knowledge puffs up the man who has it without charity.' In such a way it puffs [him] up that he thinks well of himself and despises others who cannot [do] so; and in such a way he loses what should help him best, that is, God's and man's love. Therefore know thou full well, when thou losest man's love through thy pride, it seems to thee that thou needst not honour, nor love, a man lower than thyself, or because he is not so wise as thou, or is not so rich as thou, or of so high family as thou, or not so honoured [a] man as thou in the false world, and for such things thou despisest him and omittest to call on him, or to help him in his need. Full assuredly, thou justly losest here God's love and His grace; and take this for example! Except thou hast God's and all men's love, thou canst not do any good [thing] that will ever be agreeable to God. Of this said the apostle: *Si distribuero omnes facultates meas, et cetera,* 'If I bestow all that I have for God's love, and still, over and above it,

ðanne ðu habbe ðine sennes al aboht, and all bie iclensed [1] of alle
ðine misdædes ðurh ða pines ðe ðu þolest, *and* ðurh masses *and*
bienes *and* ælmesses ðe me doð for ðe. Ðanne ðe wile sare rewen
ðat tu ðe seluen ne haddest betere iholpen ðare hwile ðe ðu 4
mihtest. Hu scolde godd, oðer ani of his halȝen, oðer ani of
ðine friend, sibbe oðer framde, hauen rewðe oðer mildce of ðe,
seððen ðu ðe seluen ne hafst nu hier none of ðe seluen ? Þis is
godes ȝiue, ȝif ðu dus ðe beþencst *and* ðar after wercst. 8

Of witte.

HIER after cumþ an oðer godes ȝiue, þe is icleped sciencia,
þ*at* is, inȝehied oðer witt. Ðurh hire ðu miht witen alle
craftes ðe on boche bieð ȝewriten. Hie ðe takð [2] gode [3] þeawes *and* 12
god lif to leden, hu ðu scalt fram ðan euele buȝen, a hu ðu
scalt gode werkes don. Ac hit bieð sume ðe bieð swiðe wise
ihealden [4] ðurh ðessere godes ȝiue, *and* want hem seluen *and* iec
sumen oðre te michele hearme, þat ðe godd hem ȝaf for here 16
michele gode. Herof sade ðe apostel: Scientia inflat, karitas
edificat. He seið þ*at* ' ðis scarpe iwitt swelð ðane mann ðe hes
haueð wiðuten charite.' On swilche wise hie swelð ðat he latt
wel of him seluen, and forhoweð oðre ðe swo ne cunnen ; *and* 20
on swilche wise he forliest ðat him betst scolde helpen, þat is,
godes luue *and* mannes. For ðan (þ*at*) wite ðu te fulle soðe,
ðanne ðu forliest mannes luue for ði modinesse, þe þingð ðat
þu naust naht to wurðin ne te luue(n) ane wurse mann ðane ðu 24
art, oðer ðat he nis alswa wis alse ðu, oðer he nis na swa riche
se ðu, oðer of swa heiȝe kenne swa ðu, oðer naht alswa wurðed
mann swa ðu on ðare lease woreld ; *and* for ðelliche þinge hine
forhowest, *and* forlatst ðat tu ne wilt to him clepiȝen, ne to his 28
niede him helpen. Fulȝewis ðu forliest hier rihtes godes luue
and his grace, *and* nem ðis to forbisne ! Bute ðu habbe godes luue
and alre manne, ðu ne miht don non god ðe æure gode bie
ȝecweme. Ðarof sade ðe apostele: Si distribuero omnes 32
facultates meas, *et* cetera, ' Gif ic deale all ðat ic habbe for
godes luue, (*and* ȝiet on-uuen ðan ȝiue mine likame to barnin

---

[1] *An erasure between* l *and* e.   [2] takd *MS.*
[3] *a letter erased after* e.   [4] *page* 40.

give my body to be burned all to dust for God's love, and I hate a single man, then I have not charity, and so I have lost all.' Now some one may say: 'Shall I love the evil man?' Listen what The Most High says to thee: *Diliges proximum sicut te ipsum* 'Love they neighbour as thyself, whatever man he be!' Be he never so much guilty, he is always thy neighbour by nature. Love the [human] nature [in him], and hate his evil! If thou canst mend it, mend it as thou wouldst wish men to mend thine, if thou wert as guilty as he, and think what the Writ says: 'Mercy should always be above righteous doom.' For such things, many very wise men lose God's love and His grace, because they neither have, nor care to have, their fellow-Christians' love, but rely upon their great wisdom; and are often deceived. Would they [only] listen to the holy apostle, they would not stand in this need! *Si quis videtur inter vos sapiens esse, stultus fiat, ut sit sapiens,* 'If any man among you,' says he, 'seemeth to be wise in this world, let him become a fool, and so he may be wise.' The wise worldling esteems it great folly for a man to leave, for God's love, house and home, wife and child, gold and silver, and all worldly wealth, and to become such a great wretch as he who had nothing; [he] says that it is better [for] him to sit in his own [house], and to give alms and to harbour blessed men, than to leave all this, and live by other men's alms. Concerning this, let us listen to Christ's own doom, and so we may be all the more sure in this conflict. It is said in the holy Gospel that a rich young man came to Christ in the days when He was dwelling here in the body, and said: *Quid faciam, Domine, ut habeam vitam aeternam?* 'Lord,' quoth he, 'what shall I do that I may have eternal life?' Our Lord answered him, and said: *Mandata nosti,* 'Thou knowest God's commandments. Thou shalt not slay, nor steal, nor rob, nor commit adultery, nor break the other commandments of God.' 'Oh, Lord,' quoth he, 'all these commandments have I kept from childhood up, and I have broken none.' Then again Christ answered him: 'Good man, thou art as he who has done no cardinal sin.' *Si vis perfectus esse, vade et*

al to duste for godes luue)[1], *and* ic hatie on-lepi mann, ðanne
ne habbe ic naht kariteð, *and* swa ic habbe all forlore*n*.' Nu
seið sum ma*n*n: 'Scal ic luuiȝe ðane euele mann?' Hlest hwat
se heiȝeste ðe seið: Ðiliges pro*x*imum sicut te ip*s*um, 4
'Luue ðine nexte al swa ðe seluen, hwat ma*n*ne swo he æure bie!'
Ne bie he næure swa swiðe forȝelt, æure he is ðin nexte after
ȝekynde. Luue ða ȝekynde, *and* hate his euel. Ȝif ðu miht hit
bieten, b(i)et hit alswo ðu woldest ðat me[2] bette þin, ȝif[3] ðu 8
wære swo forȝilt al so he, *and* þenc ðat ðe writt seið þ*at* æure bie
ðe mildce ouer ðe rihte dome. For ðelliche þinge maniȝe of ðe
wel wise me*n*n forlieseð godes luue *and* his grace, for ði ðat hie
ne habbeð, ne ne reccheð to habben, here emcristenes luue, ac 12
hopieð to here michele wisdome, *and* ofte bieð beswikene. Wolden
hie hlesten ðane hali apostel, swa hie ne ðorften! Si q*ui*s
uidet*ur* int*er* nos sapie*n*s e*ss*e, stult*us* fiat ut sit sapiens,
'Ȝif ȝeure ani,' he seið, 'is ihealde*n* for wis o*n* ðare woreld, becume 16
sott, *and* swa he mai bie*n* wis.' Ðe wise woreld-mann, he halt
michel sothade ðat mann forlate, for godes luue, hus *and* ham,
wif *and* child, *and* gold *and* seluer, *and* alle worldes wele, *and*
becume swo michel wrecche al swo he ðe naht ne hadde; seið 20
ðat him is betere to sitte*n* on his aȝen, *and* ȝiuen almessen *and*
herberȝin sæli me*n*n, ðanne he scolde al ðat late*n*, and libben bi
oðres ma*n*nes almesse. Hleste we herof Cristes aȝene dom,
and swa we muȝen bie*n* ðe sikerere of ðese iflite. Hit seið on 24
ða hali goddspelle þ*at* an riche iungman cam to Crist be ðo
daiȝe*n* ðe he hier lichamliche was wuniende, *and* seide: Q*u*id
faciam, d*omi*ne, ut habea*m* vitam eternam? 'Hlauerd,'
cwað he, 'hwat mai ic do*n* ðat ic mihte haue*n* ðat eche lif?' 28
Vre drihte*n* him andswerede, *and* seid*e*: Mandata nosti,
'Ȝecnoust þu godes bebodes. Ne sleih, ne ne stell, ne reaue, ne
forliȝe[4] ðe on hordomes, ne oðre godes forbodes ne tebrec.' 'A,
hlaueerd,' cwað he, 'alle ðese bebodes ic habbe ihealde fra*m* 32
childhade, swa ðat ic nabbe na*n* tebrocen.' Ðe ȝiet him andswerede Crist: 'God[5] man, ðu art al swo he ðe non heued-senne
ne haueð ido*n*.' Si uis p*er*fect*us* e*ss*e, vade *et* uende omnia

---

[1] *written above and on the side.*   [2] *page* 41   [3] Gif *MS.*
      [4] r *corr. from* l.   [5] *page* 42

vende omnia quae habes, etc., 'If thou wilt,' He said, 'become a perfectly good man, go and sell all that thou hast, and give it to
God's wretched [folk], and follow me!' This young man went
away sorry. Here we have learned that it is better to forsake all
that one owns, with good will, than to abide until death take it
from him, against his will. Listen now what Christ said concerning the rich man who went away sorry, and would not listen
to His counsel: 'A rich man can no more,' quoth He, 'enter into
the kingdom of Heaven, than a camel can go through the eye of
a needle.' *Vae vobis divitibus, qui habetis consolationem vestram,*
'Woe unto you,' quoth He, 'ye rich men, who have so great joy in
your great riches, that ye forget God and the salvation of your
souls!' Therefore no good seed of God's words can grow in the
mould of your hearts, through the great care ye have about your
wealth, which ye much covet, and love and like, and dread to lose.
Amongst all these thoughts the wretched heart is made so heavy,
that no word of God can spring up, nor remembrance of God, nor
of His kingdom, nor of the salvation of one's soul. But glee and
amusements, and hounds and hawks, and all the things which
here may gladden you, ye will blithely see and hear; and ye
might have all this if ye loved God more than all this which we
have spoken about. Many of you are greatly deceived. Ye fancy
that ye love God more than ye do your possessions; but let Him
tell what is most true, who is rightly called Truth: *Ubi est
thesaurus, ibi est et cor tuum,* 'Where thy hoard is, there is thy
heart,' said He. There is thy heart where thy thoughts mostly
are, and there is thy greatest love. Understand now well thyself,
and look whether thou thinkest more of God than of thy poses-
sions, and know thou forsooth: that of which thou thinkest more,
thou lovest more. Woe to the way of the man to whom God has
given understanding and wisdom, who will love more the creatures
which God created, than he does his Creator, who created him
and all things! Dear soul, I warn and beg thee eagerly, that
thou, with this gift of God's which is called *scientia*, mayst understand and learn firmly the kinds of sins, whence and when they

q*ue* habes, *et cetera*[1], 'Gif ðu wilt,' he seide, ' bien ðurhut god mann, ga *and* sell all ðat tu hafst, *and* ȝif hit gode(s) wrecchen, *and* swa folȝe me !' Ðies ȝunge mann ȝiede a-wei sari. Hier we habbeð ilierned ðat it is betere to læten all ðat te mann awh, 4 mid gode wille, þanne he abide all hwat deað hit him beneme, his unþankes[2]. Hlest nu hwat[3] C*r*ist sade be ða riche manne ðe ȝiede awei sari, *and* his ræd nolde lesten : ' Ne mai na more,' cwað he, ' ðe riche mann cumen in to heuene riche, ðanne mai ðe 8 oluende cumen ðurh ðe nædle eiȝen.' Ve uobis diuitibus, qui habetis consolationem uestram[1], 'Wa ȝeu,' cwað he, ' ȝie riche menn, ðe habbeð swa michele blisse of ȝeuer michele[4] richeise, þat ȝie godd forȝeten *and* ȝeure saule hæle !' For ði ne 12 mai wexen non god sad of godes wordes on ȝeure herte molde, for ðan michele embeðanc ðe ȝie habbeð on ȝeure michele wele, ðe ȝie michel ȝitsið, *and* luuieð *and* likeð, *and* dradeð to forliesen[5]. (A)mang[6] alle ðese embeðankes is ðe wrecche hierte swa iheueȝed, 16 þat ncn godes word upp ne mai springen, ne of godd þenken, ne of his riche, ne of his saule hale. Ac gleues *and* skentinges, *and* hundes *and* hauekes, *and* alle ðo þing ðe ȝeu hier gladien mai, þat ȝe willen bliðeliche isien *and* ȝehieren; *and* all ðis ȝe mihten 20 hauen, ȝif ȝe godd luueden mare ðanne all ðis ðe we embe hauen ispeken. Maniȝe of ȝeu bien swiðe beswikene. Weneð ðat ȝe luuen more godd ðanne ȝe den ȝeure eihte; ac læt him seggen ðat soðeste, ðe is mid rihte Soð icleped: Vbi est[7] tesaurus, 24 ibi est et cor tuum, 'Ðar ðe ðin hord is, þær is þin herte,' he sæde. Ðar is ðin herte ðarof ðe ðu mæst þenkst, *and* ðar is ðin mæste luue. Vnderstand nu wel ðe seluen, *and* loke hwaðer ðu þenke more of godd ðe of ðin eihte, *and* wite ðu te soþe : 28 hwarof ðu mare þenkst, ðat tu luuest mare ! Walewa ðas siðes, þat ani mann ðat godd hafð iȝiuen witt *and* wisdcm, scall luuien[8] more ðe scaftes ðe godd ȝescop, ðanne he do his sceppend, ðe him *and* alle þing[9] ȝescop ! Lieue saule, ic ðe warni *and* ȝierne bidde, ðat 32 tu, mid ðessere godes ȝiue ðe scientia hatte, understande *and* lierne fastliche ða ȝekyndes of sennes, hwannen *and* hwanne[10] (hie

---

[1] *Evangelista on side, red.*   [2] unstankes *MS.*   [3] hwat *twice.*
[4] i *on erasure.*   [5] an *erasure above.* n.   [6] A added red.
[7] *page* 43.   [8] liuien *MS.*   [9] þinng *MS.*   [10] w *corr. from* a.

will come, that thou mayst guard against them; and when thou
art wounded through them, that thou mayst know how to heal
thy wounds; and again, concerning those holy virtues, that
thou mayst know how to recognise them well, and to keep them
with God's help.

Of counsel.

Here comes another of God's gifts, which is called *consilium*,
that is, counsel. Of this said Solomon: *Omnia fac cum consilio, et postea non poenitebis,* 'Do all things after counsel; afterwards thou wilt not repent.' Thou hast heard and learned many
good things; accordingly take counsel, not from a wise man only,
but from one who is both wise and also God-fearing, and tried in
religion. What sort of life thou oughtst to lead best, depends
much, whether thou hast misdone much, or little; and then, one
must look after thy state, and thy body's health or sickness.
Because it is a great danger for thee, if thou undertakest such
things as thou canst not perform through sickness, which thou
hadst promised to God. Again, be aware, if thou hast promised
God to do much good, and to keep a holy life: thou canst not keep
again the less good life thou hadst before, and be saved. Concerning this says the holy Gospel: *Qui mittit manum suam ad aratrum,
et respicit retro, non est aptus regno Dei,* 'Who puts his hand to the
plough of the Gospel, and will bear Christ's yoke, and forsakes all
the world, and [then] looks back, turning to the world, is not
worthy of the kingdom of Heaven.' This is said of the man who
forsakes all the world, and follows God's voice, which says thus:
Venite ad me omnes qui laboratis et onorati estis, et cet., 'Come unto
Me,' says He, 'all ye that labour with evil works, and are heavy
laden with many kinds of sins, and I will give you rest unto your
souls; and I will lighten your burden, if ye will listen to My
counsel. Bear My yoke of obedience upon you, which is soft, and
the burden of My commandments is light to hold. With My help
ye can do everything; without Me, nothing.' For this sweet call-
ing come both good and evil, and leave all the world, and take
Christ's mark of true religion upon them, of whatsoever kind it may

cumen)[1], þat ðu muȝe bien war wið hem; and ðar ðu art ðurh hem
ȝewunded, ðat ðu cunne hes halen; and eft, of ðese hali mihtes,
ðat tu hes kunne wel ȝecnawen, and mid godes fultume wiðhealden.

4

Of rade.

HIER after cumð an oðer godes ȝiue, ðe is icleped consilium, þat
is, ræd. Herof seide Salomon: Omnia fac cum consilio,
et postea non penitebis, 'Do alle þing after rade, ðer after hit 8
ne scal þe ofþenchen.' Maniȝe gode þinges ðu hafst iherd and
ilierned; nim ðar after rad, naht at wise manne one, and þe bie
baðe [2] wis and ec goddfrihti, and ifonded of religiun. Hwilch lif
ðu betst muȝe laden, ðat auþ to benne michel after ðan ðe ðu 12
hafst michel misdon, oðer litel; and ðanne mot me lokin ðin
ikinde, and ðinne lichame(s) hæle oðer unhale. Forðan, ȝif ðu
undernimst swilch ðat tu for unhale ne miht iforðin, ðat ðu godd
haddest behaten, hit is ðe [3] michel [4] hauht [5]. Eftsones bie warr, 16
ȝif ðu behatst god michel god te donn, and heih lif te healden:
ðat lasse gode lif ðe ðu arrer hafdest, ne miht tu naht eft healden,
and bien ȝeboreȝen [6]. Hier of seið ðat hali godspell: Qui
mittit manum s(u)am ad aratrum, et respicit retro, 20
non est aptus regno dei, 'Se ðe doð his hand to ðere sull
of godspelle, and Cristes ȝoc wile beren, and forlat al ðe woreld,
and loceð abach, wændinde to ðe woreld, he nis naht wurðe [7]
heuene riche.' Dis is ȝesæd bi ða manne ðe forlat al ðe woreld, 24
and folȝeð godes stiefne, ðe ðus seið: Venite ad me omnes qui
laboratis et honorati estis, et cetera, 'Cumeð to me,' he seið,
'alle ðe swinkeð mid euele werkes, and ȝeheueȝed bieð mid mani-
kennes sennes, and ic eu wile ȝiue reste to ȝeuer saule, and ic wile 28
lihten ȝeuer berðene, ȝif ȝe mine rad hlesten willeð. Bereð min
ȝoc uppe ȝeu, of hersumnesse, þe is softe, and min berðen is liht,
of mine bebodes to healden. Mid mine fultume alle ðing ȝe
muȝen; wið-uten me, nanþing.' For ðessere swete clepienge 32
cumeð baðe gode and euele, and lateð all ðe woreld, and nimeð
Cristes marc uppen hem, of soðe religiun, hwilche kennes swa hit

---

[1] red above; the last word is written cinneri or cinnery.　　[2] bade MS.
[3] page 44.　　[4] hit is te repeated on page 44; between te and michel a
little stroke (like i) above the line.　[5] hauth MS.　[6] The second ȝ corr. from c.
[7] wurde MS.

be. The Holy Ghost warns them, who says: 'God who hath called you out of the false world into good life, doeth not force you to it, but sayeth: *Si vis perfectus esse,* 'If thou wilt,' He says, 'be a perfectly good man, forsake the world; and if thou wilt not, thou mayst dwell in the world, and also be saved, if thou well keepest thy baptism.' But if thou canst not save thyself well, or thou wilt suffer more, for Christ's love, and lead a better life : listen, I will warn thee concerning it. *Fili, accedens ad servitudinem Dei, etc.,* 'Dear son,' says He, 'if thou comest to God's house to serve Him, be well aware, and prepare thy soul against many kinds of temptations, and stand with great dread, because thou shalt be tried in the holy life as is the pot which is put into the burning oven. If it bursts in it and breaks, it is lost and soon thrown out ; if it remains whole and sound, the potter puts it where it was destined to.' The apostle says that God will not suffer one of His chosen ones to be tried more than he can bear. But they who burst within their dwellings, through the pride with which their heart is as much filled as a bladder is with wind, are thrown out through the devil's lore, not for their own sake only, but also in order to put others to flight. Then they will go again into the world, and be worse than they were before. They will cast away their counsel and their clothes, and betake themselves to the world and are apostates from Christ, forsakers, not with words, but with works, which is worse, if it may be. A monk may go out with leave into a hermitage, or to live in solitude, if he has God to witness that he does so with a pure heart, in order to do better. We find in the Writ that a hermit ought not to live in the wilderness, except he be at first tried through rule and through a master in the spiritual oven that we spoke about before. An anchorite's life is a very spiritual one. These two lives, the hermit's and a solitary life, which we now call an anchorite's, were formerly spent far from men and [those] were much loved and exalted by the holy Fathers who lived so and kept it honourably. So one may still find some— thanked be God !—who lead a very spiritual life according to the world which is now. Also one may find, among men of all kinds of

bie. Ðe hali gast[1] (hem) warneð, *and* seið : 'Godd ðe ȝeu haueð
icleped ut of ðare lease woreld i*n* to gode liue, he ne nett ȝeu naht
ðer to, ac seið : Si uis p*erfectus* esse, 'ȝif ðu wilt,' he seið,
'bie*n* ðurhut god man*n*, ðanne forlat ðu ðe woreld ; *and* ȝif[2] ðu[3] 4
nelt naht, þu miht wuniȝen o*n* ðare woreld, *and* ec bien ȝeboreȝen,
ȝif ðu ði*n*ne cristendo*m* wel hal'(d)st.' Ac ȝif ðu ne miht ðe naht
wel berȝen[4], oðer ðu wilt, for Cristes luue, more þoliȝen, *and* betere
lif laden: lhist[5], ðerof ic ðe wile warnin. Fili, acce*dens* ad 8
seruitudine*m* dei, *et cetera*[6], 'Lieue sune,' he seið, 'þanne ðu
cu*m*st to godes huse *him* to ðenin, bie wel war, *and* ȝarke ðine
saule aȝen maniȝes ke*n*nes fandinges, *and* stand mid michel dradnesse, forðan ðu scalt bie*n* ȝefonded on ða hali liue al swo is þe 12
pott ðe is ido*n* on ðe barne*n*de ofne. Gif he ðar i*n*ne bersteð *and*
brekð, he is forlore*n and* sone ut-ȝeworpen ; ȝif he belæfð hal *and*
ȝesund, ðe pottere hine deð ðar to ðe he iscapen was.' Ðe apostele seið ðat godd ne wile naht þoliȝen of none his icorene more te 16
fondin ða*n*ne he muȝe þolien. Ac ðo ðe bersteð wið-inne here
wunienge for here modinesse, hwarof here h*er*te is swa full swa is
bladdre of winde, hie bieð ut-iworpe*n* ðurh dieules lare, naht for
he*m* selue*n* ane, ac for oðre ec awei te affleien. Ðanne fareð hie 20
eft to ðare woreld, *and* bieð forcuðere ða*n*ne hie arrer wæren.
Hie forwerpeð here ræd *and* here cluðes, *and* nemeeð[7] he*m* to ðare
woreld *and* bieð apostate Criste, forsakene, naht mid wordes, ac
mid werkes, ðe werse is, ȝif hit 'mai. Munec mai ut-fare*n* mid 24
ileaue i*n* to hermitorie, oðer i*n* to onnesse te wunien, ȝif[8] he godd
hafð to iwitnesse ðat he mid hlutter h*er*te hit doð, for bett to
do*n*ne. We findeð on ȝewrite þat eremite ne owh on wilderne te
wu-[9]nien, bute he arst bie ȝefanded ðurh regule *and* ðurh maistre i*n* 28
ðan gastliche ofne ðe we ær embe spaken. Ancer is swiðe gastlich
lif. Ðese[10] twa lif, h*er*mite *and* ansæte lif, ðe we nu clepeð anker,
hie wæren hwile ferr fra*m* ma*n*nen wuniende, *and* wæren swiðe
iluuede *and* iheiȝed ðurh ða hali faderes ðe ðar i*n*ne wuneden *and* 32
hit orliche hielden. Swa me mai ȝiet sume finde*n*—iþanked[11] bie
godd !—ðe swiðe gastlich lif lædet after ðare woreld ðe nu is. Al

---

[1] *a letter erased*, hem *on the side.*   [2] ȝis *MS.*   [3] *page* 45.   [4] bergen, *MS.*
[5] lihst *MS.*   [6] Salamon *written against this at side.*
[7] *Between* neme *and* eð *a slit in the vellum.*   [8] Gif *MS.*   [9] *page* 46.
[10] s *corr. from* d.   [11] iþandked *MS.*

lives, some good and some evil. He knows it, who knows everything. If thou wilt remain in the world, and have wife and
children, and till land and weary thyself, thou shalt have all the
more toil. But if thou hast a good counsellor, thou mayst well live
there, and also earn good reward from God. Do all the things
which thou hast to do, with counsel; and let the counsel be such,
that thou doest nothing against the holy Writ. Christ warns us of
this, who says thus: *Dum es cum adversario tuo in via, etc.*,
'Whiles thou art in the way with thine adversary, grant him what
he will have done, lest he take thee and deliver thee to the dun
(creditor), and he afterwards deliver thee to the tormenters and to
the killers!' Follow this Gospel, if thou wilt. God's word, God's
counsel is thy enemy, because it does not say all that thou wouldst
wish. But if thou wilt listen to God, thou must be obedient to the
holy Writ, the little while thou art with it here in this road,
in this short life; and know forsooth, except thou agreest to
it here whatever it advises thee to do: when thou comest into the
higher way, when thou art separated from thy body, it will deliver
thee up to the dun (creditor), who will claim thee for each sin,
and maintain his right after God's own word, that thou hast to
follow him to hell, because thou hast been disobedient to God as he
[is]. Therefore listen now to what God advises thee: *Divitiae si
affluant, nolite cor apponere*, 'If the world's riches much increase
towards thee, set not thy heart upon them, but set it on Me.
Riches will fail thee, I will never fail thee. Why is thy coffer
dearer to thee than I? Did I not send to thee, saying by the writ
of the Gospel that thou shouldst make thy hoard above in the kingdom of Heaven, and not upon earth? Why wilt thou not be
obedient to Me?' Listen still further to Christ's advice, what He
says in the holy Gospel: *Cum facis prandium aut coenam, noli
vocare amicos tuos, etc.*, 'When thou wilt make a dinner,' Christ
says, 'call not thy friends, nor thy brethren to it, neither thy kins-
men, nor thy neighbours. If any of these can repay thee for thy
dinner, do not call them. But call the poor and the weak, the
blind, the dumb, the deaf, the halt, who cannot repay thee for
it; then thou art blessed: [for] thou shalt be recompensed *in*

swa me mai, maŋg alles kennes liues menn, sume gode *and* sume
euele finde*n*. He it wot, ðe all wot. ȝif ðu wilt *on* ðare woreld
beleaue*n*, *and* wif *and* childre haue*n*, *and* land teliȝen *and* weriȝ*e*n,
ðu scalt haue*n* ðas te more iswink. Ac ȝif ðu hauest godne rad- 4
ȝiue, ðu miht ðar wel libbe*n*, *and* ec at gode god lean ofearniȝen.
Alle ðo þiŋg ðe ðu hauest te donne, do it mit ræde; *and* ðe rad bie
swulch, ðat tu noht ne do aȝenes ðe holi write. Hierof us warneð
Crist, *and* ðus seið: Du*m* es cu*m* ad*u*ersario tuo i*n* ui(a), *et* 8
cet*er*a, 'Ðarhwile ðe ðu art mid þine wiðerwine on ða weiȝe, bie
him teiþinde ðat ðe he wile haue*n* ido*n*, læste he ðe nime *and*
betæche ðe ðe crauiere, *and* he seððen betache ðe ðe pineres *and*
ðe cwelleres!' Ðis godspell folȝe, ȝif ðu wille. Godes word, godes 12
ræd is ðin unwine, forðat hit ne seið noht al ðat tu woldest. Ac
ȝif ðu wilt lesten godd, þu scalt bie*n* ðe hali write buhsum, ðo litle
hwile ðe ðu art mid hi*m* her o*n* ðese weiȝe, on ðese scorte liue ;
and wite ðu te soðe, bute ðu him bie hier teiðinde hwat swa hit ðe 16
ratt¹ to donne : ðanne ðu cumst on ða hei(g)ere² weiȝe, ðanne ðu
art itwamd fram ðine lichame, hit te wile betache*u* ðe crauiere³,
ðe ðe wile crauen of elchere senne, *and* betellen riht after ·godes
awene worde, ðat tu aust hi*m* to folȝin to helle, forðan ðe ðu art 20
godd unhersum al swa he. Forði hlest nv hwat godd ðe ratt :
Diuicie si affluant, nolite cor apponere, 'Worldes eihte, ȝif
hie is swiðe rixinde to ðeward, ne do ðu naht ðine herte ðerto, ac
do hes to me. De richeise ðe scal trukien, ic ne truke ðe naure. 24
Hwi is te ðin hucche⁴ trewer ðanne ich ? Ne sente ic ðe seggen bi
ða write of goddspelle ðat tu scoldest makie ðin hord up i*n* heue*n*-
riche⁵, *and* naht upe*n* ierðe ? Hwi ne wilt tu me bie*n* buhsum ?'
Hlest ȝiet furðer Cr*i*stes rad, hwat he seið on ða hali godspelle : 28
Cu*m* facis p*r*andiu*m* aut cenam, noli⁶ uocare amicos tuos,
et cet*er*a, 'Ðanne ðu wilt makien gestninge,' seið Cr*i*st, 'ne clepe
ðu naht ðine friend, ne ðine breðren ðarto, ne ðine kenesme*n*, ne
ðine neihibures. Gif æni of ðesen ðe muȝen forȝielde*n* ðine 32
gestninge, ðane ne clepe ðu hes naht. Ac clepe ðo wrecches *and*
to unmihti, þe blinde, ðe du*m*be, ðe deaue, ðe halte, ðe ne muȝen
naht hit te forȝielden; ðanne art tu isæli: hit te scal bie*n* forȝolde*n*

---

¹ *page* 47. ² g *r*c*d above* i. ³ deuele *at side.*
⁴ u *on erasure.* ⁵ c *cor*r. *from another letter.* ⁶ *Corr. from* Nolite.

resurrectione justorum, that is, when the righteous will arise, and thou among them, on God's right hand.' If thou doest not so, the devil cannot well maintain that thou art disobedient to God. Who does this? Who keeps this? Why do men say that one cannot well be saved in the world? Why wilt thou not follow God's counsel and His teaching? This is truly one of the holy virtues which God divides among His chosen ones, that He gives them good counsel through the holy Writ, which He sends them in order to say how they may work His will, and so be saved. Let him listen and follow whoso will! *Omni petenti te, tribue*, 'Give to every man that asketh of thee, if thou hast what he has not, as thou wouldst that he should do to thee, if thou hadst not.' Therefore He says: 'If thou givest to the man who gave to thee, or whom thou knowest will give to thee, what reward oughtst thou to have from God? Do not so the sinful men who know nothing of God? If thou lovest the same that love thee : do not so the worst men of the world? Do not so the heathen? But love thy enemies for the love of God ; thou shalt have great reward for it from God ; and let Him revenge who is a righteous judge over the living and over the dead ! If a needful man will borrow from thee of thy property, lend him blithely, as to thy fellow-Christian, without any reward, and thou shalt have the reward from God.' If thou lendest him anything of thine, and thou takest again more than thou lentst him: surely thou actest against God's commandment, and deservest His wrath, except thou repairest it. For after the holy Writ, every reward is reckoned for usury; and the usurers will never come into the kingdom of Heaven ; for, though they would divide all that they have got with usury and with unrighteousness, it is not agreeable to God, who is righteous. The rich men who lend their property upon churches and upon the church-lands, or upon towns, or upon other things which yield rents, and keep them longer than until they have as much as they lent upon them, full assuredly they are doomed as usurers ; and they shall have all such reward for it as usurers, that is, the pain of hell, except they repay it. And the amendment is no other than to repay what they have taken unjustly, and with penitence. Concerning this said the prophet: *Domine, quis habitabit in tabernaculo tuo, aut quis, etc.*, 'Lord,' said he, ' who

in resurrectione i*u*stor*u*m, ðat is, ðanne ðe rih(t)wise scule*n*
arisen, *and* tu amang[1] hem, on godes swiðre.' Gif ðu naht herof ne
dest, ne mai ðe deuel betellen wel ðat tu art gode unhersum.
Hwa doð þis ? Hwa halt þis ? Whi seggeð men ðat me ne mai 4
naht wel bie*n* ȝeboreȝen on ðare woreld ? Hwi ne wilt tu folȝi*n*
godes rad *and* his lore ? Þis is iwis on of ðe hali mihtes ðe godd
scift mang his ȝecorene, ðat he ȝifð[2] hem god ræd þurh ðe haliȝe
writes, ðe he sent he*m* seggen hu hie muȝen his wille werchen, *and* 8
swa bien ȝeboreȝen. Hlest *and* folȝih se ðe wile ! Omni petenti
te, tribue[3], '*Æ*lche ma*n*ne ðe ðe bitt ðu aust to ȝiuen, ȝif[4] ðu
hafst ðat te he ne haueð, swa ðu woldest ðat he de*d*e ðe, ȝif ðu ne
hafdest.' Forðan he seið : ' ȝif ðu ȝifst ðo ma*n*ne ðe gaf ðe, oðer 12
ðe wost ðat wile ȝiue*n* ðe, whilch lean aust ðu te hauen of godd ?
Ne don swa ðe senfulle me*n* ðe of gode noht ne cu*n*nen ? Gif ðu
luuest ðo ilche ðe ðe luuiȝeð : ne do*n* swa ðe werste me*n*n of ðe
woreld ? Ne don swa ðe heðene ? Ac luue þine unwines for ðe 16
luue of godd ; ðarof ðu scalt hauen michel lean of godd ; *and* lat
him wreke ðe is riht deme ouer ðe liuiende *and* ouer ðe deade.
Ȝif nedfull ma*n*n wile borȝin at te of ðin eihte, lean him bleðeliche,
al swa ðin emcristen, wiðuten elchere mede, *and* ðu scalt hauen ðe 20
mede of god.' Gif ðu hi*m* lanst ani þing of ðine*n*, *and* tu nimst
aȝean more ða*n*ne ðu him lændest : iwis ðu art aȝeane(s) godes
bebod*e, and* his wraððe of-earnest, bute ðu hit ib(i)ete. Forðan
after ðe hali writes, ealch miede is iteld for gauele; *and* þe gaueleres 24
ne cume*n* neure i*n*to heueriche; for ðan, ðeih hie dælden all ðat hie
mid gauele biȝete*n*[5] habbeð *and* mid unrihtwisnesse, hit nis naht
gode icweme, ðe is rihtwis. Ða riche me*n*n ðe laneð here eihte uppe
chierches *and* uppe ða chirch-landes, oðer uppe tu-[6]nes, oðe uppe 28
oðre þinges þe re*n*tes ȝiueð, *and* heale*n* hes le*n*ger ða*n*ne hie
hauen al swa michel swa hie ðar uppe lænde*n*, fullȝewiss hie bieð
idemd for gouleres; *and* al swulch lean hie sculen ðarof habben alse
gaueleres, ðat is, helle pine, bute hie hit biete [7]. *And* ðe bote nis 32
nan oðer bute ȝielden ðat hie habbe*n* mid unrihte inome*n, and* mid
scrifte. Her of sæde ðe pro*f*iete : Domine, qu*i*s habitabit i*n*
tabernaculo tuo, aut qu*i*s, et cetera[8], 'Hlauerd,' he sæde, ' hwa

---

[1] amanȝ, *MS.*   [2] *page* 48.   [3] *Ewangelista at side, over a red lu or* li*f*.
[4] *Gif MS.*   [5] biȝetenð *MS*.   [6] *page* 49.   [7] *an erasure above* te.
[8] *psalm*ista *written at side, red.*

shall abide with Thee in Thy house, or who shall rest himself on
Thy holy hill of the kingdom of Heaven?' The Holy Ghost
answered him, after other things, and said: *Qui jurat proximo suo,
etc.*, 'He that sweareth truth to his neighbour, that is, his fellow-
Christian, and deceiveth him not with any bargain or with any
other thing ; and he that putteth not out his money to usury, nor
taketh reward from the *innocentes*, that is, harmless men who
intend no evil to anybody : these shall abide in God's tent, and
rest themselves on His hill.' And those who take reward, shall
never come there, if they are taken away with it. Now there are
some others who esteem themselves wise and crafty, and entrust
their money to the heathen, in order to have gain from it ; and
some lend to their fellow-Christian for half-gain, who travels with it
by land and by water in great danger of life and of soul, and with
great toil : and they [themselves] sit at home and have no trouble
for it, except in their thoughts and in their speeches. Clerics and
laymen see and hear this ; but through the evil custom it seems to
them no misdeed, but those are esteemed wise and crafty men. Of
such said God through the prophet : *Vae, qui sapientes estis in
oculis vestris, et coram vobismet ipsis prudentes,* 'Woe unto you that
esteem yourselves wise, and are prudent in your eyes ! Ye deceive
My people by your evil example, and by your sharp intellect. Ye
understand how to defend yourselves by your manifold speeches ;
ye justify the wicked for reward, and take away the righteousness
of the righteous from him !' Therefore he is now esteemed a fool,
except he gets much property ; and ye justify those who get much
property by your great property, and say that they are worthy and
good men. The prophet says still further : *Vae, qui dicitis bonum
malum, et malum bonum,* 'Woe unto you who say that it is good
to get much property, which cannot be got without unrighteousness !' Therefore it is called by God's mouth *Mammon of iniquity.*
Woe unto you who say that he is unhappy who has no worldly property, who will get none by any injustice, and who, after having

mai wunen mid ðe on ðine huse¹, oðer hwa mai him resten upe ðin
haliȝe munte of heueneriche²?' Ðe hali gast him andswerede, after
oðre þinges, and sæde: Qui iurat proximo suo, et cetera, 'Se
ðe swereð soð his nexte, þat is, his emcristenn, and him naht ne 4
beswikð mid none chiepinge ne mid nan oðre ðinge; and se ðe ne
ȝifð naht his eihte te goule, and se ðe ne nimð none mede of ða
innocentes, ðat bien uneilinde menn ðe none manne euel ne
willeð: ðese muȝen wuniȝen on gódes telde, and uppen³ his munte 8
hem resten.' And ða ðe mede nemeð, hie ne sculen ðar neure
cumen, ȝif hie bien ðar mide. ȝenomene. Nu bien sume oðre ðat
healden hem seluen wise and ȝeape, and befasteð here paneȝes ðe
haðene menn, for to habben of hem biȝeate; and sume, hi læneð 12
here emcristen te halue biȝeate, ðe fareð ðar mide be londe and
be watere on michele hahte on liue and on saule, and mid michele
swinke: and hie sitteð at ham and ne hauen ðarof non ȝeswink,
bute on here ðohtes and on here spaches. Ðis ȝesieð and ȝehiereð 16
hadede and leeavede; and for ðare euele ȝewune ne ðin(c)ð hit hem
no misdade, ac bieð ihealden for wi-⁴se menn and for ȝeape. Of
swilche sade godd ðurh ðe profiete: Ve, qui sapientes estis in
oculis uestris, et coram uobis met⁵ ipsis prudentes!⁶ 'Wa 20
ȝeu ðe healdeð ȝeu seluen for wise, and to-foren ȝeu seluen bieð
ȝeape! Ȝie beswikeð mi folk mid ȝeure euele forbisne, and mid
ȝeure scarpe witt. Ȝie cunnen ȝeu bewerien mid ȝeuere manifelde
spaches; ȝerihtwisið ðane forȝelte for medes, and ðe rih(t)wisnesse 24
of ðe rihtwise manne ȝe him benemeð.' For ðan he is iheálde nu
for sott, bute he michel eihte beȝete; and þo ðe michel eihte .
biȝeteð mid ȝeure michele eihte, hem ȝie rihtwisið, and seggeð þat
he bien auhte men and gode menn. He seið ȝiet forðer, ðe profiete: 28
Ve, qui dicitis bonum malum, et malum bonum⁶, 'Wa ȝeu
ðe seggeð ðat it is god te biȝeten michel eihte, ðe ne mai bien
biȝeten wið-uten.⁷ unrihtwisnesse⁸!' For-ði hie is icleped of godes
muðe Mammona iniquitatis. Wa ȝeu ðe seggeð ðat he is 32
unsali ðat none wordles eihte ne hafð, ðe mid nane unrihte none ne
wile biȝeten, and ða ðat he hadde mid maniȝe unrihtes biȝeten

---

¹ use on erasure.   ² riche(s) MS.   ³ the stroke above e is red.
⁴ page 50.   ⁵ t corr. from ð.   ⁶ propheta red at side.
⁷ a letter erased behind ē.   ⁸ unirht- MS.

lost what he had got by much unrighteousness, suffers it with patience, and thanks God. God says in another place: *Vae, qui ridetis, quia plorabitis*, ' Woe unto you that laugh now for the vain bliss of this world, and for your great wealth which ye have now ! Woe unto you that tax your fellow-Christian, and turn the right into wrong, and the wrong into right, and that take reward for your deceitful speeches, that speak on either side, as if ye were friend of both of them !' If thou wilt dwell in the world, and keep in mind these words of God, and follow the blessed Job, who was a good worldly man, thou canst save thyself with God's help.

Of strength.

Here follows another of God's gifts, which is called *fortitudo*, that is, strength of God. It is very needful ; be thou never so wise, nor so cunning, nor so prudent to do what thou shalt do : except thou hast this strength of God, thou canst do no good. Thou canst see many a very wise clerk, who certainly does not instruct himself, and thinks that he has enough in his knowledge which he understands, and does not beg this strength from God ; therefore he remains among them who understand no good, and is like them in works. Just as easily he sometimes will misdo, as he who understands no good. Whoso for fear of God keeps himself from all cardinal sins and from all the things which God forbids him, has this strength of God. David the king lost this holy virtue, when he committed adultery with Bath-sheba, Solomon's mother, who was wedded to Uriah. But he never ceased until he had [got] it again. *Miserere mei, Deus*, this precious psalm he made anon, and cooled God's wrath by it. 'Lord,' quoth he, ' according to Thy great commiseration, have mercy upon my great sin ! And according unto Thy manifold mercies, which Thou hast had towards mankind, do away from me this great unrighteous-ness, so that Thy tender eyes may never see in me what mislikes them ! But let the stream of Thy sweet mercy, which never ceases, run to me, so that I may understand when it comes, through the flowing tears which it brings with it unto the dried-

(he haueð forloren)¹, *and* ðat ðoleð mid ðolemodnesse, and gode
þankeð. An oðer stede he seið, godd: Ve qui ridetis, quia
plorabitis², 'Wa ʒeu ðe nu leiheð for ðese³ wordles lease blisse,
and for ʒeure michele wele ðe ʒe nu hauen! Wa ʒeu ðe beplaitið 4
ʒeuer emcristen, *and* wændeð ðat rihte te w(r)ohʒe⁴, *and* ðat wohʒe
te rihte,. *and* ðe nimeð mede for ʒeuer swikele spache(s), ðe spekeð
an aiðer half, swilche ʒie here beire friend wære.' ʒif ðu wilt on
ðare world wuniʒen, *and* ðurh ðese godes wordes war bien *and* 8
ðane eadie Iob folʒin, ðe was god worldmann: ðu miht mid godes
fultume ðe seluen berʒen⁵.

Of stren[g]ðe.

HIER after cumþ an oðer godes ʒiue, ðe is icleped fortitudo, 12
þat is, strengþe of gode. Hie is swiðe niedfull; ne bie ðu
næure swa wis, ne so ʒeap, ne swa witti to donne ðat tu scalt don:
bute ðu habbe ðese strengþe of gode, ne miht tu non god don.
Ðu miht isien sum wel wis clerec, ðe wisliche him seluen naht 16
ne wisseð, *and* þincþ ðat he hafð inohʒ on his witte ðe he cann,
ne ðese strengþe ne besekð (nauht) at gode; for ði he belæfð
among ðan ðe non god ne cunnen, and hem he is ilich of werkes.
Alswa lihtliche oðerwhile he misdoð, al swo he ðe non god ne 20
cann. Se ðe for godes eiʒhe him halt fram alle heued-sennes
and fram alle ðe forbodes ðe god him forbiet, he hafð ðese
strengþe of gode. Ðese hali mihte forleas Dauið kyng, ða ðe
he forlaiʒ mid Bersabee, Salomones moder, ðe was bewedded Vrie. 24
Ac he naure ne ʒeswoc⁶ ær he hes eft (h)afde. Miserere mei
deus, ðane derewurðe salm anon he makede, *and* godes wrað
he ðar mide acolede. 'Hlauerd,' cwað he, 'after ðat ðe ðin
mildce ys michel, haue ore of mine michele senne! And after 28
ðine manifealde mildces ðe ðu hafst ihafd to mankenne, do awei
fram me ðese michele unrihtwisnesse, ðat næure ðine milde eiʒen
ne ʒeseo on me ðat hem mislikie. Ac let ðane wellstream, ðe
næure ne trukeð, of ðine swete mildce iernen to me, swa (ðat)⁷ ic 32
muʒe understanden hwanne he cume⁸ ðurh ðe flowinde teares ðe he

¹ *On the side.* ² *Ewangelista, red at side.* ³ s *corr. from* d. ⁴ r *red above.*
⁵ *page* 51. ⁶ a *underdotted before* o. ⁷ *written above, red.* ⁸ cumen *MS.*

G

up heart. And besprinkle me with the hyssop of the holy cross, of the holy water which came out of the right side of Thy holy temple. Then shall I become cleansed from all my sins, and whiter than any snow. Lord, still I have more need! *Cor mundum crea in me, Deus*! My heart is much defiled with foul thoughts, for the sin which I first thought to do, and I know that Thou neither wilt nor canst dwell in it. But make it pure and clean, so that Thou mayst dwell within me, and renew a right spirit within me. For my spirit is grown very old, and wasted away, through the great error when it went out of Thy right way, and followed the devil's doctrine, and rejected Thine. *Ne projicias me*, because, my dear Lord, I am well conscious that I have deserved to be rejected by Thee, as I rejected Thee and Thy teaching. But now I beg Thee, through Thy great goodness, that Thou mayst not reject me from Thy face, as the lord who is wrath against his servant, and drives him from his face. And never take from me Thy Holy Ghost that Thou hast given me through Thy great goodness! Sorry and sorrowful am I, night and day, until I have Him. *Redde mihi laetitiam*, Lord, give me now again the same bliss of Thy salvation which I had before, ere I sinned! Thou hadst made me glad and blithe; but I have lost it because of my weakness. And fasten in me the spirit of strength, and make me strong through Thy power! I fancied to have strength of myself, and therefore I fell. But if Thou now wilt raise me, and bestow upon me a right and strong spirit : *docebo iniquos, etc.*, [then] will I teach the unrighteous Thy ways, and tell them how great mercy Thou hast [had] on me, who was all guilty against Thee ; and the merciless who never yet had mercy on themselves nor on others, shall turn to Thee, and believe in Thee, and praise and bless Thee, and become holy men by Thy grace, who were the devil's before. Lord, I now thank Thee above all things ! I feel my heart consoled through Thy great mercy, that Thou hast sent upon me, sinful man, the spirit of consolation, which fills my sorry heart with the sweet bliss of its dear vision, through the tears which come running,.

brinkgð mid[1] him to ðere fordruȝede hierte. And spræng me
mid tare ysope of ðare holi röde, of ðan holie watere ðe ȝiede ut
of ðe riht[2] side of ðine hali temple. Ðanne wurð ic iclansed of
alle mine sennes, *and* hwittere ðane ani snaw. Lauerd, ȝiet ic 4
habbe more niede. Cor mundum crea in me, deus[3]! Min
herte is swiðe befeld mid fule þohtes, for ðare senne ðe ic arst
þohte to donne, *and* ic wat ðat þu ne wilt ne ðu ne miht on hire
wuniȝen. Ac make hes hlutter *and* clene, þat tu muȝe wuniȝen 8
mid me, *and* rihtne gost newe inne me. For ðan min gast is
swiðe for-[4]ealded *and* forwurðen, for ðe michele dwele, ða ðe he
ȝiede ut of ðe rihte weiȝe, *and* folȝede dieules lare, *and* forwarp
ðine. Ne proicias me[3], for ði, min leue lauerd, ich am 12
wel bicnawe ðat ic habbe ofearned þat ðu scoldest me forwurpen,
swa swa ic forwarp þe *and* ðine lore[5]. Acc nu ic bidde ðe, for ðine
michele godnesse, ðat tu ne forwerp me fram ðine ansiene, al
swa ðe lauerd ðe is wrað wið his þralle, *and* drifð him ut of his 16
ansiene. And ðine hali gast ðe ðu me hafst iȝiuen for ðine
michele godnessse, ne benem ðu me næure. Sari *and* sorhfull am
ic, niht *and* dai, al hwat ic hine habbe. Redde mihi leticiam[6],
Hlauerd, ȝif me nu aȝean ðe ilche blisse þat ic (h)adde ær, ar ic 20
sineȝede, of ðire hale. Þu hafdest me imaked glad *and* bliðe; ac ich
hes haue forloren for mine wocnesse. And faste on me ðane gost
of strengþe, *and* make me strong ðurh ðire mihte. Ic wende
habben strengþe of me seluen, *and* for ði i fell. Ac ȝif ðu nu me 24
wilt aræren, *and* rihte gost *and* stronge me betachen, docebo
iniquos, et cetera[6], ic wile tacbe ðo unrih[t]wisen ðine weiȝes,
and hem kyðen hu michel mildce ðu hafst of me, ðe was all
forȝelt aȝeanes þe; *and* to orelease ðe næure ȝiete ne hadden ore 28
of hemseluen ne of oðren[7], hie sculen wænden to ðe, *and* ȝelieuen
on ðe, *and* ðe heriȝen *and* blescien, *and* mid þine grace hali menn
becumen, þe ærrer waren ðes dieules. Lauerd, nu ic ðe þanki
ouer alle þing. Ic ȝefele min herte ȝefrieured ðurh þine michele 32
mildce, ðe on me senfulle hafst ȝesænt ðane froure gost, ðe felð
mine sari herte mid ðare swete blisse of his lieue sune, ðurh ðo

---

[1] min MS. [2] page 52. [3] Psalmista *written at the side*, red.
[4] between for *and* e *a letter erased.* [5] *and* ðine lare *repeated.*
[6] Psalmista red *at side.* [7] page 53.

G 2

with great bliss, on the dried-up land.   Lord, now I would praise
Thee, and offer a sacrifice, if I had anything which would be
agreeable unto Thee.   But I know well that *bonorum meorum non
eges*, Thou hast no need of any of the goods which I have.   But if
it is Thy will that I must offer Thee a sacrifice, for Thy worship
and my salvation, then Thou must do as Thou hast always done to
all Thy people.   Thou hast sent them their sacrifice, just as the
good lord who sends offerings to his men for his own worship, and
for their service.   *Sacrificium Deo spiritus contribulatus*, according
to what Thy Holy Ghost says : "The most agreeable sacrifice which
one can offer Thee, is the spirit and the heart that are greatly
afflicted with humility and with manifold thoughts of true repentance, which make the heart sorry and sob, and the eyes wet with
running tears."   St. Peter offered this sacrifice, when he had great
guilt by forsaking Thee.   He went out, *et flevit amare*, and bewept
his sin very bitterly, and Thou forgavest it him.   Mary
Magdalene offered this sacrifice upon Thy precious feet, and she
left there all her sins.   Hannah offered Thee this sacrifice, who was
barren, and despised among the people of Israel; and she was soon
heard, and Thou answeredst her prayer, so that she might have a
child and brought forth Thy prophet Samuel.   We find written in
the Holy Scripture that everyone was heard according to his need
to whom it was Thy will to send this sacrifice.'

Dear soul, I have written this in order to console thee when thou
hast need.   Look and read ; as for this holy virtue, it will please
thee by night and by day, if thou wilt think of it with all thy heart.

Of understanding.

After this comes another of God's gifts, which is called *intellectus*, that is, understanding.   This holy virtue makes [thee] understand God and all spiritual things, as much as thou canst understand
while thou art bound in thy wretched body.   God speaks of it
through the prophet, and says to thee: *Intellectum tibi dabo, et
instruam te, etc.*, 'I will give thee understanding, and I will
instruct thee in this way which thou goest now.   Because thou
hast forsaken thy sins and thy evil customs, and learnest so

teares ðe cumeð ierninde, mid michele blisse, uppe ðe fordruȝede
londe. Hlauerd, nu ic ðe wolde wurðiȝen, *and* loc ofrien, ȝif
ic hadde ani þing *þat* ðe icweme wære. Ac ic wot wel ðat
bonor*um* meor*um* no*n* eges[1], ðu nehafst none niede of no*n* 4
ðare gode ðe ic habbe. Ac ð*an*ne hit is þin wille ðat ic ðe loc
ofri*n* mote, ðe to wurðscipe[2] *and* me to hale, ð*an*ne most þu do*n*
al swa ðu hafst aure ido*n* bi alle ðinen. Ðu hafst isænt he*m*
here ofre*n*de, al swa ðe gode hlauerd ðe sent his me*n*n ofre*n*de 8
for his aȝene wurscipe, *and* for here seruise. Sac*r*ifici*um* deo
sp*iritus* contribulat*us*[1], after ð*an* ðe ðin hali gast seið:
" Ðat icwemeste loc ðat (mann ðe) mai ofri*n*, ðat is ðe gast *and* ðe
hierte ðe bieð swiðe ȝeswæint mid eadmodnese *and* mid manifealde 12
þohtes of soðe bereusinge, ðe makieð ðe herte sari *and* sobbiende,
and ðe eiȝene wæte mid teares ierninde." Ðis lac offrede s*anctus*
Petr*us*, ða ða he was swa swiðe forȝ(i)elt ðat he hadde ðe
forsaken. He ȝiede ut, et fleu i t amare, *and* beweop hi(s) se*n*ne 16
swiðe biterliche, *and* þu hes hi*m* forȝaue. Ðis loc offrede Marie
Magdalene upe ðine derewurðe fiet, *and* alle hire se*n*ne*n* hie ðar
forliet. Ðis loc ðe ofrede Anna, ðe was unberinde, *and* unwurð
mang Israele folke; *and* hie was sone iherd, *and* hire biene ðu 20
hire teiðedest, þat hie chilt moste habbe*n and* broḥte forð ði*s*ne
profiete Samuel. On ða haliȝe write we hit findeð, hwam awo ðin
wille was te sende*n* ðis loc to ofrie*n*, he was ȝeherd of his niede.'

Lieue saule, ðis ic habbe iwrite*n* for ðe te frieurie*n* ð*an*ne ðu 24
niede hafst. Loke *and* ræd; ðis holi mihte, hit te wile likin be
nihte oðer be daiȝe, ȝif[4] ðu mid alre he*r*te hier e*m*be wilt þe*n*chen.

Of andȝet.

H IERAFTER cumð an oðer godes ȝiue, ðe is icleped intellec- 28
tu s, þat is, andȝeat. Ðies halie mihte, hie dieð understonde*n*
of gode *and* of alle gostliche þinges, swa michel swa ðu miht understonde*n* ðe hwile ðe ðu art o*n* ðine wrecche lichame ȝebunden.
Hier of spekð godd ðurh ðe profiete, *and* seið to ðe: Intellect*um* 32
t*ibi* dabo, *et* instru*am* te, *et* cete*r*a, 'Ich ðe wile ȝiue*n* an[d]ȝeat,
and ic ðe wile wissin on ðese weiȝe ðe ðu nu gost. For ði ðat tu

---

[1] Psalm*ista*, *red at side*. [2] wurd- *MS.* [3] *page* 54. [4] ȝ corr. *red from* t.

blithely these holy virtues and receivest them well: My eyes shall
be upon thee, and I will shield thee from all evil, as long as thou
art conscious that thou hast no good but from Me.' Through this
gift of God thou canst know all the thoughts which come from thy
heart; which are of God, and which are of thy flesh, and which are
of the devil. It is great need for thee to understand well the
thoughts which come from God. Concerning this said the prophet:
Audiam, quid loquatur in me Dominus Deus, 'I will listen to and
understand what my Lord God speaketh in me.' Sometimes He
will reprehend thee and make thee think thus: 'Why wilt thou
continue in thy sins until death? Why can I have no dwelling
with thee? Thy sins separate Me from thee; I can never dwell in
a foul heart. As often as thou thinkest of Me, or hearest speak of
Me: then I am with thee. Thou wast created, and afterwards
hallowed, to My use, and that I, for thy profit, might dwell in thee.
But thou drivest Me out of thee through thy manifold lusts which
thou wilt follow, against My will. Unless thou ceasest, thou wilt
repent it the more bitterly for ever!' At another time, when thou
thinkest that God has forsaken or forgotten thee, He will say:
Numquid potest mater oblivisci filium uteri sui, 'How can the
mother forget the child which she bore in her womb? Though she
forget it, I never forget thee.' At another time come many
thoughts of God's threat, concerning the pains of hell; at another
time He promises thee great joy in Heaven; at another time He
consoles thee about thy sorrow for thy sins. But that is a great
danger, except thou take much care of it, and thank Him much for
it. The thoughts which come from thy flesh are always weak,
either of meat, or of drink, or of clothes, or of sleep, or of some
idleness. God forbids us to be either anxious or full of cares. He
will find for all of us what is needful, if we first make Him rest in
ourselves. *Primum quaerite regnum Dei, et haec omnia adjicientur
vobis,* 'Seek ye first the kingdom of God,' and afterwards, says He,

hauest þine sennen[1] *and* ðine euele þeawes forlaten, *and* ðese hali
mihtes swa bleðeliche liernest[2] *and* wel undernimst : mine eieȝene
sculen bien uppe ðe, *and* ic ðe wile scilden fram alle euele, swa
longe swa ðu wilt bien icnawen ðat tu nan god ne hauest bute of 4
me.' Ðurh ðessere godes ȝiue ðu miht alle ðo ðohtes icnawe ðe
cumeð fram ðire herte ; hwilche bieð of gode, *and* hwilche of ðine
flesche, *and* hwilche bieð of ðe dieule. Ða ðohtes ðe cumeð of
gode, ðe is michel nied ðat tu wel understande[3]. Hier of sade 8
ðe profiete : A u d i a m, q u i d l o q u a t u r i n m e d o m i n u s d e u s,
' Ic wile lesten *and* understanden hwat min lauerd godd spekð in[4]
me.' Oðer hwile he ðe wile undernemen *and* ðus ðe don[5]
þenchen : ' Hwi wilt ðu ðurhwuniȝen *on* ðine sennes anon to 12
ðin(e)[6] deaðe ? Hwi ne mai ich none wuniȝenge habben mid ðe ?
Ðine sennes me[7] twameð fram ðe ; ich ne mai næure wuniȝen on
fule herte. Swa ofte swa ðu ðenchst *on* me, oðer ihierst speken
of me : þare hwile ich am mid ðe. Ðu ware ȝescapen, *and* eft 16
ȝehalȝed, to mine behofte *and* for ðine freme me ontewuniȝen. Ac
ðu me drifst ut of te for ðine manifealde willes ðe ðu folȝin wilt,
aȝeanes mine wille. Bute ðu iswik, ðe hwatliker hit te scall æure
ma rewen.' Oðerhwile, hwanne ðu ðencst ðat godd ðe hafð 20
forlaten oðer forȝeten, ðanne seið he : N u m q u i d p o t e s t
m a t e r o b l i u i s c i f i l i u m u t e r i s u i, ' Hv mai ðat moder
forȝeten ðat child ðe hie bar *in* hire wombe ? Þeih hie hit forȝete,
ic næure ne forȝete ðe.' Oðerhwile cumeð maniȝe þohtes of godes 24
þreatt of helle pines. Oðerhwile he behat ðe michele merhþe[8] on
heuene. Oðerhwile he ðe frieureð of ðine sarinesse for ðine
sennes. Ac ðat is michel hauht, bute ðu hierof neme michele
ȝieme, *and* him hierof michel ðanki. Ða ðohtes ðat cumeð of 28
ðine flesce, æure hi beð nexse, oðer of mete, oðer of drenkch, oðer
of claðes, (oðer of slape)[9], oðer of sume idelnesse. Ðis forbet
godd, þat we houhfull ne care-full ne scule bien. All he wile us
finden ðat nied is, ȝif we arst him makieð reste on us seluen. 32
P r i m u m q u e r i t e r e g n u m d e i, e t h e c o m n i a a d i c i e n t u r
u o b i s, ' Arst secheð godes riche,' *and* siððen he saið ðat alle

---

· [1] sen-nnen *MS.*   [2] liernedest *MS. with dots under* ed.   [3] understanden *MS.*
    [4] i *corr. from* o.   [5] speken *underlined between* don *and* þ.
    [6] in *corr. from* m.   [7] *page* 55·   [8] mehrþe *MS.*   [9] *on the side.*

we shall have all these things. Against such thoughts thou
shalt answer: *Non in solo pane vivit homo,* 'Man liveth not by
bread alone, but liveth by the words that proceed out of the
mouth of God.' If thou wilt know what the kingdom of God is,
which thou shalt first seek: the holy apostle instructs us, who
says: *Regnum Dei non est esca et potus, sed justitia, et pax, et gaudium in spiritu sancto,* 'The kingdom of God is not meat and
drink; but righteousness, and peace, and joy in the Holy Ghost.'
That is the kingdom of God!

Dear soul, I beg and warn thee to have no hope in thy fasting,
nor in thy watching, nor in any other good. Except thou have
these three things, God will never reign in thee, nor thou evermore
with Him, viz. that thou be righteous towards God and towards all
men. Give to each what he ought to have! Again, [it is neces-
sary] that thou have peace with God and with all men; and if thou
breakest it, may God shield thee! Do thou not so. Thou hast no
longer respite than the apostle says: *Sol non occidat super iracundiam
vestram,* 'On the same day that thou breakest [peace], see that
thou be reconciled, ere the sun goes to rest!' Take now great care
of this third thing: that is, let thy bliss not be in any earthly
thing, but in the Holy Ghost alone. Woe, Eve's children, how are
ye deceived, who seek bliss without Paradise, where no bliss is! Turn
back, turn back, and go home, otherwise you will never have any!
Even the thoughts which come from the devil are always bitter, except
thou givest way to his deceitful admonition; at first it seems sweet
to thee, but in the end it is very bitter. When thoughts of avidity, or
of luxury, or of covetousness, or of wrath, and of envy and indigna-
tion, or of vain boasting, or of haughtiness and pride come to thee,
know thou forsooth that it is the devil or his messenger. The will
of the flesh holds sometimes with him; do not love either of them!
Nolite fieri, etc., 'Be not like the horse or the mule, which have no
understanding,' but above all take heed of your heart. Every day
thoughts come to it, as flies to a sore. Let him resist who will! As
long as thou art in this poor life, thou art in a great fight. Those who
fight not, are all trodden down under the devil's feet. Be prudent

ðese þing we sculen habben. Onȝeanes ðelliche ðohtes ðu scalt
andsweriȝen: Non in solo pane uiuit homo, 'Ðe mann ne
leueð¹ naht he bread ane, ac leueð bi ða wordes ðe gað ut² of
godes muðe.' ȝif ðu wilt witen hwat bie godes riche, ðe du arst 4
scalt siechen : þe hali apostel us wisseð, and seið³: Regnum
dei non est esca et potus, seð iusticia, et pax, et gaudium in
spiritu sancto, 'Godes riche nis naht mete and drench, ac is rihtwisnesse, and sibsumnesse, and blisse in ðe hali gaste.' Þat is 8
godes riche.

Lieue saule, ic ðe bidde and warni ðat tu none hope ne haue upe
ðine fastene, ne upe ðine wæcche, ne uppe non oðre gode. Bute ðu
ðese þrie ðing habbe, ne rixit næure god on ðe, ne ðu næure mo 12
mid him. Ðat is, ðat tu bie rihtwis aȝeanes gode and aȝenes alle
mannen. Gield ælche ðat he auh te habben. Eftsones, ðat tu
haue pais aȝeanes godd and aȝeanes alle mannen; and ȝif ðu brekst,
scilde ðe godd! Ðat tu ne do. Ne hafst tu no lengere f(i)erst ðanne 16
ðe apostele seið: Sol non occidat super iracundiam uestram, 'On ðan ilche daiȝe ðe ðu tebrecst, ær ðe sunne go te reste,
loce ðat tu bie sahtled!' Of ðese ðridde þing nim nu michele ȝieme.
Þat is, ðat tin blisse ne bie of non ierðliche þinge, bute of ðe haliȝe 20
gast. Waleawa, Eve children, hu ȝie bieð beswiken, ðe secheð
blisse wiðuten paradise, ðar ðe nan nis ! Wændeð aȝean, wændeð
aȝean and fareð hom, elles ne wurð ȝew næure mo non ! Ðo ilche
ðohtes ðe cumeð of ðe dieule, æure hie bieð bitere, bute ȝif ðu 24
teiðest his swikele meneȝinge; hie ðe ðingþ arst swete, ac hie is
at ten ænde wel bitter. Ðanne ðe ðohtes cumeð of ȝiuernesse, oðer
of galnesse, oðer of ȝitsinge, oðer of wraððe, and of nið and of ande,
oðer of idel ȝelp, oðer of modinesse and priede, wite ðu to soðe ðat 28
it is dieuel oðer his sånde. Ðes flesces iwill halt oðer-h(w)ile mid
him ; ne lief⁴ þu here noðer. Nolite fieri, et cetera, 'Ne bieð
ȝelich ðe horse ne ðe mule, ðe ne habbeð non andȝet !' Ac nemeð
ȝieme ouer alle þing te ȝeure⁵ herte. Al dai ðar cumeð to þohtes, 32
al swo doð fliȝen to sare. Weriȝe se ðe wile! All ðare hwile ðe
ðu art on ðese earme liue, ðu art on muchele ifihte. Þa ðe noht
ne fihten, he bieð al te-treden under dieules fiet. Bie ȝeap aȝean

---

¹ an erasure between e and u. ² t on erasure. ³ page 56.
⁴ page 57. ⁵ to ȝeure before it, underlined.

against all the thoughts which I named to you before, and withstand them just as thou wouldst so many devils, if thou couldst see
them.   Take thy sword, that is, God's Word, and say: *Vade retro,
Satana,* 'Go back, thou Satan, with all thy cursed spirits, not
through my strength, but through His who overcame thee and
drove thee away!'

Of wisdom.

After this comes another gift of God, which is called *sapientia,*
that is, wisdom. Solomon says that *sapientia aedificavit sibi
domum, etc.,* 'Wisdom,' says he, 'reared up herself a house, and she
carved herself seven posts.'   These are the seven holy virtues which
we before have spoken about, beginning with that which is called
the fear of God, which is the beginning of this wisdom.   Here is
gathered such timber as can never rot, and this precious virtue is
work-master over it. *Vere, non est hic aliud, nisi domus Dei et
porta coeli,* 'Verily, here is nothing else among such timbering but
the house of God and the gate of the kingdom of Heaven!'   This
is certainly the holy virtue which is called God's wisdom, God's
word. He says in the holy Gospel: *Si quis diligit me, etc.,*
'Whoso loveth Me will keep My words: and My Father will love
him, and We will come unto him,' *et mansionem apud eum faciemus,*
'and We will make our abode with him.'   Courage, thou dear soul,
be now glad and blithe in the Holy Ghost, as I said before!   Because thou hast gathered fair timber of these holy virtues, and God's
own Wisdom is work-master over it, and says that He will dwell
there with thee, because thou lovest Him and His words. We must
now let thy wretched body rest, which is very weak and very frail.
Its head aches, its eyes relax, its sustenance is little, for it has nothing
but through its hand-work to live upon, and what men will give it,
for the love of God, who have pity on it.   It has toiled much
about this : may God Almighty repay it, for it has now need to
rest.

alle ðe ðohtes ðe ic ȝeu hier te-fore[1] nænnede, *and* wiðstond hem al
swa ðu woldest aȝeanes al so fele dieulen, ȝif ðu hes isien mihtest.
Nim ðin sweord, ðat is, godes word[2], *and* seiȝe : Vade retro,
satana, 'Go abach, (þu)[3] sathanas, mid alle ðine awerȝede [4]
go(st)es[4], naht þurh mine strengþe, ac ðurh his ðe ðe ouercam
and awei ðe drof!'

Of wisdom.

HIER after cumð anoðer godes ȝiue, ðat is sapiencia ȝe- [8]
namned, þat is, wisdom. Salemon seið þat sapiencia
edificauit sibi domum, et cetera, 'Wisdom,' he seið, 'ararde
hire an hus, *and* hie karf hire seuen postes.' Þat bieð ðo seuen
hali mihtes ðe we hier teforen habbeð ȝespeken, þe anginneð at [12]
tare ðe is icleped godes dradnesse, ðe is anginn of ðese wisdome.
Hier is igadered swilch timber ðe næure rotien ne mai, *and* þis
derewurðe mihte is wrihte ðerover[5]. Vere, non *est* hic aliuð,
nisi domus dei et porta celi, 'Fullȝewiss, nis her nan oðer [16]
manȝ þelliche timbringe bute godes hus *and* heueneriches gate.'
Ðis[6] is ȝewiss ðe holiȝe mihte ðe is icleped godes wisdom, godes
word. He seið on ðe holiȝe godspelle : Si q*uis* diligit me, *et*
cetera, 'Se ðe luueð me he wile lokin mine wordes, *and* min fader [20]
him wile luuiȝen, and to him we willeð cumen,' et mansionem
apud eum faciemus, '*and* mid him willeð ma[7]kien wunienge.'
Ælle, ðu lieue saule, bie nu gladd *and* bliðe in ðe hali goste, all
swo ic ær sade ! Forðan þu hauest fair timber ȝe(i)gadered of ðese [24]
hali mihte(s), *and* godes auȝen wisdom is ðar ouer wrihte, *and* seið
ðat he wile ðar mid ðe wuniȝen, for ði ðat tu luuest him *and* his
wordes. Wit mote nu læte resten ðine wrecche lichame, ðe is
swiðe unstran*g* *and* swiðe brusel. His heaued him acþh, ðe[8] eiene [28]
him trukieð, his bilif is litel, forðan he ne hafð bute ðurh his
handiswinke bi to libbenne, *and* ðat menn, for godes luue, him
giuen willeð, ðo ðe of[9] him rewðhe habbeð. He hafð michel hier
abuten iswunken, ȝielde him godalmihtin, for ði him is nied nu to [32]
resten.

---

[1] e *corr. from* i. [2] þat is godes word *repeated.* [3] *On the side.*
[4] d *underdotted before* e. [5] ð *corr. from* h. [6] D *crossed red.*
[7] *page* 58. [8] *a letter erased after* e. [9] f *crossed red.*

Now answers the soul:

I beg thee and conjure thee, too, upon the Holy Trinity, which is Father and Son and Holy Ghost, one true God, that thou leave not this work, because I have much help and good strength by it, God be thanked! Just as the body can have no strength without bones, so can I have no strength of soul, no power, without these holy virtues. Do thou not spare for our body! One cannot easily believe it; it has often deceived me. I have followed its will ever too long; I shall never [do] so again. But one ought to do with it as with the ass: *Ut jumentum factus sum apud te, et ego semper tecum,* that it may tell this truth: 'I am made as a beast toiling before Thee, that I may rest again with Thee.' Again, this same prophet said: *Sitivit in te anima mea, corpus multipliciter,* 'My soul was thirsty,' he said, 'after Thee, Lord, and my flesh much more, for the manifold labours of fasting and of its sustenance, which I got for my sins with my sweat.' Think of, and seek very willingly after these holy virtues, and put them into writ, so that they may do good to some other soul.

Reason.

Dear soul, if thou hast well understood, God's temple is reared upon thee, after what the apostle says: *Templum Dei, quod estis vos,* 'God's temple is holy; and that ye are yourselves.' But he says after this very awfully: *Si quis autem violaverit templum Dei, disperdet eum Deus,* 'Whoso defileth the temple of God with any foul sin, him shall God destroy, both body and soul.' Right belief is the ground-work of this holy temple. Concerning this the apostle says: *Fundamentum aliud nemo potest ponere, praeter idem quod positum est, quod est Jesus Christus,* 'Other foundation can no man lay than that is laid, which is Jesus Christ,' when Peter said: 'Thou art the Christ, the Son of the living God'; and all Christians who believe in Christ ought to believe and say so. The posts which

Nu andswereð þe saule:

ICH ðe bidde *and* ec halsiȝe, uppe ðare hali þrinnesse, ðe is fader *and* sune *and* hali gost, on soð godd, þat ðu þis weork naht ne forlate, for ðan ic habbe ðarof michel help *and* gode stre[n]gþe, 4 ȝeþanked bie godd! Riht alswo ðe lichame none strencþe ne mai habben wið-uten bonen, al swo ne mai ic ne no*n* saule stre[n]gþe ne mihte habbe*n* wið-uten ðese hali mihten. Ne wonde ðu naht (for) ure lichame! He nis naht lihtlich to ilieue*n*. He me hafð ofte 8 beswiken. Ic habbe ifolȝed his iwill eaure to longe; swo ne scall ic næure mo eft. Ac me scal do*n* bi him al swo bi ðan asse: Vt iume*n*tum factu*s* sum apuð te, *et* ego s[emper] t[ecum][1], þat he muȝe (ðis) soð segge*n*: 'Ich am imaked al swo a dier 12 swinkende before*n* ðe, ðat ic eft muȝe reste*n* mid ðe.' Eft sæde ðes ilke profiete: Sitiuit i*n* te a*n*ima mea, corpu*s* multipli- citer, 'Mi saule was ofþerst,' he sæde, 'after ðe, hlauerd, *and* mi*n* flesch michele swiðere, for ðo manifelde swinche(s) of faste*n* *and* of 16 his biliue, ðe ic for mine se*n*nen mid mine swote[2] biȝatt.' Ðench *and* siech well ȝ(i)erne after ðese hali mihtes, *and* sete hes on ȝewrite, ðat hie muȝe*n* sum oðre saule do*n* god[3].

Ratio.

LIEUE saule, ȝif ðu wel hafst understo*n*den, godes temple is ȝerard uppe on (ðe), after ðat ðe apostel seið: Templu*m*[4] dei, q*u*od estis uos, 'Godes temple is hali, *and* ðat ȝe bieð ȝeu seluen.' Ac he seið ðar after swiðe eisliche: Si q*ui*s aute*m* 24 uiolau*er*it templum dei, disp*er*det illum deus, 'Se ðe bifeleð godes te*m*ple mid ani full se*n*ne, godd hi*m* scal forl(i)esen, baðe licame *and* saule.' Of ðese hali temple ðe rihte beleaue is gru*n*dwall. Herof seið ðe apostele: Funda*m*e*n*tum aliuð 28 nemo potest pon*er*e, p*re*ter idem q*u*od positum est, q*u*od est Ie*s*u*s* Chri*stu*s[5], 'Ne mai no ma*n*n leiȝe*n* oðer grundwall[6] þa*n*ne ðat ðe is ileid, þat is, Iesu C*ri*st,' þar ðe Peter sade: Tu

---

[1] s. t. *MS.*   [2] *page* 59.   [3] *a letter erased between g and* o.
[4] Tempilum *MS.*   [5] īħc x͞p͞c *MS.*   [6] grunndwall *MS.*

are to bear this work are named before. Charity rises up from the foundation, and encircles all the walls, and all those who are dwelling in the holy house; and it rises up to the roof, for all the rafters of the holy virtues are fastened to it. Steadfast Hope has its place on high, because it is the roof, and covers all who are beneath it with the shingles of holy thoughts, which Wisdom finds for it. This holy virtue is wholly work-master of this blessed temple. It locks it within and without, so that He, who is King of all kings, may have His rest within. Therefore He begs that peace shall be as well in body as in soul, and that this holy virtue Peace shall be reigning in both of you; and the Justice of God shall pass sentence upon that of you who breaks it.

Now answers the body, and says:

I am very much surprised at thee, Reason, who shalt after God's ordinance instruct and direct, as well the soul as the body, that thou doest not understand that I and the soul are not of one nature, though both of us had one Creator. I am heavy, as one who is made of earth; and she is light as the air, which is called *spiraculum vitae*, that is, 'the breath of life.' She is a spirit, and I am dust; she is heavenly, and I earthly; she is of high nature as one who is God's own likeness, I am the likeness of the guilty Adam, through whom I am in great difficulties: in hunger and in thirst, in watches and in toils, and in many kinds of wretchedness, sorry and sorrowful, wailing and weeping. He knows it who knows all things, that scarcely could I write this through the tears which came running from the well-spring of repentance. Weep, weep along with me all who esteem yourselves guilty, and let us wash out the spots of our evil manners! There is no lye so good as tears: they make a face bright. Well is he who is made clean, and has the fair shroud of charity all beset with gem-stones of good works! He may come, with God's help, to the bridal before the bridegroom, and abide with Him in great joy and in great happiness. Dear Reason, this is my comfort, that I think (though you,

es *Christus*[1], fili*us* dei uiui, *and* þis sculen ilieuen *and* seggen
alle Cristene ðe on Criste belieueð. Ðe postes þat sculen beren up
ðis weorc, he bie*n* inamned hier te-foren. Cariteð arist up fra*m* ðe
grundwalle, *and* beclepð all ðe wouh, (*and*) alle ðe bieð i*n* ðo hali 4
huse wuniende ; *and* hie arist up ano*n* to ðe roue, forðan to hire
bieð ifastned alle ðe raftres of ðe hali mihtes.   Ðe faste hope hafð
hire stede[2] up an heih, for ði hie is rof *and* wrikð alle ðe hire bieð
beneðe*n* [3]mid ðe scincles of holie þohtes, þe sapie*n*tia[4] hire fint. 8
Ðies hali mihte is all wrihte of ðesen eadi temple. Hie hit belokeð
wið-i*nn*e*n* *and* wiðuten, þat he, ðe is alre kini*n*gene kyng, mu3e
hauen his reste wið-i*nn*e*n*.   For ði he bitt ðat pais bie aiðer o*n*
licame *and* on saule, *and* ðat þies hali mihte sibsu*m*nesse bie rix- 12
ende o*n* 3eu baðe ; *and* hwaðer 3u*n*ker hes tobrecð : justicia dei
scall ðar of do*n* riht.

NV andswereð[5] ðe lichame, *and* seið: 'Swiðe ich am 3ewu*n*dred
of ðe, Ratio, þe scalt[6] after godes isetnesse wissi*n* *and* stieren 16
3e ðe saule 3e ðe lichame, þat ðu ne undernemst þat ic *and* ðe
saule ne bieð nauht of one ikend*e*, ðeih wit boðe a*n*ne sceppend[7]
hadde*n*. Ic am heui, al so he ðe is imaked of ierðe; *and* hie is liht
alswo ðe left, ðat is icleped spiraculum uite, þat i*s*, ' ðe blast 20
of liue.' Hie is gost, *and* ic am dust; hie is heuenlich, *and* ich
ie(r)ðlich ; hie is of hei3e ke*n*ne al swo hie ðe is godes a3e*n* anlicnesse,
ic ha*m* ðes for3eltes Adames anlicnesse, þurh hwa*m* ic am on
muchele aruednesses, on hu*n*gre *and* on ðurste(s), on wacches *and* 24
on swinkes, *and* on mani3e(s) ke*nn*es wrecchades, sori *and* sorhfull,
woni*n*de *and* wepinde. Þat he wot ðe wot alle þing, þat unneaðe
ich mihte ðis write*n* for ðo teares ðe come*n* ierninde fro*m* ðare well-
riðe of rewnesse. Wepeð, wepeð forð mid me alle ðe healdeð 3eu 28
selue*n* for3elte, *and* waschen ðe spottes of ure euele ðeawes ! Nis
ðar no*n* swo god lei3e se teares : hie makieð scene ansiene. Wel
him ðe is clene iþrowen, *and* hafð ðat faire scrud of charite all
besett mid 3i*m*stanes of gode werkes ! He mai cumen, mid gode(s) 32
fultume, i*n* to ðe bredale to-fore ðe bredgume, *and* mid hi*m*
wuni3en on michele merhðe *and* on michele ædinesse. Lieue Racio,

---

[1] X͞P͞C *MS.*   [2] *sted on erasure.*   [3] *a letter erased before* m.
[4] *underlined, and* vvisdom *written at side by another hand.*   [5] -d *MS.*
[6] *page* 60.   [7] d *corr. from* t.

with good right, esteemed me unworthy) my hope is nevertheless
always steadfastly on Christ, God's Son, who shaped Himself after
my likeness, and became true Man ; who was, and is, and evermore
will be, true God.   Thanked be He !   He brought my nature, after
much unworthiness which He suffered here for me, to great worship, and set it very high on His Father's right hand ; and He has
promised me forsooth that, as truly as He came hither and took my
humanity and my nature, as truly shall I come to Him, and receive
of His Godhood and His nature, through His great mercy, if
I will listen to Him and follow His advice.   For His love I beg you
to forbear me and so to instruct and to guide me, that I may follow
and be obedient to both of you in all good works, the little while
that we dwell together.

Reason.

Now answers Reason, and says thus : Let it not seem strange to
thee, that I begged thee to have peace in thee and in thy soul. I know
well that God cannot abide in any soul which is in discord through
sins.   The prophet bears witness of it, who says : *In pace factus
est locus ejus,* ' In peace is made His stead, wherein He shall dwell.'
I know well what the apostle says about both of you : *Caro concupiscit adversus spiritum, et spiritus adversus carnem,* ' The flesh,'
says he, ' lusteth against the spirit, and the spirit against the flesh.'
And nevertheless ye may have peace, for he says afterwards : *Ut
non quaecunque vultis, ita faciatis,* ' Because,' says he, ' ye strive
between you, so that neither of you shall have his will.'   But ye
shall both, through this strife, follow God's will ; then there will
soon be peace over all thy land.   But help now all that thou
canst, that thy soul may have a little rest, and that this holy
temple be reared on both of you, so that God, your Creator, may
dwell therein ; then you are certainly blessed.   We must still work
a little, that it may be, with God's help, still better stored.

ðis is min froure, ðat ic þenche, þeih ȝie be gode rihte unwurð helden of me, naðeles (min [h]ope is aure fastliche) upe Criste, gode(s) sune, þe scop him seluen after mire andlicnesse, *and* becam soð mann; se ðe was, *and* is, *and* æuremo bieð, an soð godd. 4 Iþanked bie he! Mine ikynde, after maniȝe unwurðscipes ðe he for me hier þolede, he brohte to muchele wurðscipe, *and* sette hes wel heiȝe on his fader swiðer hand, *and* hafð me soðliche behoten þat, al swa soðliche swa he cam hider *and* underfeng[1] 8 mine mannischnesse *and* mine ȝekynde, swa soðliche ic scal cumen to him, *and* underfon of his goddcundnesse *and* of his ȝekynde, ðurh his michele mildce, ȝif ic him wile hlesten *and* his rad folȝin. For his luue ic ȝeu bidde þat ȝe me forberen *and* swa wissien *and* 12 swa stieren, þat ic mote folȝin *and* buhsum bien ȝing bam on alle gode werke(s), þe litle hwile ðe we tegedere wunieð.

Ratio.

NV andswereð Ratio, *and* ðu(s) seið: Ne þenche ðe no selcuð, 16 ðat ic ðe badd habben pais on ðe *and* on ðire saule. Ic hit wat wel ðat godd ne mai bien wuniȝende on none saule ðat unfrið is of sennes. Herof berð iwitnesse ðe profiete, ðe seið: I*n* pace fact*us est* loc*us* ei*us*, 'On sibsumnesse is imaked his stedel ðe he 20 on scal wuniȝen.' Ic wot wel hwat ðe apostel seið be[2] ȝeu baðe: Caro concupiscit aduersu(s) spi*ritum*, et sp*iritus* aduersus carne*m*, 'Đe flæsch,' he seið, 'hit ȝitsið aȝean ðe goste, *and* ðe gost aȝean ðe flesche.' *And* naðelas ȝit muȝen habben pais, forðan he seið after: 24 Vt no*n* qu*ecunque* uultis, ita faciatis, 'For ði,' he seið, 'ȝit winneð ȝuug betwen, ðat ȝunker noðer ne scal habben his ȝewill.' Ac ȝit sculen baðe, ðurh[3] ðese ȝewinne, folȝin godes wille; ðanne is sone pais ouer al ðine londe. Ac help nu all ðat 28 ðu miht, ðat ðin saule hadde a litel reste, *and* ðat ðis[4] hali temple (be)[5] arard on ȝinc, þat godd, ȝinker sceppend, mihte ðarinne wunien; ðanne bie ȝit iwiss isali. Wit moten ȝiet a litel swinken, ðat hit bie, mid godes fultume, ȝiet bet astored[6]. 32

---

[1] *page* 61.   [2] e *on erasure*.   [3] r *corr. from* w.
[4] *an* i *erased after* s.   [5] be *written above* is.   [6] *on erasure*.

Of peace.

Dear soul, this same virtue that is called Peace, about which we now shall speak, is very necessary for thee to keep and have, because, though thou hast toiled never so much in God's temple, He will never dwell in it, except peace be there. He brought this peace with Him from Heaven to earth, and gave it to all men who were *bonae voluntatis*, ' of good will,' that is, none save those who follow God's will. Because nobody is neither good nor righteous, but those who [are] God's and follow Him. Nobody can be full of wrath against him who has this blessed virtue. Of this says the prophet : *Pax multa diligentibus legem tuam, et non est illis scanda-lum*, ' Great peace have all who love Thy law : they are never wrath-ful.' Charity is God's law, which can hate no man, on account of any of the things one may do [against] it. Again, when Christ sent His disciples into the world, to teach them [viz. mankind] the way to the kingdom of Heaven, He then commanded them to say thus in each house where they would come : *Pax huic domui*, that is : ' Peace be unto this house !' If they found in it the man of peace, then their peace should remain there ; and if they did not, it should turn again to them.

Of prudence.

After this it behoves thee to have one of the holy virtues that well knows how, and is able to look after the gates and the doors of this holy temple. If thou couldst get *prudentiam*, [as] one [of them] is called, it [viz. prudence] would be very profitable to thee to look after this office. It is justly called Prudence. It is wise and prudent anent all thoughts, anent all words, anent all works. It will know all that they seek and that they wish for. If there comes any thought or any word on the part of God, they are very welcome to it. If they come from the devil, Prudence knows them soon, and drives them shamefully away. They can have no entrance there. If they come from men, Prudence can quickly find out, on whose behalf he is come, and receives him accordingly. For

Of sibsumnesse [1].

LIEUE saule, þies ilche mihte ðe is icleped pax, ðe we nu embe
spekeð, hie is swiðe niedfull ðe to healden and to habben,
for [2] ðan, ne haue ðu næure swo michel iswunken on godes temple, 4
bute ðær bie pais inne, ne wuneð he ðar næure. Ðas sibsumnesse
he brohte mid him fram heuene to ierðe, and ȝaf hes alle ðo mannen
ðat waren bone voluntatis, ' of gode wille,' (ðat nis non bute se
ðe folȝið [3] godes wille). For ðan non nis god ne rihtwis, bute godes 8
and ða ðe him folȝið. Se ðe hafð ðese eadi mihte, him ne mai no
mann wraðhin. Herof seið ðe profiete: Pax multa diligentibus legem tuam, et non est illis scandalum, 'Michel sibsumnesse is allen ðe luuieð ðine laȝe, ne bieð hie naure wroðe.' 12
Charite is godes laȝe, ðe ne mai nanne man hatien, for non ðare
þinge ðe me hire do. Efsones, ðo ðe Crist sente his lierning-
(c)nihtes in to ðe world, hem to tachen ðane wei to heuene riche, ðo
hiet he hem ðat hie scolden in to ælchen huse ðar hie comen, ðus 16
seggen: Pax huic domui, þat is: 'Sibsumnesse bie te ðesen
huse !' ȝif hie funden ðar inne ðane mann of pais, þanne scolde
here pais belæuen ðerinne ; and ȝif h(i)e ne deden, hie scolde aȝean
wanden to hem. 20

Of ȝepnesse.

HIER after ðe behoueð ðat tu habbe on of ðe holie mihtes ðe
wel cunne and wel muȝe ðo gaten and ðo duren wel bilokin
of ðis holi temple. ȝif ðu mihtest biȝeten prudentiam, [swa] hatte 24
an, hie ðe ware swiðe beheue ðese wike to lokin. Hie is ȝeapnesse
inamned mid gode rihte. Heo is wis and ȝeap aȝean alle ðohtes,
aȝean alle wordes, aȝean alle werkes. Hwat hie siechen and hwat
hie willen, all hie wile iwiten. ȝif ðar cumþ ani þoht oðer ani 28
word a godes half, hie bieð hire swiðe welcume. ȝif hie cumeð
fram dieule, prudencia hes icnauð sone, and drifþ hes awei
scandliche. Ne muȝen hie ðar habben non infare. ȝif hie cumeð
fram mannen, hie cann hwatliche underfinden, an hwos half he [4] 32
is icumen, and ðar after hie hine underfengð [5]. [6] Forðat hit ilimpð

---

[1] i corr. from u.   [2] page 62.   [3] folȝid MS.   [4] corrected from hie.
[5] g and ð connected.   [6] page 63.

it often happens that God sends a man to help another one, or to instruct him; and again, it happens that a man comes to another through the devil's admonition, though he may not know it. If thou wilt know a man, keep this Prudence with thee! Listen what he speaks most and oftest. If it is of God, or of things which belong to thee, he is to be loved and to be retained. If he speaks of sins and foolishness, then it is as if God said Himself: *Ex abundantia cordis os loquitur*, 'That of which the heart is full, the mouth speaketh.' The same man who is bound by a cardinal sin, and loves it, and speaks most about it, is not to be retained, unless he will listen to the words of God. If somebody comes there who asks for anything which is necessary for body or soul, advise him, help him, if thou canst! If thou canst not, have pity on him, and pray for him and all who help him. If anyone comes and brings tidings of idleness, and is speaking foolish words which raise laughter, he shall have no dwelling with thee, as thou lovest God and peace. Jesus Christ commanded us to be prudent, and said: *Estote prudentes sicut serpentes*, ' Be prudent as adders,' He said. The prudence of the adder is, that it lies down all rolled up, and its head in the middle, in order to save the head. The head is ever the beginning of all things which thou wilt do. Turn thyself all about! First think whether the thing which thou wishest to begin will be agreeable to God, or profitable to thee, or will become harmful to thy neighbour. If a righteous man has done so before thee, and if the holy Writ does not contradict thee, and bears witness to thee: do then what thou wilt do so. And [mind] that the beginning of all things be ever begun in God's name! Again, it [the adder] has another prudence, which we ought to follow: it has its hole. As soon as anything will do harm to it, it creeps into its hole, and so it saves its life. Just so do thou, after God's own counsel, when the devil, or any evil man, or anything which displeases thee, will harm thee; anon creep thou into thy hole, into Christ's open side, with thy good belief, and say unto thy Saviour: *Sub umbra alarum tuarum protege me, Domine,* 'Lord,' say, ' under the shadow of Thy wings, of Thy arms, which were fastened on the holy

ofte ðat godd sant ane man an oðer to helpe, oðer him to wissin;
and eft hit ȝelimpð ðat a mann cumþ tan oðer ðurh dieules meneȝinge, þeih he hit naht ne wite. Ȝif ðu wilt mann icnowen, haue
ðese ȝeapnesse mid ðe! Hlest hwat he speke mest and oftest. 4
Ȝif it is¹ of gode oðer of þinges ðe to ðe belimpeð, he is to luuiȝen
and to wiðhealden. Ȝif he spekð of sennes and of sothades, ðanne
hit is alswo godd sade him self: Ex habundantia cordis os loquitur, 'Of ðat ðe herte is full, ðarof spekð ðe muð.' De ilke 8
mann ðe is ibunden mid heaued-senne, and hes luneð, and mast
ðar embe spekð, nis he noht to wiðhealden, bute ȝif² he wolde
godes wordes lesten. Ȝif ðar cumþ sum ðe sehþ of aniȝere niede
ðe belemð to lichame oðer to saule, ræd him, help him, ȝif ðu miht. 12
Ȝif ðu ne miht, haue rewðe of³ him, and bide for him and for alle
ðe him helpen. Ȝif ani cumþ and bri[n]gþ tidinges of idelne(s)ses,
and is spekende sotwordes ðe aræreð up hleitres, none wunienge
ne haue he mid ðe, swa se ðu luuest godd and sibsumnesse. Iesv 16
Crist hiet ðat we scolden bien ȝeape, and sæde: Estote prudentes sicut serpentes, 'Bieð ȝeape al swa næddre,' he sade.
Dare næddre ȝeapnesse is, ðat hie lið al abuten itrand, and hire
heaued on midden, for to berȝen ðat heaued. Of alle þing ðat tu 20
wilt don, æure is ðat anginn ðat heaued. Bewænt te all abuten!
Denc arst whaðer hit wile bien gode icweme, ðat ðing ðe ðu wilt
aginnen, oðer ðe beheue⁴, oðer ðine nexte to none harme ne wande.
Ȝif rihtwis mann habbe swo ȝedon te-fore ðe, ȝif ðat hali writ ne 24
wiðseið ðe naht, and berð þe iwitnesse: ðat tu wilt so don, do hit
ðanne. And æure of alle þinge ðat ðe anȝinn bie a godes name
ȝegunnen!⁵ Ȝiet hie haueð an oðer ȝeapnesse, ðe we sculen folȝin:
hie haueð hire hol. Swa raðe swa ani þing harm hire wile don, 28
swo hie crepþ in to hire hole, and swo hie berhð hire lif. Riht
alswo do ðu, after gode(s) awene rade, ðanne dieuel ðe wile derien,
oðer áni euel mann, oðer ani þing ðat te misliki; anon crep ðu in
to ðine hole, in to Cristes opene side, mid ðine gode ileaue, and 32
seiȝe to ðine aliesende: Sub umbra alarum tuarum protege
me, domine, 'Lauerd,' seiȝe, 'vnder ðare scadewe of ðine fiðeres,

---

¹ s corr. from h.   ² gif MS.   ³ os MS.
⁴ corr. from behieue.   ⁵ page 64.

cross, shield me from all kinds of evils that come from the devil (whom Thou overcamest there), and cool my wretched heart, which is envenomed by his manifold temptations! Cool the great heat of my sorrows with the blessed stream which comes out of Thy holy side!' If thou believest this, and doest so, be sure, nothing can be of harm to thee. Though thou mayst suffer harm, all that thou sufferest for God's love will turn out to be good for thee.

Of foresight.

Providentia, that is, foresight, is another holy virtue, which thinks of and looks after all things ere they come. Therefore it repents nothing which it has done. Before the city of Jerusalem is a great hill, which is called Zion, that means 'Sight.' Upon it were the watchmen who looked after the holy city, and guarded it against all its enemies. So does this virtue upon the hill of great Consideration. It spies and looks from afar, and says thus: ' Well, thou wretched soul, which, I say, takest no heed of thyself! Couldst thou see all thy enemies who are round about thee, as I do, sorry wouldst thou be, eagerly wouldst thou cry to God to save thee! I warn thee before. Thou wilt not long be dwelling here; forsake thy sins! If thou forsakest them not here, ere thou goest out of the world, certainly they will never forsake thee, ere they bring thee to their parents. These are the cursed spirits which here above in the clouds wait for souls. If they find upon thee any of their deeds, no angel may help thee from going into pain, and paying the penalty there. *Quia nullum malum impunitum*, " No evil shall be unpunished, either here or there." It sees and hears a merry song of the good soul: *Veni, sponsa Christi, accipe coronam*, " Come, thou Christ's own bride, and receive the great worship and the great joy of the kingdom of Heaven, which He has prepared for thee to have for evermore for the good fidelity which thou borest in Him!" '

of ðine armes, ðe waren ifast(n)ed on ðare hali rode, scild me fram
alle ðes kennes eueles[1] ðe cumeð fro ðe dieule, ðe ðu ðar ouercome,
and kiel mine wreche herte, þe is iattred of his manifealde fondinges!
Kiel ðe muchele hate of mine sarinesses mid ðan eadiȝe well-streme 4
ðe cumþ of ðine halie side!' Gif ðu ðis ȝeliefst, *and* swa diest,
bie ðu siker, ne mai þe non þing to harme [bien]. Þeih ðu harm
all hit want (ðe) to gode[2] ðat tu for godes luue þolest.

Of forscea[w]nesse[3]. 8

PROUIDENTIA, *þat* is, forsceawnesse[4], is an oðer hali mihte,
ðe þencþ *and* lokeð alle þing beforen (ar ðanne hie cumen).
For ði ne rewð hire naht after hire dædes. To-foren ðare burh of
Ierusalem is an muchel dune, ðe hatte Syon, *þat* is tokned ' Scea- 12
winge.' Þærupen weren ðe sceaweres ðe lokeden ðe hali burh, *and*
warnedèn fram alle here unwines. Al swo doð ðies mihte upe ða
dune of muchel embeðanke. Hie sceaweð *and* lokeð ferrene to,
and ðus seið: ' VVelle[5], ðu earme[6] saule, ðe, ic segge, ðe none 16
ȝieme ne nemst of ðe seluen! Mihtest tu isien alle ðine unwines
ðe bieð[7] a⁸buten þe, also alse i do, sari woldest tu bien, ȝierne
woldestu[9] clepien to gode *þat* he ðe aredde! Ic ðe warni te-foren.
Ne biest ðu naht hier lange wuniȝende; forlat ðine sennen! Ȝif 20
ðu hier he(s) ne forlatst, ær ðanne ðu fare of ðare woreld, full
ȝewiss ne forlateð hie ðe næure, ær ðanne hie ðe bringen to here
eldren. Ðat bið ðo werewede gostes ðe waitið ðo soules hier
buuen on ðe wolkne. Þ(o)[10] þe hie findeþ upe ðe of here werkes, 24
ne[11] mai þe helpen non angel ðat tu ne scalt in to pine, *and* ðar
abeggen. Quia nullum m'al̨um inpunitum, "Ne scall non euel
bien unpined, oðer hier oðer ðar." Of ðare gode saule hie ȝesieð
and iherð merigne *song*: Veni, sponsa *Christi*, accipe coro- 28
nam, "Cum, ðu Cristes awen bried, *and* underfoh ðe michele
wurðscipe *and* ðe michele merhþe of heuene riche, þe he ðe haueð
iȝarked æurema to habben for ðare gode trewðe ðe ðu him
bere!"' 32

---

[1] *an* l *erased after* s. [2] ȝode *MS.* [3] w *has disappeared by the binding;*
ȝap *is written black above* scea *in another hand.*
[4] *The first* s *and* e *underdotted,* ȝ *written over* ce. [5] *The first* e *corr. from* l.
[6] wrecche (*with* w, *not* þ) *written over* earme. [7] bied *MS.* [8] *page* 65.
[9] woldest stu *MS.* [10] o *inserted after* þ. [11] *a* ð *at side and a stroke before* n.

Of righteousness.

Another holy virtue is called *justitia*, that is, righteousness. Certainly it desires that God should first pass His judgment on all His creatures, and that afterwards every creature should have its right, according to what is prepared for them. Truly, it ought to be justice within God's temple. *Justitia et judicium praeparatio sedis ejus*, this is written of it : 'Righteousness and judgment make God's seat.' *Anima justi sedes sapientiae*, 'The soul of the righteous is verily God's seat.' The same holy virtue *justitia*— that is, the justice of God's temple—asks right and judgment of all our misdeeds, because all creatures which God has created keep their nature better than man alone. Anent this said the prophet : *Non intres in judicium cum servo tuo, Domine*, 'Lord,' said he, 'enter not into judgment with Thy servant, because all that is living in Heaven and on earth could not be justified before Thee.' This same justice threw out him who was [a] bright angel in Heaven. It threw Adam out of Paradise ; it brought Christ to death, for God had said to Adam : *Morte morieris* ! There shall none escape who comes from him, so that he shall not suffer death. Since this is true, that it [justice] spared not, either the angel, or the man, or Christ Himself : how may it spare thee ? Here we are affrighted. But the holy apostle consoles us : *Si nosmet ipsos judicaremus*, 'If we sift ourselves in penitence with true repent-unce, and judge ourselves with right satisfaction, we shall never-more again be doomed.' The strength of this holy virtue takes up into Heaven and down into hell, and spreads as wide as the earth. For all the wrongs which are done on earth, it will have right. It takes no reward for holding up wrong, nor for pulling down right. Those who will revenge themselves for wrong which is done to them, take its judgment away from it, because it says : *Mihi vindictam*, 'Let me avenge, judgment is mine !' I cannot believe that anybody suffers death without the judgment of this awful virtue, be the death as it may. Neither devil nor man can have any power or strength over others, except in so much as this mighty

Of rihtwisnesse.

AN oðer hali mihte is icleped iusticia, þat is, rihtwisnesse.
Fulȝewis hie wile ðat godd a-forewarde habbe his ȝerihte of
alle his iscafte, and seððen aurich ȝescafte here rihte, after ðan ðe 4
hem iscapen is.   Hie awh wel to bene iustise inne godes temple.
Iusticia et iudicium preparatio sedis eius, ðis is ȝewriten
be hire : 'Rihtwisnesse and dom, hi makieð godes sate.' Anima
iusti sedes sapientie, 'Das rihtwises saule iwis is godes sate.' 8
Des ilche hali mihte iusticia, þat is, godes temple-rihtwisnesse, hie
acseð riht of alle ure misdades and dom, forðan alle ðe scaftes
ðat godd haueð ȝescapen, alle hie healdeð bet here ikynde þanne
mann one.   Hier aȝean sæde ðe profiete : Non intres in iudi- 12
cium cum seruo tuo, domine, 'Hlauerd,' he sade, 'ne go ðu
noht in to dome mid ðine þral'le, forðan all ðat is liues on heuene
and on ierðe ne mihte bien irihtwised onȝeanes þe.'   Dis ilche
iustise warp ut him ðe was briht angel on heuene.   Hie warp ut 16
Adam of para(d)ise; hie brohte Criste to ðe deaðe, for ði ðat
godd isæd[2] hadde to Adame : Morte morieris!   Ne scall ðar
non atbersten ðe cumþ of him, þat he deað ne scal ðoliȝen.   Seððen
þis is soð, þat hie ne wåndede, ne ðe angele, ne ðe manne, ne 20
Crist self : hu mai hie wonde ðe ?   Her we bieð offeruht.   Ac ðe
hali apostel us freureð : Si nosmet[3] ipsos iudicaremus, 'ȝif
we seiȝeð us seluen on scrifte mid soðe birewnesse, and we demen
us seluen mid[4] rihte deadbote, ne sculen we næure mo eft bien 24
idemd.'   Se strengþe of ðessere hali mihte, hie takð up in to
heuene and niþer in to helle, and spratt swo wide swo middenard.
Of alle ðe unrihte(s) þe bieð idon on ierðe, hie wile habben riht.
Ne nimð hie none miede for unriht to healden, ne for riht to leien. 28
Þa ðe willeð hem seluen wreken of unrihte ðe hem is idon, hie
benemeð hire hire dom, forðan hie seiȝeð : Mihi uindictam, 'Læt
me wreken, (d)om[5] is min !'   Ne mai ic ilieue ðat ani mann deað
þoliȝe wið-uten ðe dome of ðessere eisliche mihte, bie hit swilch 32
deað swo hit eure bie.   Ne dieuel ne mann none mihte ne none
strengþe habben ne muȝen ouer oðren, bute alswo michel swo ðis

---

[1] *page 66.* [2] a *altered to* æ. [3] með *MS.*
[4] o *underdotted before* m.   [5] d *corrected over* ð.

virtue will give them. Thou must love and follow this holy virtue, that is, be righteous in thyself and towards all others, if thou wishest to be saved.

Of strength.

Fortitudo, that is, God's strength, is another holy virtue, which is needful to shield God's temple from all enemies. The prophet said of it: *Esto nobis, Domine, turris fortitudinis,* 'Lord, be our tower of strength against all enemies!' This same holy virtue is the tower and strength to all the virtues which dwell in it, and so it is to all the chosen ones of Christ.

[Of moderation.]

Temperantia is another holy virtue, which has very great discretion and moderation in all kinds of things. It will not suffer any overdone thing; [and] on the other side, neither too little nor too much. Whoso will listen to its counsel, shall neither eat too much, nor drink too much, nor too little; nor shall he rest or sleep too much, nor too little; nor shall he speak too much, nor [be] too much silent; nor shall he be clad too proudly, nor too coarsely; nor shall he be too glad, nor too sorry. As one regulates a bath, so that it is neither too hot nor too cold, so this holy virtue regulates all the manners of the man who loves it and knows how to keep it. He is happy who keeps it! This one regulates all these blessed virtues; and those who will not listen to it, become powerless, and they shall ever repent it. It regulates all the temptations and all the displeasures and all the unwillingness, which come from man, and withholds [him] from misdoing.

Of obedience.

Another virtue is called *obedientia*, that is, obedience. This is very profitable in God's house. All who love God ought to love maini mihte hem wile ȝiuen. Đese hali mihte ðu most luuiȝen *and* folȝien, þat is, þat þu bie rihtwis *on* ðe seluen *and* aȝean alle oðren[1], swa swa ðu wilt bien iborewen.

Of stren[g]ðe.   4

FORTITUDO, þat is, godes strengþe, is an oðer hali mihte, ðe is niedfull to scilden godes temple fram alle unwines. Of hire sade ðe profiete: Esto nob*is, domine, turris fortitudinis,* 'Hlauerd, bie ure *tur* of strengþe aȝean alle[2] unwines!' Đies 8 ilche haliȝe mihte, hie is *tur and* strengþe to alle ðo mihte(s) ðe ðar inne bieð wuniȝende, *and* swa hie is alle Cristes ȝecorene.

TEMP*ERA*NTIA is an oðer hali mihte, ðe cann swiðe michel scile *and* mæðe of alle kennes þinge. Hie ne wile ðoliȝen 12 *non* ouerdon þing; an oðer halue, ne to litel ne to michel. Se ðe hire ræd hlesten[3] wile, ne scal he noðer eten to michel, ne dri*n*ken to michel, ne to litel; ne he ne scall reste*n* ne slapen to michel, ne to litel; ne he ne scal to michel bie*n* speke*n*de, ne to michel swi- 16 (g)ende; ne he ne scal to prudeliche bie*n* isc(r)edd, ne to unorne-liche; ne he ne scal bie*n* to glad, ne to sori. Al so me tempreð an baþ, ðat hit ne bie to hot ne to cold, also deð ðis haliȝe mihte alle ðes ma*n*nes ðeawes ðe hes luuiȝeð *and* healden cann.   He is isali 20 ðe hes halt ! Alle ðese eadi mihtes ðes one atempreð; *and* ðo ðe[4] hire ne wyle[5] ilesten, hie becumeð to unmihte[6], *and* eure hit hem scal rewe*n*. Alle ðe fondi*n*ges *and* alle ðe unluste(s) *and* alle[7] un-willes ðe cumeð of ðe ma*n*ne, ðies hes atempreð, *and* wiðhalt te 24 misdo*n*.

Of hersumnesse[8].

AN oðer mihte is ȝehoten obedie*n*cia, ðat is, hersumnesse[9]. Đies is swiðe behieue on godes huse. Alle ðe godd luuiȝeð 28

---

[1] odre*n* *MS.*   [2] *page* 67.   [3] leshten *MS.*
[4] ne *MS.*   [5] *over erasure,* w = w, *not* p. *Also an erasure on the margin.*
[6] *a letter erased after* e.   [7] *The first* l *on erasure.*   [8] buh *is written above* her *in another hand, black.*   [9] her *underdotted,* i-buh *written above it.*

and keep it. As all mankind had death through disobedience, so it came to life through obedience. This holy virtue makes the man pliant and obedient to God and to his parents; and afterwards, to old and young and every man. After this, as to what he can perform, he takes no heed whether it is fair or loathsome, or hot or cold, or heavy or light; he thinks all to be good, for His love who was obedient to His Father even until death, Jesus Christ. This is very profitable to every man whoever will be saved, that he be obedient to God, and, for His love, to the bishop, and to his priest, and to his lord. But one ought not to be obedient except in good [things]. If a man commands or bids to do a sin, one ought not to be obedient to it. Where God gives this virtue, it soon shows itself. A man may be of never so high a family, it makes him become a servant. Just as it does these monks, who are obedient to a mortal man as if it were God Himself, so it does them who dwell in the world. They are very eager to learn God's laws, and then to work after them, and they beseech him who knows well how to instruct them, and listen blithely to and follow his counsel, lest they fall with the blind into the pit which Christ Himself spoke of. He called them dumb dogs through the prophet, who said: *Canes muti, non valentes latrare,* 'They are the dumb dogs which cannot or may not bark.' For the love of God I beg, do not look unworthier on this account, because thou knowest who it is. Through this holy virtue and through his good belief Abraham was blessed by God, and it was promised to him that One should come of his kind through whom all mankind should be blessed. Thus spoke God to Abraham : *Exi de terra tua, etc.,* 'Go,' quoth He, 'out of thy land and out of thy kindred and out of thy father's house, and come into the land that I will show thee.' Abraham believed what God said to him, and was obedient to Him. This same says God to them whom He wishes to be obedient to Him : 'Go out of thy land!' Thy land is thy flesh, which is nothing but earth. Go out of the lusts of thy flesh and follow them no more. 'And out of thy kindred!'

hes aȝeð to luuien *and* to healden. Al swa al mankinn ðurh unhersumnesse hafden deað, al swa ðurh hersumnesse hit cam to liue.
Ðies holi mihte makeð ðane mann leðebeih *and* hersum gode *and*
his eldren; *and* ðar after ealde *and* ȝunge *and* alle manne. After 4
.ðat, ðe he iforðen mai, ne nimþ he none ȝieme hwaðer hit bie fair ðe
loðlich, ðe hot ðe cold, ðe heui ðe liht; all him ðiugð god, for
his luue ðe was hersum his fader anon to ðe deaðe, Iesv Crist.
Ðies is swiðe [1] behene æurilch mann ðat æure i-boreȝen scal bien, 8
þat he bie hersum gode, *and*, for his luue, ðe biscope, *and* his prieste,
and his louerde. Ac me ne auh to bien hersum bute of gode. Ȝif
mann hat oðer bitt [2] senne [3] to donne, þar to ne awh me naht to
bien hersvm. Whar ðe godd ȝifð ðese mihte, hit kydh hit sone. 12
H(i)e makeð ðane mann—nis he of swo heie kenne, þat hie him
ne makeð—þreall. Al swa hie deð ðese munekes, ðe bieð hersum ane
deadliche manne al swa hit wære godd self, swa hie dieð hem ðe
on ðare woreld wuniȝen. Hie bien swiðe ȝiernfull godes laȝe to 16
liernin, *and* ðanne ðar after werchen, *and* him ðe hem wel cann
wissin hie bBesekeð, *and* his ræd [4] bliðeliche hlisteð *and* folȝið, ðe
laste hie falleð mid ða blinde in to ðan [5] pette ðe Crist self embe
spak. He hem clepede dumbe hundes ðurh ðe profiete, ðe sade : 20
Canes mu(ti), non ualentes latrare, 'Hie bieð ðe dumbe
hundes ðe ne cunnen oðer ne muȝen berken.' For ðe luue of godd
ic bidde, ne latt tu herfore non ðe unwurþere, for ðan ðu wost
hwo it is. Ðurh ðesse holi mihte *and* ðurh [6] his gode ileauen [7] was 24
Abraham iblesced of godd, *and* him behoten ðat on scolde cumen
of his kenne ðurh hwam all mannkenn scolde bien iblesced. Ðus
spak godd to Abrahame : Exi de terra tua, et cetera, 'Ga ut,'
cwað he, 'of ðine lande *and* ut of ðine kenne *and* ut of ðines fader 28
huse, *and* cum in to ðo londe ðe ic ðe wile sceawin.' Abraham
iliefde ðatt godd [8] him sæde, *and* was him hersum. Ðis ilche seið
godd to hem ðe he wile ðat bie him hersum : 'Ga ut of ðine lande!'
Þin land ðat is ðin flesc, ðe nis bute ierðe. Ga ut of ðines flasches 32
lustes, ðat tu [9] hem na [10] more ne folȝe. 'And ut of ðine kenne!' Þat
bieð alle ðine euele ðeawes ðe ðu mide ware iboren *and* ec ifedd.

---

[1] page 68.   [2] oðer bitt *double, the first time crossed with red colour.*
[3] senne *MS.*   [4] *or* rad ?   [5] *or* ðæm ?   [6] *an erasure above* r.
[7] *or* ileaue ? *The little line over* ue *very short and curved.*   [8] g *corr. from* d.
[9] *an erasure over* t.   [10] *page* 69.

That are all thy evil manners wherewith thou wast born and also
fed. 'And out of thy father's house!' The while the man lies in
cardinal sins, he is the devil's son, as the good man is God's son
when he loves and follows God. All this world was the devil's
house ere Christ came, who cast him out. Thereof He said: *Nunc
princeps mundi hujus ejicietur foras,* 'Now shall the prince of this
world be driven out.' Here God teaches thee that thou shalt forsake the world voluntarily, ere death takes it from thee against thy
will, and come to the land which He will show thee, that is, the
land of the heavenly Jerusalem. Again He tried him [viz.
Abraham], and found him true. *Tolle filium tuum, quem diligis,
Isaac,* 'Take thy son, whom thou lovest so much, and offer him
to Me on the hill which I will show thee!' Abraham had no
son by his right spouse but one, and that was begotten in his great
age. Therefore he was called Isaac, that is, Bliss. So says God to
thee: 'Offer me thy son Isaac, that is, the thing which thou lovest
most!' Understand now well what that may be, and look
whether thou couldst be obedient in this respect to God Almighty.
If thou lovest thy own will most of all, it is very wholesome for
thee to offer this to thy Lord God, because it is a very agreeable
sacrifice to Him that thou forsakest thy own will and followest His.
This thou shalt offer upon the high hill of Obedience. There is no
virtue in God's temple which has not lot and part with this blessed
virtue.

Of mercy.

Another holy virtue is called *misericordia,* that is, mercy, which
is very agreeable to God. He showed it Himself to all the needful
who besought Him. So were Mary and Martha, who besought
Him for their dead brother, Lazarus, whom He soon raised from
a double death, [viz.] of the soul and of the body. So He soon had
pity on the adulterous woman, who was to be stoned to death, after
the old law. He forgave her the death, and all her sins He forgave.
So He did St. Peter, who had forsaken Him. Anon, when He
looked upon him, he began to weep, and his sins were forgiven him.
How [did] the thief, who never had done good? This mercy made
him come from the cross anon into Paradise. There is none who

'*And* vt of þines fader huse!' Ðar hwile ðe mann lið *on* heaued-
sennes, he is ðes dieules sune, al swo ðe god*e* mann ðe is godes
sune þanne he godd luueð *and* folʒeð. All ðis woreld was ðes
dieules hus ær Crist come, ðe hi*m* ut warp. Ðerof he sade : N u n c 4
princeps mu*n*di huiu*s* eicietu*r* fora(s), 'Nu scal ðe alder
of ðis woreld ut bien ʒedriue*n*.' Hier ðe lærð godd ðat tu scule
ðe woreld forlaten ðines aʒenes þankes, ær ðe deað hes te benime
þines unþankes, *and* cume*n* to ðo lande ðe he ðe wile sceawin, þat 8
is, ðat lond of ðare heue*n*liche Ierusalem. Efsones¹ he hi*m* fondede,
and fond him treuwe. Tolle filiu*m* tuu*m*, qu*e*m diligis,
Isaac, 'Ni*m* ðine sune, ðe ðu luuest swa michel, *and* offre hine
me upe ðare dune ðe ic ðe wile sceawi*n*!' Abraam ne hadde 12
na*n*ne sune be his rihte spuse bute ænne, *and* ðat was biʒete*n* o*n*
his michele ielde. For ði he was icleped Isaac, þat is, blisse. Al
swo seið godd to ðe : 'Offre me þine sune Ysaac, þat is, þat þing
ðe ðu mast luuest!' Vnderstond nu wel what ðat bie, *and* loke 16
hwæðer ðu muʒe ðerof bien he*r*sum goddalmihtin. ʒif ðu luuest
ðin aʒene wille alre mast, þanne is ðe swiðe holsu*m* ðat ðu þis
ofri ðine louerde² god, forðan hit is (him) swiðe ʒecweme loac
ðat ðu lat ðine aʒene wille and folʒe his. Ðis ðu scalt ofrien upe 20
ðare (heiʒe)³ dune⁴ of hersumnesse. Nis no*n* mihte *on* godes
temple ðat ne hafþ lott *and* dole mid ðessere eadiʒe mihte⁵.

Of milce.

MISERICORDIA hatte an oðer hali mihte, ðat is, milce, 24
ðe gode is (swiðe) icweme. Ðat he sceawede hi*m* selu to
alle nied-fulle ðe hi*m* besohte*n*. Also was Marie *and* Martha, ðe
hi*m* besohte*n* of here deade broðer, Lazaru*m*, ðe he sone arearde of
tua deaðes, of saule *and* of lichame. Swa he hadde sone mildcé of 28
ðe forleiene wiue, ðe scolde bien ofsteand te deaðe, after ðare
ealde la(u)ʒe. He forʒaf hire ðane deað, *and* alle hire si*n*nen he
forʒaf. Swa he dede seinte⁶ Petre, ðe hine hadde forsaken. Anon,
ðo ðe he lokede upe*n* him, he aga*n*n to wepen, *and* his se*n*nen hi*m* 32
wære*n* forʒiuene. Hu ðe ðeof⁷, ðe næure god nadde ido*n*? Ðis

---

¹ *an erasure between* E *and* f.　² o *corr. from* d.　³ *on the margin.*
⁴ ðune *MS.*　⁵ *page* 70.　⁶ seintre *MS.*　⁷ o *corr. over another letter.*

could know all the mercies which God has done, and does still, ever
through this blessed virtue. Of this Jesus Christ reminds us, who
says : *Estote misericordes,* 'Be merciful, as your Father is in
Heaven !' Again, He says Himself : *Beati misericordes, quoniam
ipsi misericordiam, etc.* 'Blessed are the merciful, for they shall
have mercy from God, as they have mercy on men.' Of this holy
virtue is written in the Psalter : *Misericordia et Veritas obviaverunt
sibi,* 'God's Mercy and Truth, that is, God, met together.' All that
ever is in the holy Writ, is all a prefiguration of God. It says that
these two, Mercy and Truth, met one another, and I shall write as
if Mercy spoke with Truth ; and thus she says : 'Tell me, Truth,
what is thy counsel concerning guilty Adam, and all his offspring ?
Can he nevermore come back ? Wherefore was he ever shaped to
man ? Why was he not shaped to have ever, with the angels, the
joy of the kingdom of Heaven ?' Then answered Truth : 'No
injustice is done to him. I warned him, and said forsooth, that the
day on which he would break God's commandment, he should
suffer death ; and he had [his] own choice to do whichsoever he
would. The devil used no force against him.' Then answered
Misericordia again : 'Consider that just as thou saidst that he
should suffer death, so thou saidst [also] : "Let us make man in
our own image, after our likeness !" After thy likeness thou
shapedst him. Never let thy own likeness perish, but let him
come, through thy great goodness, to the happiness for which he
was created, although his great evilness has not earned it !' Truth
was compliant, as her custom ever is, and said to Mercy : 'Let us
go before God and His Justice and His Judgment and-before all His
holy Virtues, and complain there. All that I can do to help thee
I will [do] blithely.' *Misericordia* took with her *Pietatem* and
Pacem, and they came before God, and very meekly besought Him,
and the happy Mercy soon stretched herself down before God, and
said thus : 'Holy, holy Lord, have mercy and pity on Adam, Thy
guilty man, who so many hundred years has suffered the darkness

mildce him dede cumen fram ðare rode anon in to paradise. Nis
non ðe mihte witten alle ðe milcen ðe godd hafð idon, and ȝiet
dieð, æure ðurh ðessere eadi mihte. Herof us meneȝeð Iesu Crist[1],
and seið : Estote mi(sericordes), 'Bieð mildciende, al swo ȝeuer 4
fader is on heuene!' Eft he[2] seið him self : Beati[3] misericordes,
quoniam ipsi misericordiam[4], et cetera, 'Eadi bieð ðe milde,
forðan hie sculen hauen milce of gode, swo swo hie habbeð milce of
mannen.' Bi ðessere holi mihte is iwriten on ðe saltere : Miseri- 8
cordia et Uerita(s) obuiauerunt sibi, 'Godes Mildce and Soð,
þat is, godd, ȝemetten hem to gedere.' All ðat æure is on ðe hali
write, all[5] hit is forbisne of gode. Hit seið þat ðese two, Mildce and
Soð, hem imetten, and ic write swilch[6] Mildce speke wið Soðe, and 12
ðus seið : 'Sei me, Soð, hwat is ðin rad of ðe forgilte Adame, and
of all his ofsprenge ? Ne mai he nauere mo aȝean cumen ? Hwarto
was he aure iscapen te manne ? Hu ne was he iscapen for to hab-
benne forð mid ðo aingles heueneriches merhþe ?' Ða andswerede 16
Soð : 'Nis him idon non unriht. Ich him warnede, and soð sade,
hwilche dai ðe he tobreke godes forbode, he scolde[7] deað poliȝen ;
and he hadde auȝene kere te donne hwaðer swo he wolde. Ne dede
dieuel him none strengþe.' Ða andswerede ȝiet Misericordia : 'Be- 20
þenc þat alswa swa ðu sadest ðat he deað scolde poliȝen, alswa ðu
sadest : Faciamus hominem ad ymaginem et similitudi-
nem ! After ðine anlicnesse ðu hine scope. Ne latt ðu naure
forfaren ðine aȝen anlicnesse, ac to ðare eadinesse ðe he to was 24
iscapen, lat him ðarto cumen, for ðire muchele godnesse, þei his
miche[le] euelnesse hit nabbe noht ofearned !' Soð was leðebei, alse
hire iwune is aure, and sade to Mildce : 'Cume we te-fore gode and
his Rihtwisnesse and his Dome and beforen alle his holi mihtes, and 28
bemæn ðe ðar ! Al ðat ic mai ðe bien te fultume ich wille bleðeliche.' Misericordia nam mid hire Pietatem and (Pacem),
and comen before gode, and swiðe eadmodliche him besohten, and se
eadiȝe Mildce hire astrehte sone teforen gode, and ðus sæde : 'Hali, 32
hali lauerd, haue are and milce of Adame, ðine forgilte manne, ðe
swo maniȝe hundred wintre hafð iðoled þo ðesternesse of helle, ðe

---

[1] jħu crist in luca written above ðapostel.   [2] h on erasure.
[3] in Math qc. written above.   [4] m written over the following &.
[5] a over &.   [6] an e erased after h.   [7] page 71.

I

of hell, who was shaped to the great happiness of Thy kingdom!
But the devil has not him alone, but all his offspring so in his
power, that none can come into the kingdom for which they were
shaped; but he brings [them] all into hell, both good and evil.
Lord, have mercy and compassion and pity on Thy handiwork!
Ever they have hope that thou wouldst have pity and mercy upon
them.' Anon Pity complained, and said: ' Ay, Thou, Lord, beginning and source of all goodness, have mercy and pity on
wretched Adam's soul, that was shaped after Thy likeness, and on
Thy patriarchs and on Thy prophets, and on many thousand holy
souls, which all suffer pain through Adam's guilt, with good right, for
his disobedience! They all weep and wail, and hope in Thy great
mercy and look to Thee, until Thou shalt send them some release.
I am so sorry for them that I cannot have rest.' ' Lord, if it is Thy
will,' said Peace, ' this cannot be in Thy kingdom. Thy peace is
so very great that not a single thought can exist there except with
all softness and with all meekness. Make reconciliation between
Mercy and Justice, and make Judgment and Pity [to do] well
together! Nevertheless, I know well that Thou wilt have pity on
mankind. Thy goodness cannot help it.' Then said Justice: ' With
much right Adam suffers what he suffers, for he was disobedient to
his Creator. He disdained God when he allowed His adversary to
overpower him, without force. To his Lord he did first great
harm, he slew first himself, and since all mankind, and for his
disobedience he bereft God's kingdom of himself and of all his offspring, so that he nevermore can come again [here] by right doom.'

Then said Truth : ' That is right that God's mercy is ever higher
and more than His right judgment. Lord, it is truth that Thou
promisedst to Abraham, Thy dear friend, that through One of his
kin all mankind should be blessed. Afterwards, thou promisedst
to David, the righteous king: *De fructu ventris tui ponam super*

was iscapen to ðare muchele eadinesse of ðine riche ! Ac noht
he one [1], ac all his ofsp(r)eng hafð dieuel swo on his walte, ðat non
ne mai cumen into ðare riche ðe hie to waren iscapen ; ac alle he
bringþ in to helle, baðe gode *and* euele.   Hlauerd, haue ore *and* 4
rewhþe *and* mild(c)e [2] of ðin handiwerc ! Æure hie habbeð hope
ðat tu scule habben ore *and* milce of hem.'

Anon hire bemande Rewðe [3], *and* sade : 'Ælle, ðu, lauerd, angin
and welle of alle godnesse, haue rewðhe *and* milce of ðe wrecche 8
Adame(s) soule, ðe was iscapen after ðine andlicnesse, *and* of ðine
patriarches *and* of ðine profietes, *and* mani þusend hali saules, ðe
alle þolieð pine for Adames gelte, mid gode rihte, for his un-'hersumnesse !   Alle hie wepeð *and* wonið, *and* hopieð to ðire 12
muchele milce *and* to ðe lokið, all hwat ðu send hem sume
aliesendnesse.   Hi me reweð (swa) [5] swiðe ðat ic reste ne mai
habben.'

'Lauerd, ȝif hit is ðin wille,' sæde Sibsumnesse, 'þis ne mai noht 16
bien on ðine riche.   Ðin sibsumnesse is swo (swiðe) michel ðat on
lepi þoht [6] ne mai ðer bien bute mid alle sof[t]nesse *and* mid alle
eadinese.   Make seihte betwen Milçe *and* Rih[t]wisnesse, *and* Dom
and Rewðe make wel to-gedere ! Naðelæs, ic hit wot [7] wel ðat tu 20
wilt hauen ore of mankenne.   Þin godnesse [8] hit ne mai noht læten.'

Ðat sede Rihtwis-nesse : 'Mid michel riht ðoleð Adam ðat he
ðoleð, for ðan he was his sceppend unhersum.   Godd he unwurðede
ða þa he ðolede ðat his wiðerwine him ouercam, wið-uten strencþe. 24
His louerd he dede arst michel harm, he slou arst him seluen, *and*
seððen all mankenn, *and* for his unhersumnesse he bereauede godes
riche of him seluen *and* of all his ofsprenge, þat naure mo he ne
mai aȝean cumen be rihte dome.'   28

Ða sade Soð : 'Ðat is riht ðat godes milce bie aure heier *and*
more ðanne his rihte dom.   Hlauerd, hit (is) [9] soð ðat tu behete
Abraham, ðine lieue frend, þat þurh an of his kenne scolde bien
iblesced all mankenn.   Eft ðu behete Dauiðe, the rihtwise kyng : 32
De fructu uentris tui ponam super sedem tuam, "Of ðo

---

[1] *an erasure above* o.   [2] e *over two erased letters.*
[3] pieta(s) *written on the margin.*   [4] *page* 72.   [5] *on the margin.*
[6] ne mai ðoht *erased.*   [7] *a letter erased after* t.
[8] *an erasure before* g.   [9] *red above* t.

sedem tuam, "Of the fruit of thy body will I set upon thy throne."
Again, he says in another place: " The Lord hath said unto me:
Thou art My Son; [this day have I begotten Thee]." '

Then spoke Almighty God, and said: ' This day has ever been
with me and evermore will [be]. It is true that thou sayest:
" On this day have I begotten Thee in Heaven, without mother."
So Thou shalt be begotten on earth, without father, by a mother.
Thus Thou shalt become a true Son of Man as Thou art the true
Son of God. I demand no other sacrifice for Adam's guilt but
Thee. *Postula a me,* and ask of Me as much folk as Thou wilt
long for, and I shall give [it] Thee for Thine inheritance, and Thou
shalt rule all the earth and all what therein is.'

Tunc dixi: ecce, venio! Then said Truth: ' Lord, Father, Thou
wouldst no other sacrifice nor other offering but that I accepted
man's body and soul, and that I offered Thee here for their guilt.
Ecce venio, look, I am ready to work Thy will, and to release
mankind.'

That said God's Justice: ' Now Thou wilt become man, Thou
shalt suffer death after Thy own doom, if that wonder can be
true that Eternal Life may suffer death; and Thou shalt in every
way atone for what he has broken. Hail Thy goodness!'

That said Truth: ' For this I am all ready, to be obedient to
God even until death in order to release mankind.' *Justitia et Pax
osculatae sunt;* the prophet says that ' Justice and Peace have
kissed each other.' When this was done, Truth sprang out of the
earth, and as true kind of earth. Our earth was cursed through
Adam's guilts. *Maledicta terra in opere tuo,* ' Cursed be the earth
in thy work,' quoth God to Adam. Now says the prophet: ' Lord,
Thou hast been favourable unto Thy land.'—*Benedicta tu in mulie-
ribus, et benedictus . . .* ' Blessed be thou,' said the angel, ' on God's
behalf among all women, and blessed be the fruit of thy womb,
which is true God and true Man!' Through this Man Jesus
Christ, who was of Adam's kind, the earth became blessed, which
was before cursed. He paid for all the harm which had come
through Adam, very wisely as He who was Wisdom Himself.
Through Eve, who was still virgin, all mankind was lost; through

wastme of ðine wombe ic wille setten uppe ðine setle." Eft he
seið an oðer stede : Dominus dixit ad me : filius meus.'

Da spac almihti godd, *and* sade : ' Ðies dai haueð aure ibien mid
me *and* æure ma wurð. Hit is soð ðat tu seiest : " On ðese daiȝe 4
ic ðe habbe istriend *on* heuene, wið-uten moder." Swa ðu scalt *on*
ierðe, wið-uten fader istr(i)end of moder. On ðelliche wise ðu
scalt becume*n* soð mannes sune swo swo ðu art soð godes sune [1].
Ne bidde ic no*n* oðer loc for Adames gelte bute ðe. Postula a 8
me, *and* besiech at me swo muchel folc swo ðu wilt after ȝiernen,
and ic ðe wile ȝiuen to ðin eruename, *and* ðu scalt wealden all
middeneard *and* all ðat ðar inne is.'

Tunc dixi : ecce, uenio. Ðo sade Soð : ' Hlauerd, fader, ðu 12
ne woldest no*n* oðer loac ne oðer ofrende bute ðat ic underfenge
mannes lichame *and* his saule, *and* ðat ic ðe her offrede for here
gelte. Ecce venio, loke, ic am (i)radi ðine wille to werchen, *and*
manke*n*n to aliesen.'   16

Ðat sad*e* godes Rih[t]wisnesse : ' Nv ðu wilt mann becume*n*, ðu
scalt deað þolie*n* after ðine auȝene dome, ȝif ðat wunder mai bie*n*
soð þat eche lif mai ðoliȝen deað; *and* ðu scalt *on* alle wise bieten
ðe he haueð tebroken. Hoal ði godnesse ! '   20

Ðat sade Soð : ' Hierto ic am all iradi, te bie*n* hersu*m* godd ano*n*
to ðe deaðe for manke*n*n to aliese*n*.' Iusticia *et* Pax osculate
su*n*t ; ðe profiete seið ðat ' Rih(t)wisnesse *and* Sibsumnesse
kesten hem to-gedere.' Ðo ðis was ȝedon [2], Veritas de terra orta 24
est, and swo swo soð ȝekynd of ierðe. Vre ierðe was ȝewerȝed
ðurh Adames geltes. Maledicta terra i*n* opere tuo, 'ȝewerȝed
bie ðe ierðe o*n* ðine werke,' cwað godd te Adame. Nu seið ðe
profiete : Benedixisti, domine, terram tuam.—Benedicta tu 28
i*n* mulieribu*s, et* benedictu*s*, ' Iblesced bie ðu,' seide ðe angel, ' o*n*
godes half mang alle wiues, *and* iblesced bie ðat wasme of ðine wombe,
þe is soð godd *and* soð mann ! ' Ðurh ðese manne Iesu Crist, ðe
was of Adames kenne, warð se ierðe iblesced, ðe was arer iwerȝed. 32
All he ȝeald ðane harm ðe was ȝecumen ðurh Adam, swiðe
wisliche al swo he ðe was wisdom him self. Ðurh Eue, ðe was
ȝiet maide*n*, was all manke*n*n forlore*n*; ðurh Marie, ðe eadi

---

[1] *page* 73.   [2] ȝedo*n* and *MS.*

Mary, the blessed Virgin, it became saved again. Through the tree
and its fruit all mankind was doomed to death; through the tree
of the dear holy cross and through the blessed fruit which hung
thereon, it came again to eternal life.   Through obedience concerning the tree, the devil overcame Adam; through obedience
Christ overcame the old devil on the holy cross.   Because He was
obedient to His Father until death, although He Himself had not
deserved it, for He never did a sin; and nevertheless He suffered
the cross, as if He were guilty.   Adam saw with his eyes the fruit
of the tree which he liked, but Christ suffered that one blind-folded
Him. His feet bore him [Adam] to the forbidden tree, but Christ's
feet were bored through with iron nails to the cross.   His hands
took the fruit of the tree, but Christ's hands were nailed through
to the holy cross.   The fruit in his mouth seemed sweet to him,
but God received the bitter gall in His mouth.   Adam's heart was
poisoned through the devil's admonition, so that he both liked it
well and also yielded, but Christ suffered that one stung through
His heart; and for the two great [sins of] liking and granting,
two great blessings came to us from the holy wound, that was,
water and blood.   In the water we are washed from all sins;
by the fruit which hung on the holy cross, and by the blood
which came out of it, we taste on [our] palates all kinds of
poison of the devil, and so we cool our wretched heart, which is
often scorched by the great burning of the devil's temptations.
Thus our Saviour Jesus Christ healed us, thus our Redeemer redeemed us; and afterwards, He arose from the dead as He who was
true life, and bore our sacrifice and our offering up to Heaven, His
holy body, which He took of our kind, and offered to His Father a
very agreeable sacrifice, by His own witness who said: *Hic est
filius meus dilectus, in quo mihi bene complacui*, 'This is my
beloved Son, in whom I am well pleased.' He has opened the gate
of the kingdom of Heaven to all who believe in Him and will

maiden, hit warð eft ȝeboregen. Đurh ða trowe *and* his wastme
werð al mankenn idemd to deaðe[1]; þurh ðe trowe of ðe lieue halie
rode *and* ðurh ðare iblescede wastme ðe ðar on heng, hit cam eft
te ðan eche liue. Đurh unhersumnesse of ðe trowe ouercam ðe 4
dieuel Adam; þurh hersumnesse of ðe hali rode ouercam Crist
ðane ealde dieuel[2]. For ðan he was hersum his fader anon to ðe
deaðe, swa swa he him self hit ne hadde noht ofearned, forðan
he neure senne ne dede ; *and* naðelæs þolede o[3] ðe rode, swilch he 8
ware forȝ(e)ilt. Aȝeanes ðat Adam mid his eiȝene iseih ðat[4] wastme
of ðe treuwe ðe him likede, aȝeanes ðat þolede Crist ðat me blind-
fallede his(e)[5]. Aȝeanes þat his fiet him baren to ðe forbodene
treuwe, aȝeanes ðat waren Cristes fiet ðurhborede mid .isene nailes 12
to ðare rode. Aȝeanes ðat his honden namen ðas trewes wastme,
aȝeanes þat waren Cristes handes ðurhnailed te ða hali rode.
Aȝeanes þat him ðuhte swete ðat wastme on his muðe, aȝeanes þat
underfeng godd ðe bit(r)e ȝalle on his muðe. Aȝeanes ðat Adames 16
hierte was i-attred ðurh dieules meneȝinge, swa ðat him baðe hit
wel likede *and* ec teiþede, ðolede Crist ðat me þurh-stong his
hierte ; *and* aȝeanes[6] ða twa michele likinge *and* teiþinge, us
comen twa michele gode[7] of ðare hali wunde, þat was, water *and* 20
blod. On ða watere we bieð iwascen of alle sennes; of ða wastme
ðe hangede on ðe hali rode, *and* of ða blode ðe ðar[8] utȝiede, we
notieð on ȝomes alles kennes attre of dieule, *and* swa we kylieð
vre wreche hierte, ðe his ofte forswald of ðan michele brene of 24
dieules costninges[9]. Đus us halde ure halend Iesu[10] Crist[11], þus us
aliesde ure aliesend, *and*[12] seððen aros of deaðe, alswo he ðe was
soð lif, *and* bar up to heuene ure loac *and* ure ofrende, his hali[13]
lichame, ðe he nam of ure ȝekynde, *and* ofrede his fader swiðe 28
icweme loc, be his aȝene iwitnesse ðe sade: *Hic est filius meus*
dilectus, in quo mihi bene complacui, 'Đis is mi leue sune, on
him me likeð swiðe.' Heueneriches gate he haueð iopened alle ðe
on him (leueð)[14] *and* him folȝin willeð. Alle his ikorene he hafð 32

[1] *page* 74. [2] *an erasure above* d. [3] o *red inserted.* [4] treu *underlined.*
[5] e *is red inserted.* [6] *Here begins another hand.* [7] ȝode *MS.*
[8] dar *MS.* [9] costninȝes *MS.* [10] jhu *MS.*
[11] *end of second hand, old hand goes on.* [12] þu *underdotted.*
[13] his hali *once more, underlined.* [14] *Added red on the margin.*

follow Him. He has promised to all His chosen, as truly as He
arose from the dead, that they shall dwell so with body and with
soul, both with the holy angels and with Him evermore. Amen.

Of penitence.

When Christ first began to preach, that was, when He went from
the river Jordan, He said: *Poenitentiam agite, appropinquabit enim
regnum coelorum,* 'Repent of your sins, the kingdom of Heaven
approacheth.' Full surely a clean soul is Christ's kingdom. Therefore our Lord admonishes us first of all things about this
blessed virtue, that we should repent of our sins, and so look to us
with His help, that we may not fall into sin again. That says
St. Jerom: *Est autem poenitere peccata ante acta deflere, et flenda
non repetere,* ' So shall,' says he, 'a man repent of his sins, that he
do not again what he again needs to repent of.' This says St.
Austin: *Poenitere est poenam tenere,* 'That is true repentance,'
says he, ' to hold oneself ever in some pain.' Again, we find in
the holy Writ that neither the knight who bears weapons unlaw-
fully, nor the chapman who buys and sells with unrighteousness,
can ever do true repentance, the while they defile this office ; nor
he who perseveres in wrath, nor he who habitually lies in whoredom,
nor gleemen, nor usurers, nor witches, nor unjust judges, nor any of
those men who lie in cardinal sins and love them. Let a man who
will be very repentant, not only repent of his sins, but moreover
repent that through his carelessness he has not done good in the
time which he nevermore will recover again, and [which] is gone
by. Those who are in a religious order are ever under penance,
as it also behooves us.

Of confession.

Here follows another holy virtue, which is called *confessio,* that
is, confession ; that is, when the man opens his heart, and tells his
confessor his sins through his mouth, which were before concealed

bihoten, swa soðliche[1] swa he aros of deaðe, þat hie sculen al swo mid lichame *and* mid saule, *and* mid ðe hali angles *and* mid him aure mo wunizen. Am*en*.

Of scrifte. 4

Ð A ðe Crist gann (arst) to spellen, ðat was, ðo ðe he ziede fram flumen Iordan[2], ða sade he : Penitenciam agite, appropinquabit enim regnum celorum, 'Nimeð scrifte of zewer sennes, hit neiheð[3] heuene riche.' Fullzewis is clene saule Cristes[8] riche. For ði us menezeð allre þinge arst ure lauerde of ðesre eadi mihte, þat we scolden beon rewsende[4] ure sennen, *and* swa hus l(o)kin[5] mid his fultume, þat we eft ne befallen on senne. Ðat seið *sanctus* Ieronimus : Est au*tem* penitere peccata[12] ante acta deflere, *et* flenda non repetere, 'Swa scal,' he seið, 'mann his senne berewsen, ðat he eft ne do ðat he eft ðurue be-riwsin.' Ðis seið *sanctus* Augustinu*s* : Penitere est penam tenere, 'Ðat his,' he seið, 'soðe berewsinge, ðat mann him healde eure on[16] sumere pine.' Eft we findeð on ða hali writt ðat ðe cniht ðe weapne berð unlawliche, ne chapmann ðe beið *and* selð mid unri[h]twisnesse, ne muzen neure soðe scrifte don, ðare [h]wile ðe hie ðese wike befeleð ; ne he (ðe) ðurhwuneð on wraðþe, ne he ðe[20] wuneliche lið on hordome, ne glewmen, ne gau(e)leres, ne wi(c)chen, ne unriht domesmann, ne non ðare manne ðe on heaued-senne lið *and* ða luuieð. Mann ðe wel wile bien riwsinde, ne rewe him nauht ane hise sennes, ac zet ðat (he) for [h]is zemelaste ne hafð[24] god[6] zedon on ða time ðe he naure mo eft nacoureð, *and* is forð zegan. Ða ðe bieð on religiun, hie bieð aure under scrifte, swa bihoueð[7] us alswa.

Of andetnesse. 28

H IER after cumeð an oðer hali mihte, ðe is icleped confessio, ðat his, andetetdnesse ; ðat is, ðanne ðe mann undett [h]is herte,[8] *and* seið his scrifte his sennes ðurh his muðe, ðe

[1] *page 75.*   [2] *Here begins a new hand which goes on to end.*
[3] *Some letters erased behind ð.*   [4] *s corr. from h.*
[5] *o corrected above i.*   [6] *a half g before z underdotted.*
[7] bihoued *MS.*   [8] *and* seið *twice, the first time underdotted.*

in his heart. Of this said God: *Dic tu iniquitates tuas, ut justi-
ficeris,* 'Tell thou thy unrighteousness, if thou wilt be justified.'
Concerning it said St. Austin: *Qui per vos peccatis, per vos erubescatis,* ' Ye who sin of your own accord, be ashamed of yourselves.
And know ye forsooth that same shame is a lot of the forgiveness.'
*Fit enim veniale per confessionem, quod criminale fuerat per opera-
tionem,* ' It is a pardonable sin through confession what was before
a cardinal sin through work.' But it behooves it to be well clear,
and that no venom be concealed. Of this said the prophet: *Confi-
temini Domino, quoniam bonus,* 'Confess your sins,' he said, 'to God
Almighty, because He is good, because His mercy is here in the
world.' He who gets God's mercy not here will never get it
elsewhere. We find in the holy Writ that if a man were suddenly
upon his death, and he could have no priest, he ought to confess
his sins to him who is nearest to him, and he should have mercy,
except it were that he contempted the priest; or if he were alone,
then he must [confess] to God only. And let every man look that
he never mistrust in God's grace nor in His mercy, nor, again, be
no man too bold to sin, and say: ' More can God forgive than we
can sin.' *Non adjicies peccatum super peccatum et dices: quoniam
misericordia Domini magna est !*

Of cleanness.

Another blessed virtue is called *munditia,* that is, cleanness,
which is much loved within God's house. It cannot suffer any un-
cleanness in God's temple, neither beneath in thy body, nor
above in thy soul, neither in thoughts—for it knows well that
thoughts are more open before God than speeches are before man—
nor can it suffer aught of foul speeches—for it knows that God
hears them and mislikes them all—nor can it dwell near to evil
works, for God bids to shun them. *Mundamini qui fertis vasa
Domini,* ' Make yourselves clean who bear God's vessels !' Cleanse
thy heart, because it ought to be God's vessel. One shall bear in

waren arrer ȝedett on his herte. Hier of sade godd: Dic tu iniquitates tuas, ut iustificeris, 'Sei ðu þine unrihtwisnesses,
ȝif ðu wilt bien irihtwised[1].' Herof sade *sanctus* Avgustinus:
Qui *per* uos peccatis, *per* uos erubescatis, 'ȝie ðe seneȝin be ₄
ȝew seluen, doð scame ȝew seluen. *And* wite ȝie to soðe ðat ilke
scame is on lott of ðare forȝifnesse.' Fit enim ueniale *per con*-
fessionem, quod criminale fuerat *per* operacionem, 'Hit is
forȝiuenliche senne ðurh andettednesse ðe was arrer heaued-senne ₈
ðurh weorke.' Ac hit be[h]oueð ðat hie bie wiel (h)lutter, *and* ðat
ðar ne bie forholen non atter. Hier of sade ðe profete: Confi-
temini d*omi*no, q*uonia*m bonus, 'Andettið ȝewer sennen,' he
sade, 'goddalmihtin, for ðan ðe he is god[2], for ðan his mildsce is ₁₂
hier on world.' Se ðe her godes mildsce ne beȝett, ne wurð hie
him naure mo ealles hwer. We findeð on ðe hali write ðat ȝif
ma*n*n ware firliche[3] uppen (h)is deaðe, *and* he prest ne mihte
habben, andette his sennen him ðe ware necst him, *and* he scolde ₁₆
habben mildsce, bute ȝif hit ware ðat he ðane prest forhowede;
oððer ȝif he ware all hone, ðanne most he to godd ane. *And*
belokie elch ma*n*n ðat he naure nortriwi godes are ne his mildsce,
ne eft sones ne bie no ma*n*n to þrist to seneȝin, *and* segge: 'Mare ₂₀
mai godd forȝiuen ðanne we muȝen seneȝin.' Non adicies
peccatu*m* super peccatu*m et* dices: qu*onia*m misericordia
d*omi*ni magna est!

Of clennesse. ₂₄

A̶N oðer eadi mihte his ȝehaten mundicia, þat is, clannesse,
ðe is inne godes huse swiðe ȝeluued. Ne mai ȝie iðolien none
unclannesse on godes temple, ne beneðen on ði likame, ne abuuen
on ðire saule, ne on ðouhtes, for ðan hie wat wel ðat openlicor ben ₂₈
þouhtes to-foren gode ðanne beð spaches be-foren manne; ne of
fule spaches hie ne mai nauht ðolien, for ðan h(i)e wot ðat god his
ȝehiereð *and* alle mislikið; ne euele workes hie ne mai nieh
wunien, for ðan ðat godd his hat scunien. Mundamini qui ₃₂
fertis uasa d*omi*ni, 'Makieð ȝew clane ðe bereð godes faten!'
Clanse þine hirte, for ðan þe hie owh to be*n*ne[4] godes fatt. On

---

[1] *page* 76.   [2] ȝod *MS.*   [3] *The 1st* i *corr. from* a.   [4] *page* 77.

it God's message, God's word. *In corde meo abscondi eloquia tua, ut non peccem tibi,* 'In my heart I hid Thy words, Lord, lest I should sin against Thee.' So did St. Mary; she bore God's words in her heart, that she often might think of Him whom she loved much, *conferens in corde suo.* She bore in her heart what God said : *Beati mundo corde, quoniam ipsi Deum videbunt,* 'Blessed are the pure in heart, for they shall see God.' God cannot be seen with any other eyes but with the heart's. Wash and wipe well clean the eyes, because it is true what they tell thee. If thou wilt know which eyes the heart may have, they are named *intellectus et ratio.* These can see about as well at mid-night as at mid-day. Intellect and reason are the two eyes. Through intellect thou understandest all things, and through discernment thou shalt discern the evil from the good. All that thou thinkest thou seest with these eyes. But ever too many are short-sighted with the one of these eyes, and too many with both. Of all the blessings which God promised in His preaching, there is none so high as is 'who is pure in heart.' May he get it whoso can ! I warn thee, thou never gettest it clean whilst thou doest not care what thou thinkest, nor what thou speakest, nor what thou hearest speak. And except thou gladly makest it clean as much as possible, with God's help, thou shalt never see God Almighty with these eyes with which thou seest sun and moon. Love this holy virtue *munditiam,* and it will make thee pure in heart. Amen.

Of lore.

Disciplina is another holy virtue, which God Himself bids us to take through the prophet, who says : *Apprehendite disciplinam, etc.,* 'Take discipline of all the misdeeds which ye do, lest God be angry, and ye perish from the right way!' Except thou doest justice to thyself for the misdeeds which thou misdoest, with fasting, or with watching, or with wailing and sore repentance, or with weary-

hire me scal beren godes sande, godes word. In corde meo
abscondi eloquia tua, ut non peccem tibi, 'On mine hierte
ich hedde þine wordes, hlauerd, þat ich nolde naht seneȝin aȝeanes
ðe.' Swa dede *sancta*[1] Maria; hie bar godes wordes on hire 4
hierte, þat hie ofte mihte þenken on him ðe hie michel luuede,
conferens in corde suo. Hie bar on hire hierte þat þe godd
sade: Beati mundo corde, q*uonia*m ipsi deum uide*bu*nt,
'Eadi bieð ða clane-hierte menn, for ðan hie sculen gode ȝesen.' 8
Godd ne mai ben ȝesiȝen mid none oðer eiȝen ðanne mid þare
hierte. Wassce *and* wipe wol clane ða eiȝene, for ðan soð is ðat
hie ðe siggen. Gif[2] þu wilt witen wilke eiȝene ðe hierte muȝe
habben, hie bieð ȝenamned intellect*us* et racio. Ðese muȝen 12
ȝesen alswa wel onbuten mid-niht alswa on mid-daiȝ. Andȝeat *and*
skele bieð ða twa eiȝene. Đurh andȝeat þu unde(r)stanst alle þing,
and ðurh scadwisnesse þu scalt skilien ðe euele fram ðe gode. All
ðat ðe þu þencst þu ȝiesichst mid þese eiȝen. Ac aure to fele bieð 16
bisne mid þan onen of þese eiȝen, *and* to fele mid baðe. Of alle
ða edmodnesses ðe godd[3] behet on his spelle, nis ðar non swo heih
swa is 'ðe is[4] clane-hierte.' Beȝiete se ðe muȝe! Ich[5] þe warni,
ne beȝiethst ðu his naure clane ðar wile ðat þu ne recst wat þu 20
þenche, ne wat þu speke, ne wat ðu ȝehire speken. And bute þu
his ȝier[n]e make clane after þine mihte, mid godes helpe, ne scal tu
naure ȝesen mid ðase eiȝene ðe þu mide ȝesiest sunne *and* mone,
godd almihtin. Luue ðese hali mihte mu*n*diciam, *and* hie ðe 24
makeð clane-hierte. Amen.

Of lore.

Disciplina is on oþer hali mihte, ðe goddself us hat neme*n*[6]
ðurh[7] ðe *p*rophete, ðe seið: Apprehendite disciplinam, 28
et cet., 'Nemeð discipline of alle ðe misdades ðe ȝe deð, þe las te
godd him wraðþi, *and* ȝie forfaren of ða rihte weiȝe!' Bute ðu neme
riht of ðe seluen of ðe misdades ðe ðu mis-dest, mid fasten, oððer mid
wake, oððer mid wope *and* sare beriwsinge, oððer mid weringe[8], 32

---

[1] *an i underdotted after the 2nd s.*   [2] G *with a j inserted above.*
[3] gode *MS.*   [4] ðeies *MS.*   [5] ic *inserted red above between* ich *and* þe.
[6] *page* 78.   [7] *and* ðurh *MS.*   [8] þeringe *MS., a letter erased between* r *and* i.

ing [thyself], or with kneeling, or with toil, or with pure prayer, or
with pure alms, with the counsel of thy confessor: God's wrath
will come upon thee, so that thou losest the one right way which
goes to Heaven. That is a great wrath of God that man is so blind
that he goes to hell laughing. Though he much misdo, he is therefore not more sorry, than if he had not misdone. *Excaeca cor
populi hujus, ne videant et intelligant.* Of them said God: 'Blind
the heart of this people, lest they see or understand the right way
to the kingdom of Heaven.' Their hard heart and their evilness
have deserved it that the blind leads the blind. That is, he who
should instruct him, does the same sins and gives an example of them,
and he also teaches him and says that [neither] for eating nor for
drinking nor for woman, whom God has shaped as companion to
man, anybody ever shall be lost. Woe to this lore and this deed!
Do thou not so, dear soul. But when thou feelest that thou
hast neither God's love nor His fear as thou shouldst, cry to Him
and say with the prophet: *Illumina oculos meos, Domine,* 'Lord,
open my eyes and lighten them with the true light, so that I never
be sleeping in the soul's death, nor that the devils may boast that
they had the upper hand over me.' *Bonitatem et disciplinam et
scientiam doce me, etc.,* 'But Thou, Lord, teach me goodness,
through which I may be good, and teach me such discipline, that
I may soften Thy wrath, and such knowledge, that I may know and
please Thee!'

Of patience.

Patientia is a holy virtue, that is, patience, which God Himself
taught us with word and also with example. In His Gospel He
said: *Qui te percusserit in maxillam, praebe ei et aliam,* 'Whosoever
shall smite thee under the ear, suffer it for My love, and turn to him
the other. Whosoever shall take away thy coat, give him thy
mantle. Whosoever shall compel thee to go with him two miles,
go with him three.' This seems foolishness to the fool, but nevertheless Wisdom said it. The blessed man who has this virtue will
suffer, for God's love, all kinds of things which one may do him,

oððer mid cnewlinge, oððer mid swinke, oððer mid clane bede,
oððer mid hlutter almesse, mid ðe rade of þine scrifte : godes
wraððe cumþ uppen ðe, swa þat ðu forliest ða ane rihte weiȝ þe
gað to heuene. Ðat is michel godes wraþþe þat mann is swa blind 4
ðat he farð to helle leiȝinde[1]. Þeih he michel mis-do, nis for ði na
mare sori, þanne ȝif he nadde naht mis-don. Exceca cor populi
hui*us*, ne uideant *et* intelligant. Of hem sade godd : 'Bland
ðies folkes hierte, þat hie ne sien ne understande ðe rihte weiȝe to 8
heuene riche.' Heare harde hierte *and* here euelnesse hit haueð
of-earned þat ðe blinde latt ðane blinde. Þat is, se ðe him wissin
scolde, deð ðo ilke sennes *and* haueð ðar of forbisne, *and* ec he him
lareð *and* seið þat for ates ne for drenches ne for wifmanne, ðe 12
godd haueð ȝescapen manne to ȝemoane, ne scal man naure ben
forloren. Walawa þessere lare *and* ðesere dade ! Swa ne do þu
naht, lieue saule. Ac þanne ðu ȝefelst þat ðu godes luue ne his
eiȝe ne hafst swa swa ðu scoldest, clepe to him *and* seih mid ðe 16
prophete: Illumina oculos meos, domine, 'Hlauerd, opene
mine eiȝene *and* liht his mid þe soðe lihte, þat ich naure ne bie
slapinde on ðare saule deaðe, ne ðat ðe dieule(s)[2] muȝen beȝelpen
þat hie hafden ðe heiȝere hand ouer me.' Bonita*tem*[3] *et* disci- 20
plina*m et* scienciam doce me, *et cetera*, 'Ac ðu, hlauerd, tach
me godnesse, ðurh wan ich god muȝe bien, *and* tach me swilche
discipline, þat ich þine wraððe muȝe softin, *and* swilch andȝet,
ðat ich ðe muȝe ȝecnawen *and* ȝecwemen !'   24

Of ðolemodnesse.

PACIENCIA is an hali mihte, ðat is, ðolemodnesse, ðe godd[4]
self us tahte mid worde *and* ech mid forbisne. On his
spelle he sade: Qvi te *pe*rcusserit in maxillam, prebe ei 28
et aliam, 'Se ðe smit þe under ðat (e)are, þole[5] hit for mine
lune, *and* wand him to þat oðer. Se þe benimð ðe þine kiertel[6],
ȝif him þine mantel. Se ðe net þe to *gon*ne mid him twa milen,
ga mid him þrie.' Þis þincð ðe sott sothade, ac naðelas wisdom hit 32
sade. De sali mann þe ðese mihte hafð, alleskennes þing ðe

---

[1] *an erasure under* de.   [2] s *inserted above, red.*   [3] *page* 79.
[4] goðð *MS.*   [5] e *corr. from* a.   [6] kie *on erasure.*

except sin only. That said Solomon : *Melior est patiens viro forti,* 'Better is,' he said, 'the patient man than the strong who taketh castles.' Because to do evil is no strength, but is impotence, for he is esteemed as stronger who overcomes his own mood, than he who slays and takes castles. Dear soul, all the while thou dwellest in the smoke-house of thy body, whence many kinds of smokes of impatience come, it is very great need to thee to have this virtue with thee ; and full surely it will bring thee to the kingdom where thou never more shalt find anything which thou mayst dislike.

Of maidenhood.

Virginitas is a very precious virtue, that is, maidenhood, which follows the holy Lamb, and is nearest to it. For the great purity this same holy virtue is hallowed in Christ, St. Mary's Son, who was and is evermore maiden. She promised to keep [her] maidenhood, and she performed it well; and after her many thousands, through her good example, kept their purity and suffered therefore many kinds of martyrdom. Neither God nor the apostle bade [anyone] to keep this maidenhood, except those who would vow it with their good will. But when it is vowed, it must be kept, if they will be saved. It is angelic life of Heaven whoso humbly keeps maidenhood on earth. *Qui potest capere, capiat,* 'Whosoever can have it, let him receive and keep it !' He is certainly blessed.

Of chastity.

Castitas is also [a] very holy virtue, that is, chastity. Without maidenhood man can be saved, but without chastity or right spouse no man can be saved. Of this said the apostle : *Pacem et sanctimoniam diligite, sine qua nemo videbit Deum,* 'Love peace and holiness, that is, this chastity ; without it man never shall see God.'

mann him maiȝ don, wið-uten senne one, he wile þolieȝen for
godes luue. Ðat sade Salemun: Melior est paciens uiro
forti, 'Bettre his,' he sade, 'ðe þolemode mann þanne þe stronge
þe nimð casteles.' For þan euel to done nis non strencþe, ac 4
is unmihte, fo(r)[1] þi he is ihealden strengere ðe ouor-cumþ his
auȝen mod, þanne he ðe slecð *and* casteles nemð. Lieue[2] saule,
al ðe (h)wile[3] ðe þu wunest on ðe smec-huse of ðine likame,
hwanene cumeð[4] manies kennes smekes of unþolemodnesse, ðe is 8
swiðe michel nied ðat ðu þese mihte mid þe habbe; *and* full-
ȝewis hie þe bringð to ðare riche ðar ðu naurema ne scalt finden
(no)ne[5] (þinge) þe ðe misliki.

Of maiden-had.   12

UIRGINITAS is an swiðe derwurðe mihte, ðat is, maidenhad[6], ðe folȝið ðe hali lombe, *and* him his neȝest.   For
þare michele clannesse ðies ilke hali mihte is ȝehalȝed on Criste,
seinte Marie sune, þe was *and* is aurema maiden.   Hie behet 16
maidenhad to healden, *and* hie wel it ȝelaste; *and* after hire
mániȝe þusend, for hire gode forbisne, here clannesse ihelden *and*
manieskennes martirdom ðar fore ðolede.   Naðer ne godd ne þe
apostel ne hieten þis maidenhad to healden, buten ðo þe wolden 20
mid here gode wille hit behaten.   Ac seððen hit is behaten,
siðþen hit is to healden, alswa hie willen ben iborȝen.   Hit is
angelich lif of heuene, se ðe eadmodliche halt maidenhad on ierðe.
Qvi potest capere, capiat, 'Se ðe hit mai habben, he hit neme 24
and healde !'   He is iwiss isali.

Of clannesse.

CASTITAS is ech swiðe hali mihte, þat is, clannesse.   Wið-
uten maidenhad mann mai bien ȝeborȝen, ac wið-uten 28
clannesse oððer rihte spuse nan mann (ne)[7] mai ben ȝeborȝen.
Hier of sade ðe apostel: Pacem *et* sanctimoniam diligite,
sine qua nemo uidebit deum, 'Luuieð sibsumnesse *and* hali-

---

[1] *r added, red.*   [2] *Before* l *another one by another hand.*   [3] h *inserted red.*
[4] ð *corr. from* t.   [5] nan ðare *underdotted.*   [6] *page* 80.   [7] *red above the line.*

This holy virtue has three gifts from the Holy Ghost, that is, that the devil never can overcome it, where it reigns, by any kind of lechery, [neither] working with limbs, nor speaking with ill-mannered speeches, nor thinking with foul thoughts; but anon if they come they are driven out of the heart with sorry mood and with running tears. So one shall do with them who will not [keep] peace.

———————

Pudicitia is her sister, [a] maiden holy in thoughts, and pure from all filth. That says St. Austin: 'If a maiden has this holy virtue in her thoughts, though she became deflowered against her will, she is before God nevertheless maiden;' and afterwards: 'She who is a pure maiden in body, and has not this holy virtue in her thoughts, but willed what she may not, she is no maiden before God.' *Pudicitia* is the pure maidenhood of the thoughts, as *castitas* is the purity of the body.

Of continence.

Continentia is continence concerning fornication. It is very much loved by all those who hope in God's mercy. Because the apostle has well promised them that, if they keep and love these three holy virtues together: *castitatem, pudicitiam, continentiam,* though they have lost their bodily maidenhood, he has espoused them to Christ, and says thus: *Despondi enim vos uni viro, virginem castam exhibere Christo,* 'I have wedded you to one husband [as a] chaste maiden, that is, to Christ,' that is [a] right spouse to every good soul. For all Christ's chosen are Christ's limbs, and He is the head of all of us, and with right belief we are all one with His flesh and with His blood, so that nothing can divide us. *Quis nos* dom, þat is, þes clannesse; wiðuten hire ne scal naure mann isien godd.' Þies hali mihte haueð of ðe hali gaste þrie (ʒiues)[1], þat is, þat naure deuel ne mai hes ouercumen, þar hie rixið, mid naneskennes galnesse, mid lemes werchinde, ne mid unðeaufulle [4] spaches specinde, ne mid fule þowtes þenkinde; ac anon ʒif hie cumeð hie bieð idriuen ut of þare hierte mid sari mode and mid ierniende teares. Swa me scal don of hem ðe grið ne willeð[2].

PVDICICIA is hire suster, hali maiden of þanke, *and* clane [8] of alle felðes. Ðat seið *sanctus* Augustinus: ' Gif maiden hafð þese hali mihte on hire þanke, þeih hie wurðe hire unðankes forleiʒen, hie is to-foren gode naþelas maiden '; *and* eft: ' H[i]e ðe is clane maiden on likame, *and* ðese mihte ne hafð on hire [12] ʒeþanke, ac wolde þat hie ne mai, hie nis naht maiden to-foren gode.' Pudicicia is ðe hlutter maiden(h)ad of þe þanke, alswa castitas is þe clannesse of ðe likame.

Of wið(h)ealdnesse[3]. [16]

CONTINENCIA is wið[h]ealdnesse[3] after þe forleire. Hie is swiðe ʒeluued of alle ðe hopieð to godes mildsce. For þan þe apostel hem hafð[4] wel behaten þat, ʒif hie healdeð *and* luuieð þese þrie halie mihtes to-gedere: castitatem, pudiciciam, [20] continenciam, þeih hie here likamliche maiden-had habbe forloren, he [h]is haueð ʒespused to Criste, *and* þus seið: Despondi enim uos uni uiro, uirginem castam exibere *Christo*[5], ' Ich ʒew habbe bewedded ane were clane maiden, þat [24] is, to Criste,' *þat* is riht spus ta alchere gode saule. For þan alle Cristes ʒecorene bieð Cristes lemen[6], *and* he is ure alre heaued, *and* mid rihte ʒeleuen mid his flesce *and* mid his blode we bieð all an, swa ðat nan þing ne mai us twammen[7]. Qvis nos separa- [28]

---

[1] *Written above* þinges, *which is underlined.*   [2] *page* 81.
[3] wið- *MS.*   [4] hafd *MS.*   [5] xp̄o *MS.*
[6] m *partly on erasure.*   [7] *The first* m *on erasure.*

separabit a caritate Christi? Full certainly these holy virtues bind us also together.

Of harmlessness.

Innocentia is another holy virtue, that is, harmlessness. He is certainly *innocens*, that is, harmless, who never yet did harm to himself or to any other. Such was none except Christ. The holy children who were martyred for Christ are rightly called *innocentes*, because they never yet did harm either to God or to man, either in thoughts or in words. Therefore they are blessed. Follow this holy virtue in thoughts, in words, in works, and think that first thou doest harm to thyself, if thou thinkest amiss, or speakest or doest anything in another way to thy fellow-Christian, than as thou wouldst wish that he did to thee. Think hereof! Again, says the holy Writ about this: *Manus in manus non erit innocens malus,* '[Though] hand [join] in hand, the evil man is not guiltless.' That is said about the man who has done evil against God and against his neighbour, and thinks and deceives himself that he does no more evil, than the man who sits idle and holds his one hand in his other, and does evil to nobody. Yet, though this man do so, he is not *innocens*, except he atones for what he has broken before. Ever too few men think about to have this holy virtue, and [yet] without it no man can please God well.

Honestas is called another virtue, which is needful to every good man. That is, that he looks decent with all the limbs of his body. It (honesty) withholds his eyes, lest they be too much looking hither and thither; the ears, lest they blithely listen to vanities, and therewith prevent the soul hearing good thoughts of good words; the tongue, lest he become the unworthier for it, and when it shall speak with God in its prayers, the more disagreeable. It makes the man look decent who loves it, both with his hands and his feet. It does not let the hands play with [a] stick or with

bit a karitate *Christi* ! Fulȝewis ðese haliȝe mihtes us bindeð
ec to-gedere.

Of vneilindnesse.

INNOCENCIA is an oððer hali mihte, þat is, uneilind[ness]e. 4
He is iwis innocens, þat is, uneilinde, þe. nauerȝete him
seluen ne eilede ne nan oððer. Þat nas nan wiðuten Criste. Ða
hali children ðe waren ȝemartired for Criste, hie bieð mid rihte
icleped innocentes, for ðan hie ne eileden nauerȝiete ne 8
gode[1] ne manne, ne a þoutes ne a wordes. For þi hie bieð
eadi. Folȝe ðese hali mihte on þouhtes, on wordes, on workes,
and þenc þat arst þu eilest ðe seluen, ȝif ðu misþencst, oððer
spekest oððer dest auht oðerliker onȝeanes þin emcristen, þanne 12
ðu woldest *þat* he.dede ðe. Þench hier of ! Ȝiet[2] seið þat hali
writ herof: Man*us* in manus non erit innocens malus[3],
' Hande on hande nis naht ðe euele man gylt-leas.' Ðat is iseid[4] bi
ðo manne ðe euele haueð ȝedon aȝean godd *and* aȝean [h]is nexte, 16
and beþeincð him *and* beswicð þat he namare euel ne dieð, þanne
ðe man ðe sitt idel *and* halt [h]is on hand in oðer, *and* none
manne euel ne deð. Ȝiet[2], þeih ðis mann swa do, nis he nauht
innocens, bute ȝif he biete[5] ðat he harrer hafde tobroken. Aure 20
to feawe men bien abuten to habben ðese hali mihte, *and* wið-[6]
uten hire ne mai non ma*n*n godd wel ȝecweme*n*.

HONESTAS is cleped an oðer mihte, ðe is niedfull alche
gode manne. Þat is, ðat he worðliche him loki mid alle hise 24
lemes of his likame. Hise eiȝene, þat hie ne bien to swiðe
gawrinde hider *and* ȝeond ; þo earen, ðat hie bliðeliche ne hlesten
ydelnesses, *and* ðare mide benime ðare saule gode þohtes of gode
wordes to ȝe(he)ren[7] ; þe tunge hie wiðhalt, þat he ne wurðe for 28
hire ðunworðere, *and* þanne hie wið gode scall speken on hire
benes, þe uncwemer. Wurðliche hie deð lokin ðe manne ðe hes
luuieð, baðe his handen *and* hise fett. Ne lat hie nawht ðe hande

---

[1] *page* 82.   [2] G *is altered into* ȝ *by inserting a* j *above.*
[3] I*n* libro sapiencie *red, at side.*   [4] d *corr. from* ð.
[5] beȝiete *MS., the* ȝ *underdotted.*   [6] wið *MS.*   [7] he *written above* a, *red.*

[a] straw—that is no good token of a mature man, the heart is not yet steadfast—nor [a man] sit tottering with [his] foot, nor throw the one over the other. Blessed is that man who takes good heed of himself, and thinks that nobody lives for his own behoof alone, but is an example either of good or of evil to all who see him or hear of him. If thou takest heed hereof, thou wilt be honoured before God and before man.

Of abstinence.

Another holy virtue is called *abstinentia*, that is, abstinence. Concerning the man who withholds himself not only from eating and drinking, but from all the things which God forbids to do, said the apostle : *Abstinete vos a carnalibus desideriis, quae militant adversus animam,* 'Abstain,' said he, 'from the lusts of the flesh, which war against the soul.' That is that wholesome abstinence. Again, he said for it : *Haec est enim voluntas Dei, sanctificatio vestra,* 'This is verily the will of God,' said he, 'that ye be holy,' *ut abstineatis vos a fornicatione,* 'and that ye should abstain from fornication,' *ut sciat unusquisque vas suum possidere,* 'and that ye should know how to hold the vessel of your body with great worthiness and with great purity, as the same vessel wherein ye bear the precious treasure, that is, the Holy Ghost.' When a great lust comes to thee after a thing, do not yield to it anon, but bethink thyself well eagerly and abstain firmly. If it comes often smiting to thy heart, know thou forsooth that it is of the devil. If thou yieldest to it, thou makest thyself [a] slave, and not [a] man's, but the devil's. If thou doest something else, and refrainest this lust, and overcomest it with prayer, thou shalt have great reward from God, and make thyself free.

pleiȝende mid stikke, ne mid strawe—nis þat non god tocne of
ripe manne [1], nis ðe hierte nauht ȝiet stedefast—ne mid fote sitten [2]
toterinde, ne ðen enne worpen ouer ðan oðre. ȝesali [3] is ðe ilke
mann ðe gode ȝeme nimð (of him seluen), and þencð þat no mann [4]
ne leueð to [h]is aȝene be[h]ofte ane, ac is forbisne oðre of gode
oððer of euele to alle ðe hine ȝeseð oððer of him hiereð. ȝif [3] ðu
herof ȝieme nemest, þu best ȝewurðed to-foren gode and to-foren
manne.   8

Of wiðheldnesse [4].

ABSTINENCIA hatte an oðer hali mihte, þat is, wið[h]eald-
nesse. Ðe mann þe him wiðhalt naht one of ates and of
drenches, ac fram alle ðo þinges ðe godd forbett to donne, herof 12
sade ðe apostel : Abstinete uos a carnalibus desideriis, que
militant aduersus [5] animam [6], 'Wiðhealdeþ,' he saide, 'ȝew wið
þa flesches (h)lustes [7], ðe winneð aȝean ðare sawle.' Þat is ðat
halsume wið[h]ealdnesse. ȝiet [8] he sade for ðare : Hec est enim 16
uoluntas dei, san[c]tificatio uestra [6], 'Ðis is iwis godes
wille,' he sade, 'þat hie ben hali,' vt abstineatis uos a forni-
cacione, 'and þat ȝie wið[h]ealden ȝew fram galnesse,' vt sciat
unusquisque uas suum possidere [6], 'and ðat ȝie healden 20
cunnen ȝewer fatt of ȝewer likame mid michele wurscipe and mid
michele clannesse, alswa ðat ilke fatt ðe [8] ȝie bereð inne þat der-
worðe tresor, þat is, ðe hali gast.' Ðanne ðe cumð a michel lust
after ane þinge, ne teiþe þu him naht anoan, ac beðenc ðu ðe wel 24
ȝerne and fastliche wið[h]eald [9] þe. ȝif [8] hitt cumð ofte smitende
to ðin hierte, wite þu to soðe ðat hit is of dieule. ȝif ðu him tei-
þest, þu makest ðe seluen þrall, and noht mannes, ac deules. ȝif [8]
ðu dest sumþing elles, and dwellest þisne lust, and mid ibede hine 28
ouercumst, þu scalt habben michel lean of godd [10], and ðe seluen
makest frie.

[1] page 83.   [2] an erasure between s and i.   [3] a j inserted above in G.
[4] wiðhelðnesse MS.   [5] deum underdotted.   [6] apostolus, red on the margin.
[7] (h)lustess MS., the last s underdotted.   [8] de MS.   [9] wid eald MS.
[10] page 84.

Of fasting.

Jejunium is another virtue which has often cooled God's wrath, that is, holy fasting. Through fasting God's wrath became assuaged against Nineveh, the great city which took three days to go [round it]. All the people that dwelt therein were to be destroyed through God's right doom, if they had not fasted. Then this holy virtue helps much in all the needs which man has to do. It gets forgiveness for the sinful, rest for the toilful, gladness for the sorry. Christ Himself hallowed this fasting when He fasted forty days in the wilderness, [away] from all men. There He gave to anchorites and hermits who love loneliness [a] good example to flee the world and to love loneliness, since He, whom nobody could hinder, nevertheless flew from men when He would fast. So did Moses. He fasted forty days when he took the law from God Himself, upon the Mount of Sinai. So did Elijah, the prophet, in the wilderness; forty days he fasted. All these three fasts were as wonderful as no others, viz. without all kinds of meats. God is ever fasting. Therefore ought all who think to dwell with Him to love fasting much, just as one can suffer it. In great trouble we are while we shall strive and care about meats. But there are some who think too much of them, and give their heart ever too much to them. So strongly they are deceived, and so sweet it seems to them and pleases them so [much], that they have no other bliss, nor care to have, but of eating and of drinking and of their body's lusts. When they shall fast at all, they fast scarcely all the noon; then after noon they drink all the day, and some still by night. They do not understand that it is as great a sin to break fasts by drinking after noon without great need, as it is before noon by eating without just as much need. Such unhappy men bemoans the apostle weeping sorely, who says : *Quorum Deus venter est,* 'Of their belly they make their God.' For the good man is thinking night and day how he may please God, and obey Him best. So is this deceived man thinking night and day how he may fill his unhappy belly with sweet meats and drinks. *Quorum finis interitus,* 'They are certainly lost who end in this.' *Quoniam*

Of fasten.

IEIVNIUM is an oðer mihte ðe godes wraðþe hafð ofte ikeled,
þat is, hali fasten. Ðurh fasten warð godes wraðþe ȝeleid of
Niniue, ðare muchele burȝh ðe ȝelaste ðrie daiȝes fare. All ðat folk 4
ðe þerinne was scolde ben forfaren þurh godes rihte dome, ȝif here
fasten nare. To alle ðo nedes ðe mann hafð[1] to donne þanne is
(þes)e[2] hali mihte swiðe helpinde. Hie beȝiet ðe senfulle forȝifnesse, ðe swinkfulle reste, ðe sari gladnesse. Crist self halȝede 8
ðis fasten þo þe he faste fowerti daiȝes on ða wilderne, fram alle
mannen. Dar he ȝaif ancres *and* hermites ðe luuieð onnesse gode
forbisne ðe world to flene *and* onnesse to luuien, seððen he, ðe no
mann ne mihte letten, fleih naðelas menn, ða ðe he fasten wolde. 12
Swa dede Moyses. He fastede fowerti daȝes þar (ðe) he þe laȝhe
nam of godd self, uppe ðe munte of Synay. Swa dede Helyas, ðe
prophete, on þe wilderne; fowerti daiȝes he faste. Alle þese þrie
fasten waren swa selcuðliche swa non oðre, wið-uten alles kennes 16
metes. Godd is haure fastinde. For ði aȝen alle ðe mid him
þenken to wunien, michel to luuien fasten, swa swa me hit þolien
mai. On michele ȝeswinke we bieð ðar [h]wile ðe we abuten
metes sculen striuen[3] *and* hoȝiȝen. Ac hit bieð sume ðe to michel 20
þar of þenceð, *and* aure to michel her hierte þar to doð. Swa
swiðe hie bieð beswiken, *and* swa swete hit hem þincð *and* swa
him likeð, þat. hie nan oðer blisse ne habbeð, ne[4] ne reccheð to
habben, buten of ates *and* of drenches *and* of here likames hlustes. 24
·Þanne hie alles fasten sculen, ðane fasteð hie all þat none uneaðe;
ðanne after non drinkeð all daiȝ, *and* sume ȝiet benihte. Ne
understandeð hie naht þat alswa michel senne hit is to breken
fasten mid drinke after none wið-uten michele nede, a(l)swa hit is 28
to-foren non of aten wið-uten alswa michele niede. Of ðelliche
unsali menn bemaneð ðe apostel sore wepinde, *and* seið: Q*vorum*
deus uenter est, 'Of here wombe hie makieð here godd.' For
ðan ðe gode mann is niht *and* daiȝ þeinkinde hu he muȝe gode 32
icwemen, *and* him betst hersumen; alswa is ðies beswikene mann
niht *and* daiȝ þeinkinde hwu he muȝe fellen [h]is unȝesali beli mid
swete metes *and* drenches. Quor*um* finis interitus, 'Hie bieð

---

[1] h *corr. from* i.   [2] þes *written above* ðe.   [3] steruin *MS.*   [4] *page* 85.

ebriosi regnum Dei non possidebunt, 'Great drinkers shall never, never forsooth, enjoy the kingdom of Heaven.' Thou who committest this and wilt not be deceived, go to the burying-place of him who committed this with thee or before thee, and think how lonely he lies from all his fellows with whom he was wont to drink and to play, and how dark he lies there who was accustomed to the fair fire and to the bright candles, and think that the foul belly is crawling full of worms, which he was wont to fill with good meats and sweet drinks, and try; if thou doest not shudder hereof, thou art not in the life which thou shouldst live. Woe be to the same man who sees and hears this and never is the better !

Of sobriety.

Sobrietas is another virtue, that is, sobriety. This makes the man sober who was too greedy. Of this said the apostle: *Sobrii estote et vigilate, etc.,* 'Be sober and watch with thoughts, because your adversary goeth about every man whom he might swallow with some cardinal sin. As the lion who goes about the animals to swallow them, so does the devil about you.' Beware whoso will! *Sobrietas est nimii cibi et potus repressio.* This virtue makes the man who will follow it sinless and free from shame before God and before man as for eating and drinking. There are some who know no moderation in feeding themselves, as there are ever too many other men who give without distinction as well the things which they should not give, as those which they should give. That this virtue wills that thou givest those things gladly which shall be given rightly. *Quia hilarem datorem diligit Deus,* 'God loveth a cheerful giver.' And those things which shall not be given, are to be withheld with great discretion. One ought to give [neither] church-things, nor tithes, nor offerings, nor alms anywhere but where great need is and where he nevermore in this life seeks to have reward or meed. Think hereof ye who love the world's love !

iwis forlorene ðe hier on andieð.' *Quoniam* ebriosi regnum dei non possidebunt, 'Ðe michele drinkeres soðliche naure, naure heuene riche ne sculen bruken.' Ðu ðe þis befelst *and* ne wilt [bien] beswiken, ga to his berieles ðe ðis beuall mid þe oððer ₄ beforen ðe, *and* þenk hu anliche he lið fram alle hise felawȝes ðe he was bewune mide to drinken *and* to pleiȝen, *and* hu ðiester he lið ðar þe was bewune to ðe faire fiere *and* to ðe brihte kandeles, *and* þench ðat ðe fule wombe is crewlinde full of weormes, ₈ þe he was bewune[1] to fellen mid gode metes *and* swete drenches, and fonde ; ȝif þe herof noht nagrist, nart þu naht liues þar ðe ðu[2] libben scoldest. Wa mai bien ðe ilke mann ðe þis ȝesikþ *and* ȝehiereð *and* na ðe bettre ne bieð !   ₁₂

Of ȝe-meðe.

SOBRIETAS is an oðer mihte, þat is, maðe. Ðies makeð þanne mann maðfull ðe was to grady. Her of sade ðe apostel : Sobrii estote *et* uigilate, *et cet.*, 'Bieð imeðfull *and* ₁₆ wakieð mid þoutes, for ðan ȝewer wiðerwine gað abuten alche manne (w)ham he mihte forswoleȝen mid sume [h]eaued-senne. Alswa ðe lyon ðe gað abuten þe dier hem to forswoleȝen, swa deð deuel abuten ȝew.' Bie war se ðe wile ! Sobrietas est nimii[3] ₂₀ cibi *et* potus repressio. Ðies mihte, hie makeð þanne mann ðe hire wile folȝin senne-leas *and* scameleas to-foren godd *and* to-foren manne of ates *and* of drenches. Hit bieð sume þat non imeðe ne cunnen of hem seluen to feden, alswa bieð aure to fele ₂₄ oðre menn ðe ȝiueð wið-uten schele alswa ða þinges ðe hie naht ne scolden ȝiuen, alswa ða ðe hie scolden ȝiuen. Ðat wile þies mihte þat þu ȝiue ða ðinges þe sculen bien mid rihte iȝiuen, gladliche. Qvia hillarem datorem diligit deus, 'Gladne ȝiuere luueð ₂₈ godd.' *And* ða þinges ðe ne sculen ben iȝiuen, þa bieð to wið- [h]ealden mid michele skele. Chierche-þinges, tiȝeþes, ne offrendes, ne almesses ne awh me nauhwer to ȝiuene buten ðar þe michel nied is *and* ðar he naure ma on ðese liue lean ne mede ne secð to ₃₂ habben. Þeinkeð hier of ȝie þe luuieð worldes luue !

page 86.   [2] bewune*n MS.*   [3] *The second* i *is half erased.*

Of conscience.

Again, there is another virtue—very happy [he] who may get it !—which is called *pura conscientia*, that is, pure conscience. It dwells so concealed in the heart that nobody can see or know it but God alone. It bears good witness of all kinds of good deeds, because it is glad and blithe of them, [and] of all kinds of evil works, words, or thoughts which come before it—so they must all, evil and good. All these it receives blithely or sorrily. All which are agreeable to God are very welcome to it. Of those which are not so and come before it, it is very sorry, and reprehends the heart strongly and accuses [it] before God. Concerning this said the blessed apostle St. John : *Si cor nostrum non reprehenderit nos,* ' If our heart,' he said, ' does not reprehend nor accuse us of any sin which God hates and thou lovest : whatsoever we beseech God for, He will soon grant us.'

Of prayer.

Now we have quite come to this blessed virtue which one calls *oratio sancta,* that is, holy prayer. It is not right that we leave it, without saying something of it. When we read in the book, God speaks with us ; when we say our prayer, we speak with God. If thou wouldst beseech the king for any thing, and thou camest into his hall where he sat among his rich men, and thou shouldst speak alone before all his men, thou wouldst speak with great dread and with great consideration. With much more fear and love thou oughtst to come before God, who is King of all kings, and beseech Him very humbly for thy need, so that thou shouldst say at the end of each petition what Christ said Himself as an example for us, because we do not know whether we beg what is agreeable to God and useful for us, or is not so : *Non sicut ego volo, sed sicut tu vis,* ' Lord,' He said, ' do not as I will, but as Thou wilt.' Christ

Of inȝehied.

GIET is an oðer mihte—swiðe eadi ðe hes beȝeten mai!—þe[1] is
icleped pura *consciencia*, þat is, hlutter inȝehied. Hie
wuneð swa derneliche on þare hierte, ðat[2] no mann hes ne mai isien 4
ne witen bute godd one. Hie berð gode ȝewitnesse of alleskennes
gode dades, for ðan hie is ðer of glad *and* bliðe; of alles kennes
euele workes, wordes oðer þoutes ðe cumeð toforen hire, swa hie
moten alle, euele *and* gode. Alle hie his underfongð[3] bliðeliche oððer 8
sariliche. Alle ðe gode beð icweme, hie bieð hire swiðe welcume.
Ða ðe swa ne bieð *and* cumeð toforen hire, hie is ðarof swiðe
sari, *and* swiðe ða hierte undernimð *and* wreiȝeð toforen gode.
Herof sade ðe eadi apostel *sanctus* Iohannes: Si cor *nostrum* 12
non reprehenderit nos, 'ȝif[4] ure hierte,' he sade, 'us ne under-
nemeð naht ne ne wreihð of nane senne ðe godd hateð *and* ðe
luuieð: hwat so we beseceð at gode, he us wile sone teiþin.'

Of biene. 16

NU we alles bieð ȝecumen to ðessere eadi mihte ðe me clepeð
oratio sancta, þat is, hali bede. Nis hit naht riht þat we
hie forlaten, þat we of hire sum ðing ne seggen. Danne we on
boke radeð, ðanne spekeð godd wið us; ðanne we ure bede 20
seggeð, þanne speke (we) wið gode. Gif þu woldest at te (k)inge[5]
ani þing beseke*n*, *and* ðu come into his [h]alle, ðar he sate mang
(his) riche mannen, *and* ðu scoldest ane speken to-foren alle hise
mannen, mid michele dradnesse *and* mid michele embeþanke ðu 24
scoldest speken. Mid muchel mare eiȝe *and* luue þu auȝhst to
cumen to-foren gode, ðe is alre kinge king, *and* him swiðe eadmodliche besechen of ðiere niede, swa þat[6] þu hat alchere bede
sende [scoldest] seggen þat Crist sade himself us to forbisne, 28
forðan we ne witen hweðer we bidden ðat godd be ȝecweme *and*
us biheue, oððer hit ne bie: Non sicut ego uolo, set sicut tu
nis, 'Hlauerd,' he sade, 'naht alswa ich wille ne do ðu, ac alswa
ðu wilt.' Crist self us tahte hu we scolden don, *and* sade: Tu 32

---

[1] *page* 87.   [2] ðar *MS.*   [3] fonȝð *MS.*   [4] G *with* j *inserted.*
[5] k *corr. above* þ.   [6] page 88.

Himself taught us how we should do, and said : *Tu autem, cum oraveris, intra in cubiculum tuum, etc.*, ' When thou wilt pray,' He said, ' go into thy bed-room and shut the door upon thee, and pray so to thy Father, God Almighty. And He who knoweth and seeth all things will hear thee.' Go into thy bed-room, that is, into thy heart—there ought to be thy rest—and shut the door, so that thou lettest no other thoughts into thee but of God and of thy need. Thus He taught with word and showed with works that we should seek loneliness and a private place for such a need. The Gospel says of Him : *Ascendit Jesus in montem solus orare.* It says that ' He went up into a mountain apart to pray.' All the men of the world were about Him ; they could not prevent Him to think one thought but as He would. But [He did so] in order to give an example to hermits and anchorites, who ought to love and to keep loneliness more than all other men. And those who cannot dwell in loneliness, however, when they will pray their prayer to God, may do it as secretly as they can. For all the needs which ever come to man he always ought to beseech God first of all things, and then it will speed him always the better. This holy prayer is very agreeable to God, if it is sent forth with tears, with clean heart, and with burning love. Of this said the prophet : *Dirigatur, Domine, oratio mea, etc.*, ' Lord,' said he, ' so may go upwards my prayer before Thee, as the incense doeth out of the censer !' All the goods which one ought to have, must all be got through holy prayer and through good works. *Multum valet deprecatio justi assidua.* This said St. James, the holy apostle : ' The prayer of a righteous man availeth much,' and he gives such an example of it : ' There was a man, mortal as we are, and he besought God that it should not rain, to chasten the people. God heard him—that was Elias—and withheld all the rains three years and six months, so that they were all overcome through hunger and with thirst. And so they turned to God and begged forgiveness ; and again, this

autem, cum oraueris, intra in cubiculum tuum, et cet.,
'Ðanne ðu wilt ӡebidden ðe,' he sade, 'ga into þine bedde, and
s(c)ette þe d(ure)[1] uppen ðe, and bidde þe swa to þine fader,
godd almihtin. And he þe wat and isikð alle þing, he ðe 4
wile ӡeheren.' Ga into þine bedde, þat is, in to þine hierte—
ðar ah to bene þine reste—and scete ðe dure[2], swa ðat þu ne lat
none oðre þauhtes[3] in to þe bute of gode and of þine niede. Ðus
he tahte mid worde, and mid workes he sceawede þat we annesse 8
and senderlicne stede scolde scechen to þelliche niede. Ðat
godspell seið of him : Ascendit Iesus in montem solus orare.
Hitt seið þat 'he steih uppen ane dune ane him to bidden.' Alle
ðe menn of ðare world waren abuten him ; ne mihten hie him 12
benemen anne þouht to þenken buten alswa he walde. Ac for to
ӡiuene[4] forbisne her(e)mites and ancres, ðe annesse aӡen to luuen
and to healden ouer alle oðre manne. And ðo þe on annesse
wuniӡen ne muӡen, hure and hure, ðanne hie willeð here ibede to 16
godde bidden, swa[5] derneliche swa hie muӡen, swa don hie! To
alle ðo niedes ðe aure cumeð to manne aure hie awh gode to
beseken alre ðing arst, and ðanne scal him aure ðe bettre ӡelim-
pen. Ðies hali ӡebede, hie is gode swiðe ӡecweme, þan hie mid 20
clane hierte and mid barninde luue forð mid teares bieð ӡesant.
Dar of sade ðe prophete : Dirigatur, domine, oracio mea,
et cet., 'Hlauerd,' he sade, 'swa go upp mine ӡebede to-foren ðe,
swa ðat stor dieth ut of storf(a)te[6] l' Alle ðe gode ðe mann awh 24
to habben, alle hie moten bien beӡeten þurӡh hali bede and þurh
gode workes. Multum ualet deprecacio iusti assidua.
Ðis sade sanctus Iacobus, ðe hali apostel : 'Swiðe michel
helpð þas rihtwismannes bede,' and ðar of he seið ðelliche 28
forbisne : 'Hit was (on) mann, dedlich alswa we bieð, and he
besohte at gode þat naht ne scolde reinin, for ðe folke to kastin.
Godd him ihierde—þat was Helyas—and wið[h]eld alle reines
þrie hier and six moneþes, swa ðat hie waren ðurh hunger and 32

---

[1] *Two letters have been scratched out,* ure *is written above, and* ur *inserted on the erasure by a later hand.*
[2] *One or two letters erased.*   [3] a corr. from o.
[4] ac for to ӡ *is written twice, but the second time underdotted.*
[5] *page* 89.   [6] *Corrected from* storafte.

same Elias besought God for rain, and all joy came to them.'
Again, it is written: *Qui avertit aurem suam ne audiat legem,*
oratio ejus erit execrabilis, 'From him that turneth away his ears
from God's law, will God also turn away, when he beseecheth Him
for aught.' Again, God Almighty Himself says: *Antequam vocetis,*
dicam : ecce assum, ' Ere thou shalt cry to Me, I shall say: Look,
here I am, beg what thou wilt.' When thou wilt beseech God for
anything, kneel down before His feet, and think as if He were right
there before thee, and say as he did who esteemed himself all guilty
and got forgiveness : *Deus, propitius esto mihi peccatori,* 'Lord God,
have mercy upon me sinful !' I am well conscious that I am all
guilty as he who has lost and despised the happiness of the kingdom of Heaven, and deserved the pain of hell. But I believe that
Thou art the Highest God, and graceful and willing to forgive, and
that Thou wilt, through Thy great goodness, and that Thou canst,
because Thou art almighty, make sinful me righteous, and that
Thou canst make me, who am all guilty, one of Thy chosen ones,
if I have true repentance, so that I would sin nevermore again.
But I cannot have this, except Thou wilt give it me through Thy
great goodness and through Thy great mercy. And I believe and
know it well that as good and as merciful Thou art to-day, so
Thou wast that day when St. Peter forsook Thee. But as soon as
Thou lookedst at him he quickly repented that he had done so, and
he bewept it with bitter tears, and so Thou forgavest it him. So
Thou didst to the guilty thief who hung on Thy right [hand]. So
Thou didst to guilty Mary Magdalene. Thou madest her, sinful
as she was, [a] thoroughly holy [one]. So Thou hast done to all
to whom it was Thy will to give true repentance in their hearts.
Now, my dear Lord, I beseech Thee, through Thy great goodness,
to look upon me as Thou didst upon St. Peter, and send a drop of
Thy sweet mercy to my wretched, dry heart, so that it might soften
and melt and send out some tears. Then I may hope that Thou

OF PRAYER. 145

mid ðurst all ouercumen. *And* swa hie wanten to gode *and*
forȝifnesse beden; *and* eft ðies ilke Helyas besohte godd of reine,
and heom cam alle winne.' Eft is ȝewriten: Qvi auertit aurem
suam ne audiat legem, oracio eius erit execrabilis, 'Se [4]
ðe want his earen fram godes laȝhe, alswa wile godd wanden fram
him, þanne he him awht besekeð.' Eft seið goddalmihti [1] him
self: Ante-qua*m* [*] uocetis, dicam: ecce assum, 'Ar ðanne
ðu clepiȝe to me, ich segge: loke, hier ich am, bide þat ðu [8]
wilt.' Ðanne ðu wilt at gode ani þing beseken, cnyle ðar niðer
to-foren hise fet, *and* þinc swilch he bie riht ðar to-foren ðe, *and*
seiȝe alswa he dede ðe him [h]eald all forgelt *and* forȝifnesse
beȝat: Deus, *propicius* esto m*ihi* peccatori[2], 'Hlauerd godd, [12]
[h]aue are[3] of me senfulle!' Ich am wel becnawe ðat ich am all
forgelt alswa se ðe haið forloren *and* forgaud ðo eadinesse of
heuen-riche, *and* of-earṇed helle-pine. Ac ich ilieue þat þu art
łreiȝest godd, *and* orefull *and* forȝiuenlich, *and* ðat þu wilt, for [16]
þine michele godnesse, *and* ðat þu miht, for ði þat þu art almihti,
of me senfulle maken rihtwis, *and* of me allforgelt miht makien
on of þine ȝecorene, ȝif ich hadde soðe berewnesse, þat i(c)h nauerma
eft seneȝin nolde. Ac ich þis ne mai habben, bute ðu for ðine [20]
michele god-nesse *and* for þire michele mildsce[4] hit me ȝiuen wille.
And ich ilieue *and* wel hit wot þat alswa god[5] *and* alswa milde
þu art nu to daiȝ, alswa ðu ware ðas daiȝes ðe seinte Peter þe
forsoch. Ac swa· raðe so ðu to him lokedest, sone him rewh þat [24]
he hadde swa ȝie-don, *and* mid bittere teares hit bewop, *and* swa
ðu hit him forȝaue. Swa þu dedest ðe (al)[6]-fo[r]gelte þieue þe
he(ng) on þire[7] swiþere. Swa ðu dedest ðe forgilte Marie
Magdaleue. Ðu makedest of hire senfulle ðat hie was, þurȝhali. [28]
Swa ðu hauest ȝedon alle þar þin wille was soðe berewsinge to
ȝieuene on here hierte. Nu, min leue hlauerd, ich ðe besieke, for
þire michele godnesse, þat þu lokie to me swaswa þu dedest to
seinte Petre[8], *and* sand aṇe drope of þire swete mildsce to mire [32]
wrecche, fordruȝede hierte, þat hie mihte nexxin *and* mealten *and*
ut-sanden sume tear. (Ðanne mai ic hopien) ðat tu wilt of me

---

[1] almihtin *MS.*   [*] *page* 90.   [2] *Ewangelista red at side.*
[3] *an erasure before* a. [4] *an erasure above* ld. [5] *the second* d *underdotted.*
[6] *the second* l *erased.* [7] *page* 91.   [8] *corrected above* Marie.

L

wilt have mercy upon me as Thou hadst upon them upon whom
Thou lookedst and to whom Thou gavest tears.

Of tears.

Know thou forsooth that these tears which we speak about are
certainly God's gift, and very needful to the needy ones who shall be
heard by God.   Of them said the prophet: *Fuerunt mihi lacrimae
meae panes die ac nocte*, 'My tears,' said he, 'were my bread day
and night ; so good they seemed [to be].'   Of other kinds of tears
he said: *Lacrimis meis stratum meum rigabo*, 'I shall water my
bed with my tears.'   This bed betokens the *conscientia*, that is, the
conscience within.   Where the good soul has its rest, there the evil
soul has its pain.   Therefore he said that he would wash with tears
the conscience from that of which his heart accused him.   We find
nowhere that God denied anything for which any man besought
Him with tears.   God sent to Hezekiah, the king, by His prophet,
and said: *Dispone domui tuae, quia morieris tu, et non vives*,
'Bequeath thy legacy,' He said, 'for thou shalt be dead, and
thou shalt not live.'   The King became sorry, as it is loathsome to leave riches, and very dear to live.   He then turned
to the wall, and did the best.   'Oh Lord God,' said he, 're-
member now that I have loved Thee and have done blithely
for Thy love, and give me still a little respite through Thy
goodness !'   This was a good conscience, that he could show forth
his good deeds when he had need.   Therefore God heard him and
said to His prophet, who was homeward: 'Turn again,' quoth He,
'and say to the king: *Vidi lacrimam tuam*, 'I saw,' quoth He,
'thy tears, and I heard thy prayer.   Thou shalt still live fifteen
years ; so much I have increased thy life.'   When thou in great need
wilt beseech God it is very good for thee that thou canst draw forth
some good deeds ; thy heart is the gladder, and thou mayst beg
the more assuredly.   Let us now say with the prophet: *Ciba nos
pane lacrimarum*, 'Lord, feed us with the bread of sweet tears,' *et*

habben are[1] swa swa ðu hauest ʒe[h](a)fd[2] of hem ðe ðu to lokedest
and teares ʒe(a)ue.

Of teares.

WITE ðu to soðe ðat þese teares ðe we embe spekeð[3] hie bieð[4]
iwis godes ʒiue, *and* swiðe niedfulle to ðan inede[4] þat iherd
sculen-[bien] of gode. Of hem sade ðe *prophete*: Fuerunt m*ihi*
lacrime me panes die ac nocte, 'Mine teares,' he sade, 'me
waren bred daiʒ *and* niht; swa gode hie þouhten.' Of oþres[8]
kennes teares he sade: La*cr*imis meis stratum meum rigabo,
'Ich scal watrien min bedd mid mine teares.' Ðies bedd tacneð þe
consciencia, þat is[5], þat inʒied wið-innen. Þar ðe gode sawle
haueð hire reste, þar haueð se eule sawle hire pine. For þi he sade 12
þat he wolde mid teares wascen þat inʒied[6] þar of ðe his herte him
wreiʒede. Ne finde we nawher þat godd wernde ani þing ðe ani
mann mid teares him besouhte. God sante to Ezechie, þe kinge, be
his *prophete*, *and* sade: Dispone domui tue, quia morieris 16
tu[7], *et* non uiues, 'Becweð þine[8] cwide,' he sade, 'for ðan þu scalt
bien dead, *and* naht ne scalt tu libben.' Ðe king warð sari, alswa
richeise is lað[9] to laten, *and* swiðe lef to libben. He wante þo to
ðe wauʒe, *and* dede þat [10] betste. '(A) hlauerd godd,' sade he, 20
'þench nu ðat ich ðe habbe ʒe-luued *and* for þine luue bliðeliche
idon, *and* ʒif me ʒiet a litel ferst, for þine godnesse!' Ðies was
god inʒied, þat he mihte his gode dade forðsceawin þa þe he niede
hadde. For þi him ʒeherde godd *and* sade to [h]is *prophete*, ðe 24
was ham-ward: 'Wand aʒean,' cwað he, '*and* sai to þe kinge: Vidi
lacrimam tua*m*, 'Ich iseih,' cwað he, 'þine tear, *and* ich iherde
þine bene. Þu scalt ʒiet libben fiftene ʒear; swa michel ich habbe
ieiht þi lif.' Ðanne ðu on michele niede gode wilt beseken, þanne 28
is ðe wel god þat þu muʒe forðdraʒen sume gode dade; þin
hierte bieð ðe gladdere, *and* ðe sikerliker ðu miht bidden. Segge
we nu forð mid þe *prophete*: Ciba nos pane lacrima*r*um,

[1] *a letter erased before* a.
[2] ʒefadd *MS.*; a *is underdotted, and an* a *is put above* e.
[3] speked *MS.*   [4] n *corr. by erasure from* h.   [5] is *corr. from* þ.
[6] d *corr. from another letter.*   [7] et tu *MS.*
[8] *page* 92.   [9] ð *corr. from* d *by a later hand.*
[10] at *on erasure.*

potum da nobis in lacrimis in mensura, 'and give us to drink of other kinds of tears, and that in measure.' I will that thou be well warned that, if God gives thee these sweet tears, no wine in the world is so sweet. And as a man may drink too much wine, so a man may weep too much, though they [viz. the tears] are sweet; and therefore it is good for thee that thou beseechest God for one virtue which is called *discretio*, that is, discretion.

It is very useful among all the other virtues. Thus say the holy Fathers: ' She is mother of all the other virtues; where she reigns man can never perish who wills her to reign and will follow her.' It is said in *Vitas patrum* that the holy Fathers were gathered together in some room, and were speaking among themselves in which way one might come to God most rightly and most surely. Some said: through fasting, some: through vigil, some: through prayer, some said: through obedience, some said: through loneliness, some said: through harbouring wretched men and feeding and shrouding [them], some said: through looking after sick men; and in manifold ways they mentioned according to what the holy Gospel says. Then said one of the oldest and one of the wisest: ' Through all these we have seen and heard a great many saved, and many by all these named virtues perished, because *discretio* failed them, that is, discretion and discernment. For some did much more than they could well complete, some did too little, some did evil and fancied to do well, some began well and ended badly. But we never saw that a man who had this holy virtue with him ever fared amiss.' Get it whoso can !

One holy virtue is called *perseverantia.* It is not to be disregarded, because it makes the man to whom God sends it persevere in his goodness. In the old law it was bidden anent all the animals which

'Hlauerd, fed us mid ðo breade of swete teares,' *et potum* da
nobis in lacrimis in mensura, 'and ȝif us drinken of oðres-
kennes teares, and ðat mid imete !' Ðat ich wile þat ðu wel be
iwarned, ȝif[1] godd ðe ȝifð þese swete teares, þat non win in ðare 4
world nis swa swete. *And* alswa alswa man[2] to michel mai drinken
of ðare wine, alswa mai ðe mann to michel wepen, þeih hie
swete bien ; *and* for ði þe is god þat þu beseke at gode one mihte
ðe hatte discrecio, þat is[3], sckelewisnesse.   8

HIE is swiðe beheue mang alle ðe oðre mihtes. Ðis ðe hali
faderes seggeð: 'Hie is moder of alle ðe oðre mihtes; ðar ðe
hie rixið ne mai naure[4] man forfaren þe hire wile rixin *and* folȝin.'
Hit seið in Vitas patrum ðat at sume sal waren ðe hali faderes 12
to-gedere igadered, *and* waren spekinde betwen hem on (h)williche
wise me mihte rihtist *and* sikerest to gode cumen. Sum sade :
þurh fasten, sum : þurh wacchen, sum : ðurh bede, sum sade :
þurh hersumnesse, sum sade : ðurh annesse, sum sade : ðurh her- 16
borȝin[5] wrecche menn *and* feden *and* screden, sum sade : ðurh seke
menn to lokin ; *and* on manieskennes wisen hie namden after ðan
þe þat hali goddspell seið. Ða sade on of ða eldest[6] *and* on of ða
wisest : 'Ðurh alle ðesen we habbeð iseȝen *and* iherd swiðe maniȝe 20
ȝeborȝen, *and* manie of alle ðesen inamde mihten forfaren, for þi
ðat hem trukede discrecio, þat is, scadwisnesse and skele. For
ði[7] sume deden michel mare þan hie mihtin wel andin, sume deden
to litel, sume deden euele *and* wenden wel don, sume wel a-gunnen 24
and euele andeden. Ac naure ne ȝeseiȝe we manne þat hadde þese
hali mihte mid him, þat he aure misferde.' Beȝete se ðe muge !

PERSEUERANCIA hatte an hali mihte. Hie nis naht[8] to
laten, for ðan hie makeð ðanne man ðe godd (h)is to-sant 28
þat he þurwuneð on his godnesse. On ðare ealde laȝe hit was
i[h]oten[9] þat alle dier ðe me gode scolde offrin, þat hie lokeden wel

---

[1] Gif *MS.*, *with a* j *inserted in* G.   [2] *a letter erased after* n.
[3] *page* 93.   [4] *two words erased.*   [5] ȝ *on erasure.*
[6] t *destroyed by a hole.*   [7] ði *on erasure.*   [8] *page* 94.
[9] io *corr. from two other letters by erasure.*

one should offer to God, to care well that the tail were on every
animal. That betokens that each man who offers God any service
persevere therein. In this new law said Christ: *Qui perseveraverit
usque in finem, hic salvus erit,* 'He that endureth in his goodness
which he has begun, shall be saved and not otherwise, for no good
which he has done, whatsoever it is.'

Ratio dicit animae:

Dear soul, I have made this little writ with sore toil—He knows
it who knows all things!—in order to instruct thee, to warn thee,
and to help thee and to save thee. If thou wilt understand it well
and learn and follow and keep [it] without any doubt, thou mayst
save thyself with God's help and surely gain the joy of the kingdom
of Heaven with these holy virtues.

Nunc auctor loquitur finaliter:

Let us now thank and praise our Lord, Almighty God, for
this knowledge and for this wisdom which we have here gathered
from His hoard and from many a holy man's labours, who worked
much for the love of God and in order to teach us! It is right
that we praise and thank and bless Father and Son and Holy Ghost
in the Holy Trinity, which is one true God in unity, who liveth
and reigneth evermore world [without end]. Amen. Never forget
thou to praise God and to thank [Him] for all good things. Just
as we have need to beg Him by day and by night, and often and
frequently, so it is need to praise Him. Amen.

ðat ðe[1] tail ware on auriche netene. Þat tocneð ðat ilke mann
ðe gode ani seruise offreð, þat he þar on þurȝwunie.   On ðessere
newe laȝe sade Crist: Qvi perseuerauerit usque in finem,
hic saluus erit[2], 'Se ðurȝ-[3]wuneð on his godnesse ðe he hafð 4
agunnen, he worð iborȝen and naht elles, for none gode þe he don
hafð, hwat (hwat)[4] it is.'

Ratio dicit anime:

L IEUE (saule)[5], ðis little writt ic (habbe)[6] sare beswonken—he it 8
wat þat[7] wot alle þing !—for[8] ðe to wissin, for ðe to warnin,
and for ðe to helpen and for ðe to berȝin. ȝif[9] ðu wilt wel hit
understonden and liernin and folȝin and [h]ealden wið-uten alche[10]
twene, þu miht mid godes felste ðe berȝen and heuneriches merchþe 12
mid þese halie mihtes sike(r)liche[11] iwinnen.

Nunc autor loquitur finaliter:

H VTE we nu þ(a)nkin[12] and herien ure hlauerde, almihtin gode
of ðese witte and of ðese wisdome ðe we hier habbeð 16
igadered of (h)is horde and of maniȝes[13] haliȝes mannes ȝeswinkes,
þe michel sw(u)nken[14] for ðe luue of gode and for us to wissin !
Hit is riht ðat we heriȝen and þankin and bledscin fader and sune
and hali gast on ða hali þrinnesse, se ðe is on soð godd in onnesse, 20
se ðe l(i)ueð[15] and rixeð aure ma a woreld. Amen. Ðat ne forȝeit[16]
ðu naure, þat ðu godd ne heriȝe and þanke of alle gode. Alswa
swa we habbeð niede him to bidden be daiȝ and be nihte, and ofte
and ȝelome, alswa hit is niede him to heriȝen. Amen.   24

Veni, creator spiritus, mentes tuorum uisita; implet
superna gracia que tu creasti pectora[17].

---

[1] ðe was written twice, the first erased.
[2] Ewangelista, red on the margin.   [3] durȝ MS.
[4] written above on erasure.
[5] red, corr. above ratio, which is red underlined.
[6] corr. above write.   [7] þa MS., with underdotted a.
[8] f is later inserted.   [9] G with inserted j.   [10] c corr. from l.
[11] r corr. above l.   [12] a corr. above e.   [13] page 95.
[14] u correction above i.   [15] i written above an underdotted e.
[16] i over erasure.   [17] the Latin verses are written in a much larger type.

EXTRA SERIES.

Early English Text Society.

The Subscription, which constitutes membership, is £1 1s. a year (and £1 1s. additio[n] for the EXTRA SERIES), due in advance on the 1st of JANUARY, and should be paid eithe[r] the Society's Account at the Head Office of the Union Bank, Princes Street, London, E[..] or by Cheque, Postal Order, or Money Order (made payable at the Chief Office, Londo[n] to the Hon. Secretary, W. A. DALZIEL, Esq., 67 Victoria Road, Finsbury Park, Londo[n] N., and crost 'Union Bank.' (United States Subscribers must pay for postage 1s. 4d. year extra for the Original Series, and 1s. a year for the Extra Series.) The Society's Tex[t] are also sold separately at the prices put after them in the Lists.

ORIGINAL SERIES.

The Publications for 1887 are :—

87. Early English Verse Lives of Saints (earliest version), Laud MS., ed. Dr. C. Horstmann. 20s.
88. Hy. Bradshaw's Life of St. Werburghe (Pynson, 1521), ed. Dr. C. Horstmann. 10s.

The Publications for 1888 will be :—

89. Vices and Virtues, from the unique Stowe MS., ab. 1200 A.D., ed. Dr. F. Holthausen. Part I. 8s.
90. Eadwine's Canterbury Psalter, from the Trin. Cambr. MS., ab. 1150 A.D., ed. F. Harsley, B.A. [At Pres[s]
91. Bede's Liber Scintillarum, edited from the MSS. by — Rhodes, B.A. [At Press.

The following Texts are preparing for Issue :—

Parallel-Text of 10 Psalms from all the Anglo-Saxon Psalters, ed. Dr. H. Logeman.
Sir David Lyndesay's Works. Part VI. and last, ed. W. H. S. Utley. [At Press.
Cursor Mundi. Part VI. Introduction, Notes, and Glossary, ed. Rev. Dr. R. Morris. [Part printed.
The Lay Folk's Catechism, by Archbp. Thoresby, ed. Canon Simmons and F. D. Matthew. [Text printed.
Capgrave's Life of St. Katharine, from the unique MS., ed. Dr. C. Horstmann. [At Press.
Melusine, the prose Romance, ed. from the unique MS., ab. 1500, by W. H. S. Utley. [At Press.
Aelfric's Metrical Lives of Saints, MS. Cott. Jul. E 7, Part III. ed. Prof. Skeat, Litt. D., LL.D. [At Press
Vices and Virtues, from the unique Stowe MS., ab. 1200 A.D., ed. Dr. F. Holthausen. Part II.

EXTRA SERIES.

The Publications for 1887 are—

XLIX. Guy of Warwick, 2 texts (Auchinleck and Caius MSS.), Part II, ed. Prof. J. Zupitza, Ph.D. 15s.
L. Charlemagne Romances :—12. Huon of Burdeux, by Lord Berners, ed. S. L. Lee, B.A. Part IV. 5s.
LI. Torrent of Portyngale, from the unique MS. in the Chetham Library, ed. E. Adam, Ph.D. 10s.

The Publications for 1888 will be chosen from—

LII. A Dialogue against the Fever Pestilence, 1573. By W. Bullein. Ed. A. H. & Mark Bullen. [At Press
LIII. Thos. Vicary's Anatomie of the Body of Man, 1548, ed. 1577, edited by F. J. & Percy Furnivall.
Bp. Fisher's English Works, Pt. II, with his Life and Letters, ed. Rev. Ronald Bayne, B.A. [At Press.
Early English Pronunciation, by A. J. Ellis, Esq., F.R.S. Pt. IV, the present English Dialects. [At Press.
Hoccleve's Minor Poems, from the Phillipps MS., ed. F. J. Furnivall, M.A., Ph.D. [At Press.
Hoccleve's Complaint, from the Cosin MS. at Durham, ed. F. J. Furnivall, M.A., Ph.D.

☞ *The Large-Paper Issue of the Extra Series is stopt, save for unfinisht Works of it.*

Preparing :—

Barbour's Bruce, ed. Rev. Prof. W. W. Skeat. Part IV.
Lonelich's Holy Grail, ed. F. J. Furnivall, M.A., Ph.D. Part V.
Robert of Brunne's Handlyng Synne, A.D. 1303, re-edited by Dr. Furnivall.
Caxton's englishing of the Eneydos, A.D. 1590, with its French original, ed. M. Culley, M.A.
Caxton's Book of the Ordre of Chyualry, ab. 1484, with Loutfut's Scotch copy of it, ed. W. Bayne, B.A.
Caxton's Englishing of Alain Chartier's Curial, ed. F. S. Ellis.

The Publications for the years 1878 to 1886 (one guinea each year) are :—

XXX. Lonelich's Holy Grail, ed. F. J. Furnivall, M.A., Ph.D. Part IV. 15s.   1878
XXXI. The Alliterative Romance of Alexander and Dindimus, ed. Rev. W. W. Skeat. 6s.   ,,
XXXII. Starkey's "England in Henry VIII's Time". Pt. I, Starkey's Life and Letters, ed. S. J. Herrtage. 8s. ,,
XXXIII. Gesta Romanorum (english ab. 1440), ed. S. J. Herrtage, B.A. 15s.   1879
XXXIV. The Charlemagne Romances :—1. Sir Ferumbras, from Ashm. MS. 33, ed. S. J. Herrtage. 15s.   ,,
XXXV. Charlemagne Romances :—2. The Sege off Melayne, Sir Otuell, &c., ed. S. J. Herrtage. 12s.   1880
XXXVI. Charlemagne Romances :—3. Lyf of Charles the Grete, Pt. I., ed. S. J. Herrtage. 16s.   ,,
XXXVII. Charlemagne Romances :—4. Lyf of Charles the Grete, Pt. II., ed. S. J. Herrtage. 15s.   1881
XXXVIII. Charlemagne Romances :—5. The Sowdone of Babylone, ed. Dr. Hausknecht. 15s.   ,,
XXXIX. Charlemagne Romances :—6. Rauf Colyear, Roland, Otuel, &c., ed. S. J. Herrtage, B.A. 15s.   1882
XL. Charlemagne Romances ;—7. Huon of Burdeux, by Lord Berners, ed. S. L. Lee, B.A. Part I. 15s.   ,,
XLI. Charlemagne Romances :—8. Huon of Burdeux, by Lord Berners, ed. S. L. Lee, B.A. Part II. 15s.   1883
XLII. Guy of Warwick : 2 texts (Auchinleck and Caius MS.), ed. Prof. Zupitza. Part I. 15s.   ,,
XLIII. Charlemagne Romances :—9. Huon of Burdeux, by Lord Berners, ed. S. L. Lee, B.A. Pt. III. 15s.   1884
XLIV. Charlemagne Romances :—10. The Four Sons of Aymon, ed. Miss Octavia Richardson. Pt. I. 15s.   ,,
XLV. Charlemagne Romances :—11. The Four Sons of Aymon, ed. Miss O. Richardson. Part II. 20s.   1885
XLVI. Sir Bevis of Hamton, from the Auchinleck and other MSS., ed. Prof. E. Kölbing. Part I. 10s.   ,,
XLVII. The Wars of Alexander, ed. Rev. Prof. Skeat, Litt.D., LL.D. 20s.   1886
XLVIII. Sir Bevis of Hamton, ed. Prof. E. Kölbing. Part II. 10s.   ,,

LONDON: N. TRÜBNER & CO., 57 & 59 LUDGATE HILL.
BERLIN: ASHER & CO., 53 MOHRENSTRASSE.

additional
d either to
idon, E.C.,
e, London)
k, London
e 1s. 4d. a
ety's Texts

20s.

t I. 8s.
.A. [At Press

t printed.
Text printed.

vst.
). [At Press
II.

Ph.D. 15s.
art IV. 5s.
. 10s.

n. [At Press
irnivall.
[At Press.
[At Press.

yne, B.A.

rtage.

15s.
s. 15s.
6s.
15s.
A. 15s.
I. 15s.
I. 15s.
5s.
II. 15s.
I. 1s.
. 20s.
I. 10s.

LL.

CPSIA information can be obtained
at www.ICGtesting.com
Printed in the USA
LVHW010145011118
595580LV00008B/98/P